Praise for Antidisestablishmentarianism

"...Great book if you want to know the truth about the Christian foundation our country was built ... "

" ... Great overview of the religious nature of the State Constitutions which were never barred from establishing religion by the U.S. Constitution."

"I enjoyed it!"

"Must Read!"

What Is an Establishment of Religion? (Serial Antidisestablishmentarianism Part One)

by

Michael J. and Mary C. Findley

What Is an Establishment of Religion? (Serial Antidisestablishmentarianism Part One)

by Michael J. and Mary C. Findley

"Speaking the truth in love. "

Table of Contents

Preface: Disestablishmentarianism

... When they knew God, they glorified him not as God, neither were thankful; but became vain in their imaginations, and their foolish heart was darkened. Professing themselves to be wise, they became fools...
Romans 1:21, 22

The most religious people on earth are those who claim not to have any religion. Dogmatic, intolerant, and bigoted, they refuse to allow anyone to so much as speak their opposition. Yet these same people demand political power and tax support. The mildest opposition, such as the mere mention of Intelligent Design (not God), has blacklisted tenured professors. Just two parents in a middle school in Texas made the national news by objecting to Gideon Bibles placed, without comment, on a table outside the school office.[1] Such people dishonestly claim that they are not religious and "religion" is a group of mythologies. The truth is that they are the ones promoting mythology. In every aspect of life they promote this mythology with unproven dogmatic assertions under the guise of "Science" vocabulary. After hijacking the word "Science," they use the courts to elevate their misuse of the term to an established religion.

Science is the study of the world around us, the use of the experimental method and the improvement of our lives through the application of technology. It is divided into various academic disciplines such as Chemistry, Physics, Mathematics and Biology. However, what the federal courts, the Academic community and the mainstream Western media mean by science is uniformitarianism. It is the cosmological foundation of the religion of Secular Humanism. "Since the fathers fell asleep, all things continue as they were from the beginning of the creation" (II Peter 3:4). This concise description of Uniformitarianism clearly shows that it is completely and entirely a religious belief in antiscientific myths.

Secular Humanists use words which have been in the English language for hundreds of years but give them "new" meanings. However, "there is no new thing under the sun" (Ecclesiastes 1:9, KJV). The words believe, faith and trust are all historic judicial terms and they also form the foundation of the true scientific method. What Secular Humanists promote as their version of the scientific method consists of preconceptions, presuppositions and assumptions. It is the opposite of an open mind.

A true open mind is founded in belief, faith and trust. The historic meaning of believe is to perceive or understand with the mind and then make an informed decision.[2] The most basic use of the word believe which the average American would understand is that of a juror in court. Which witness do you believe? Which piece of evidence is believable? A synonym would be the word credible. When we believe something or someone and then act on that belief, that is faith. The active part of belief is faith. The passive part of belief is trust. Suppose your brother says that he will drive you to the doctor. If you believe him, then you understand what he says and you make a decision to get ready. If you get in the vehicle with him, that is faith. You act on your belief. When you sit in the vehicle as he drives, that is trust, a passive reliance on what you have proven true. You trust in his driving skills. You trust in the vehicle. You trust the roads, etc. Everything we do is a combination of belief, faith or trust. By restoring their historic definitions, belief, faith and trust re-emerge as the clear language of true experimental science. These terms were deliberately segregated from science to deceive people into believing Secular Humanism.

Liberals, Secular Humanists and materialists, however, use the word "belief" as a synonym for a philosophical position, just an opinion. Faith and trust to them are metaphysical words which mean different things to different people. And this is just the tip of an enormous iceberg. Secular Humanists have redefined hundreds of words to support their religion, such as sin, judgment and anthropology. A conversation with them can be very difficult since they use historical English words but mean something entirely different.

The traditional role of religion is to place priesthood as intermediary between God and man. The traditional role of an establishment of religion places the government in that intermediary role between God and man. In the Middle Ages the Roman Catholic Church put itself between man and God, as other religions have in the past. Johann Tetzel, a "professional pardoner," sold indulgences representing forgiveness for sins in Germany. Indulgences were based on the "storehouse" of good works believed to exist because of the sacrifice of Christ and the good deeds and prayers of past saints. Tetzel was said to promise that, "As soon as a coin in the coffer rings, a soul from purgatory springs."[3]

Selling indulgences was the final act of many which brought on the Reformation. People wouldn't have bought them if they hadn't believed the Catholic Church alone could placate God on their behalf. Martin Luther convinced the princes of Germany that they did not need to send their money to Rome because they could go to God directly. Rome sent armies to collect the money.

Even Modern Roman Catholics who do not believe that their church today claims to stand between them and God have to admit that the medieval Roman Catholic Church did.

The combined power of Church and State restricted personal worship, scientific study and access to historical truth. Today Secular Humanism has done the same by removing foundational truths from education. It excludes study and discovery that contradicts uniformitarianism. It rewrites history to undermine morality and freedom of expression.

The union between the medieval Romanist church and the state came to an end in two ways. In Southern Europe during the Renaissance, art, architecture, literature, and learning opened up to all men, not just those who were part of the church and state system. The Renaissance left the power intact, however. In Northern Europe, the Reformation abolished the need for a church like Rome through the great affirmations of the Reformation: The Scriptures are the absolute authority; Justification is by faith alone apart from works; and every believer is his own priest with direct access to God. The Reformation made a special priesthood class unnecessary because men could pray directly to God and read His Word on their own.

The medieval Roman Catholic Church kept the Scriptures almost exclusively in Latin to prevent ordinary people from studying them, forcing people to come to the priest. The priest would not only tell them what the Scriptures said, but he also mingled that with the church's interpretation. In order for ordinary people who did not know Latin to read the Bible for themselves, the Scriptures had to be translated into the language of the ordinary people. Translation work by Reformers was essential to enable ordinary men to read the Scriptures for themselves, even though it was punishable by death under the Church-State system. The Renaissance and the Reformation worked together in the development of moveable type to make printing and distribution of translations of the Scriptures easier. Renaissance scholars revived interest in studying forgotten manuscripts and making translations into the vernacular. Erasmus's Greek New Testament provided a basis for more accurate translations of the Scriptures.

The Medieval Romanist Church-State system took away freedom by forcing man to rely on and accept its teachings. The Renaissance and the Reformation restored freedom by returning art, science, and all forms of learning to ordinary people. In particular the people were able to worship God as the Scriptures taught, without Church-State control. Modern western culture, and American culture in particular, was founded on this religious freedom. American culture is more Christian than European cultures, but neither of these cultures can survive if the foundation of religious freedom is destroyed.

It is this Christian foundation of religious freedom which is the real target of Secular Humanists. These Secular Humanists have taken outrageous liberties in their unrelenting quest to replace religious freedom with their established religion of Secular Humanism, which they incorrectly call science or Natural Law. Their major tool is the US court system. Sympathetic US courts have consistently supported Secular Humanism by using every possible opportunity to replace the word religion with the ancient concept of Natural Law. However, since Natural Law has been used so many different ways, the courts had to standardize the term Natural Law. Their version of Natural Law goes back to Plato's *Republic.* Though Plato never used the phrase "natural law" in his *Republic,* translator Benjamin Jowett's notes state that, "Plato among the Greeks, like Bacon among the moderns, was the first who conceived a method of knowledge... "[4] Plato's *Republic* is at least the foundation of modern Natural Law, if not the detailed finished product. Together with Aristotle, Plato is supposed by secularists to have laid the foundation for learning and development of the Sciences. This is really is essence of Natural Law.

Jowett goes on to say that Plato provided for a means to spread his method of acquiring knowledge. "In the ideal State which is constructed by Socrates, the first care of the rulers is to be education."[4] Jowett makes it clear that Socrates meant to impart much more than mere academic knowledge, just as Natural Law means to teach more than mere Science. Socrates promoted "the conception of a higher State, in which 'no man calls anything his own,' and in which there is neither 'marrying nor giving in marriage,' and 'kings are philosophers' and 'philosophers are kings;' and there is another and higher education, intellectual as well as moral and religious, of science as well as of art, and not of youth only but of the whole of life."[4]

Many know that Plato in his *Republic* based his state on a philosopher/king. Few, however, are aware that he believed in communism and free love and that these two "natural" principles were to be foundational principles of the state.

Though the preceding condensation by Benjamin Jowett is an excellent job, as you can read for yourself, the actual words of Socrates, as quoted by Plato, are much longer and more difficult to understand. "None of them will have anything specially his or her own." "... Their legislator, having selected the men, will now select the women and give them to them [the legislator gives selected women to selected men]... they must live in common houses and meet at common meals ... they will be together ... And so they will be drawn by a necessity of their natures to have intercourse with each other..." "...

Until philosophers are kings, or the kings and princes ... have the spirit and power of philosophy, and political greatness and wisdom meet in one ... cities will never have rest from their evils."[5]

The philosopher/king, according to Socrates, was to lay these foundational ideas through education. Though he did not use the phrase "establishment of religion," Plato clearly advocated an established religion. It was to be put in place by a philosopher/king through education based on a state where "no man calls anything his own" and where there is neither "marrying nor giving in marriage." Though this education would begin with children, it would continue throughout a person's entire life. This is the Natural Law which the US Court system has imposed.

The US needs to disestablish its Establishment of Religion and reestablish religious freedom. In the 1800's churches which tried to break away from the Church of England were called disestablishmentarians. The people who fought against the disestablishment of those churches within the Church of England in the 1800s were called Antidisestablishmentarians. Today, the mainstream media, liberal politicians, the academic community, the liberal courts and all others who file lawsuits, blacklist, fire, refuse to hire, tax, legislate against, libel, slander and do whatever is necessary to maintain their positions of privilege and power are modern Antidisestablishmentarians.

---

1 (No author) "Parents Fuming as Texas Schools Let Gideons Provide Bibles to Students," Tuesday, May 19, 2009, *Fox News.com*. "A spokeswoman for the school district said that a number of materials are made available to students this way, including newspapers, camp brochures and tutoring pamphlets. College and military recruitment information is available all year

long. The Gideon Bibles were made available for just one day. 'We have to handle this request in the same manner as other requests to distribute non-school literature – in a view-point neutral manner,' Shana Wortham, director of communications for the district, wrote in an e-mail to *FoxNews.com.*

2 Alexander Hamilton, in an 1802 letter to James Bayard. "I have carefully examined the evidences of the Christian religion, and if I was sitting as a juror upon its authenticity I would un-hesitatingly give my verdict in its favor. I can prove its truth as clearly as any proposition ever submitted to the mind of man."

3 Philip Schaff, *History of the Christian Church,* Volume 7, "The Reformation," Charles Scribner's Sons, 1910.

4 Plato, *The Republic* (c. 360 B.C.), translated by Benjamin Jowett over a period of 30 years until his death in 1893, completed posthumously by Lewis Campbell. (Introductory material (in double quotes) and paraphrases of Plato's ideas (in single quotes) were written by Jowett.)

5 Plato, *The Republic*, Book Five Dialogue excerpts among Socrates, Adeimantus, Glaucon and Thrasymachus have been placed in parentheses within Jowett's introductory material.

Introduction

Facts are stubborn things; and whatever may be our wishes, our inclinations, or the dictates of our passion, they cannot alter the state of facts and evidence.[1]
John Adams

Sometime in the early twentieth century, Secular Humanist indoctrination convinced almost everyone in the United States that "an establishment of religion" in the first phrase of the first amendment of the United States Constitution is vague and can mean just about anything. "The state of the facts and evidence," as John Adams so eloquently put it, is the exact opposite.

Section One of this work documents what the founders meant by the phrase "an establishment of religion." The Founding Fathers made as clear a statement as the English language permitted. The Constitution of the United States is founded on English law and to a lesser extent, various European laws, especially German and Dutch. In each of these countries, an Establishment of Religion was the collection of taxes to support education, welfare and public worship. The various governments appointed the teachers, welfare workers and pastors and expected these people to support the government in turn.

The original state constitutions not only permitted, but openly encouraged establishments of religion, especially in the areas of welfare and education. The foundation of the US Constitution is the fact that federal government was to have no control whatsoever in these areas. Their concept of a separation of Church and State was the exact opposite of what the courts have rammed down our throats for the past hundred years. The church should have the right to pray and teach without any federal intervention whatsoever. Judges should have the right to post any Scriptures they want. The courts should have no authority whatsoever to comment. Removing a state judge from office for posting the Ten Commandments is not merely an Establishment of Religion. It is the Inquisition.

Section Two documents the foundations of Secular Humanism and how it grew to become America's Establishment of Religion. The words "Secular Humanism" come from various groups in the 1950's. The phrase "Secular Humanist" is found in court documents to describe this set of beliefs. Secular Humanism is as old as civilization, but the primary foundation of twenty first century Secular Humanism is Plato's *Republic*. In America, Secular Humanism can be said to have originated with Thomas Paine. Secular Humanism has specific beliefs which are written down in various manifestos. Like Christianity, Islam and Judaism, Secular Humanism has many variations. Though Secular Humanists do not like the term, the most accurate words to describe these variants are "sects" or "denominations." Like Christians, Muslims and Jews, many Secular Humanist denominations do not get along with one another. Therefore, we have attempted to point out the beliefs which have the greatest agreement.

Section Three defines science, since Secular Humanists claim that science separates them from all other religions. Since true science is founded in the belief, faith and trust of the Bible, all of these words are defined carefully and in detail. In the Bible, belief, faith and trust are legal terms. Believe means to examine the evidence and come to a reasoned conclusion. Action taken on that belief is faith. Trust is the passive version of faith.

The Scientific Method is the biblical version of belief, faith and trust applied to the material world which God created for us. In the Bible, the Scientific Method recognizes that God is the creator, that we are required to be responsible managers of the material world God has given us, and that there is a final judgment after death which will include how well we managed the gifts God allowed us to use.

Our book concludes with Section Four, the results of having Secular Humanism as an Establishment of Religion. With the exception of America's founding documents and the ancient documents such as Plato, Plutarch and Genesis, hundreds of other quotes could easily be substituted for the quotes that appear here. There is nothing new or unique in this book. It is a combination of what used to be common knowledge in America before Secular Humanism took over and destroyed the education system and current events. If we were to start over today, we would pull different stories from the daily news. Though the individual stories would be different, the points would be the same. "There is nothing new under the sun" (Ecclesiastes 1:9). Or to state the same thing another way, the more things change, the more they stay the same.

America's Established Religion is Secular Humanism. This work is dedicated to exposing, defining and disestablishing it.

---

1 John Adams, "Argument in defence of the [English] soldiers in the Boston Massacre trial," December 1770.

2 "Alabama's Judicial Ethics Panel removed Chief Justice Roy Moore from office Thursday for defying a Federal judge's order to move a ten commandments

monument from the State Supreme Court building." Friday, November 14, 2003. Posted 6:56 AM Eastern time. *CNN.com*

Section One: What Is an Establishment of Religion?

1. Why Go to The American Wilderness?

Blessed are they which are persecuted for righteousness' sake. Blessed are ye, when men shall say all manner of evil against you falsely, for my sake. Rejoice, great is your reward in heaven.
Matthew 5:10-12 KJV

If you were born in the Middle Ages, you would be locked into a rigid class system with little hope of escape. If you were a Gypsy or a Jew, you would have little or no chance of owning land or even obtaining a job. If you were a minor noble, you would live where you were born, with the same job your father had. You might even be given a chance for an education. Most of all, you would be thankful you weren't a serf. At least you would have clothes.

A serf was lower than a slave. A slave was at least valuable property. A serf was considered part of the land. A serf was never educated, had various cruel nobles lording over him during his very brief life. His only real hope was a life after this one.

The Medieval European Church, however, forced everyone to come to it to find out what the Bible said. The only Bible available was handwritten and in Latin. The average Medieval European Church did not even have a Latin translation. The few churches with a Latin Bible had the massive book chained to the front of the church. It really did not matter, since only the clergy could read it anyway.

Only the Established Religion could "properly" interpret the Scriptures and the Established Religion took every measure possible to retain their position of power and prestige. This restricted access to God. The Established Religion put itself between God and man. At the height of her power, the Roman Pope Innocent III even interdicted England, telling every man, woman and child in England that they could not speak to God unless their king, King John, submitted to Rome.

Almost two hundred years later, one poor English parson, John Wycliffe, recovering from a near-fatal illness and realizing how short life could be, changed that by translating the Bible into the language of his people. His translation of the Bible into English from Latin brought the wrath of the established church of England down on him.

> *[When]... Wickliffe ... set about ... the translation ... he published a tract, wherein he showed the necessity of it. The zeal of the bishops to suppress the Scriptures greatly promoted its sale, and they who were not able to purchase copies, procured transcripts of particular Gospels or Epistles. Afterward, ... it was a common practice to fasten about the neck of the condemned heretic [before burning him at the stake] such of these scraps of Scripture as were found in his possession, which generally shared his fate.*[1]

Oxford Professor John Wycliffe was called the morning star of the Reformation. Wycliffe impressed even a devout Catholic like Geoffrey Chaucer. In *The Canterbury Tales*, Chaucer based his Poor Parson character on Wycliffe, contrasting him with the fat and flourishing members of the Church who thrived on what Wycliffe condemned. Chaucer was not afraid to point out the flaws and hypocrisy of the Church using people like the Pardoner, the Prioress and the Friar. The following is a modern English version of Chaucer's prologue description of the Poor Parson.

There was a good man of religion, too,
A country parson, poor, I warrant you;
But rich he was in holy thought and work.
He was a learned man also, a clerk,
Who Christ's own gospel truly sought to preach;
Devoutly his parishioners would he teach.

...

There is nowhere a better priest, I trow.
He had no thirst for pomp or reverence,
Nor made himself a special, spiced conscience,
But Christ's own lore, and His apostles' twelve
He taught, but first he followed it himself.[2]

Wycliffe's basic translation of the Bible from the Latin Vulgate was completed. He went home to be with his Lord in heaven before he could be burned at the stake. Although Rome, the established church of the time, was restrained in his lifetime from harming him, the Church could not let his bones rest in peace. On October 8, 1427, on order of the Council of Constance (the same Council that burned John Hus at the stake), Wycliffe's body was exhumed, his bones burned, and the ashes strewn on the River Swift.

> *They burnt his bones to ashes and cast them into the Swift, a neighboring brook running hard by. Thus the brook conveyed his ashes into the Avon, the Avon into the Severn, the Severn into the narrow seas and they into the main ocean. And so the ashes of Wyclif are symbolic of his doctrine, which is now spread throughout the world.*[3]

Foxe also gives an account of William Tyndale, an Englishman living in Antwerp during the reign of the English King Henry VIII 150 years later. He was the first man to translate the Bible into English from the original Greek and Hebrew.

> *... The English clergy (... should have been the guides ...) [but instead tried] to drive the people from the knowledge of the Scripture, which neither they would translate themselves, nor yet abide it to be translated of others; ... that the world being kept still in darkness, they might [control] the ... people through ... false doctrine, to satisfy their ambition [to be] above king and emperor.*
>
> *[Tyndale] was condemned by ... the emperor's decree, ... at Augsburg. ... He was ... consumed with fire, at the town of Vilvorde, A.D. 1536; crying ... "Lord! Open the king of England's eyes."*
>
> *During the time of his imprisonment ... he converted, it is said, his keeper, the keeper's daughter, and others of his household.*[1]

Later the English Queen Mary Tudor (reigned 1553-1558), daughter of Henry VIII, known as Bloody Mary, executed everyone in positions of leadership who refused to convert to Roman Catholicism. By the grace of God, she only reigned five years. However, during this brief reign, about three hundred were burned at the stake and thousands imprisoned.

This is the world into which William Bradford was born. His diary, Of Plymouth Plantation, written c. AD 1630, encompasses the whole of his experiences with the pilgrims: their resolution, their preparations, and their journey and early settlement years. It continues the thread of Foxe's chronicles and echoes his account of persecutions that forced the faithful to flee England. It includes the deadly enemies of "contention" and "discord" within the churches of the Reformation.

... He [Satan] then began another kind of war ... contention and ... discord and bitter enmity amongst the ... reformed ... When he could not prevail ... against the principal doctrines ... he bent his force against the holy discipline and outward regiment ... by which those holy doctrines should be conserved [among the] people of God.

... Besides those worthy martyrs ... burned in Queen Mary's days ... 800 ... became several congregations at Wesel, Frankfort, Basel, Emden, Markpurge, Strasburg and Geneva, etc. Those at Frankfort began that bitter war ... about the ceremonies and service book, and other popish and antichristian stuff... Which the better part sought, according to the purity of the gospel, to ... abandon. ... The other part ... for their own ... advancements, sought ... to ... defend.

The one side labored to have the right worship of God and discipline of Christ ... without the mixture of men's inventions; ... ruled by the laws of God's Word, ... by those officers of Pastors, Teachers and Elders ... according to the Scriptures. The other party, ... endeavored to have the episcopal dignity ... with all those courts, canons and ceremonies, ... with ... revenues ... [which] upheld their antichristian greatness and enabled them ... to persecute the poor servants of God. ... Neither the honor of God, the common persecution, nor the meditation of Mr. Calvin ... could prevail with those thus episcopally minded; ... to charge ... their chief opposers with rebellion and high treason against the Emperor....

> *... Many of them being preferred to bishoprics and other promotions [when returning under Elizabeth] ... that inveterate hatred against the holy discipline of Christ in His church hath continued ... incensing the Queen and State against it [the more biblically-based system of reform] ... as dangerous for the commonwealth; ... it was most needful that the fundamental points of religion should be preached ... to win the weak and ignorant they might retain divers harmless ceremonies.*[4]

Under the 1559 Act of Uniformity, it was a crime to miss a Sunday church service or a holy day in an Established Church. Only the Church of England provided formal education or welfare to the poor. This was so important to the English monarchy that Queen Elizabeth's successor, James VI of Scotland, when he ascended the English throne in 1603 and became James I, said, "No Bishop, no King." The fines might seem small to us, but to these extremely poor Englishmen, paying these often meant going hungry. Failure to pay the fine meant imprisonment. The fines increased and imprisonment lengthened for conducting unofficial services. Two pastors of the English Separatists, Henry Barrowe and John Greenwood, were executed by Queen Elizabeth for sedition in 1593.

Her successor, James I, intensified persecution of Separatists. One Separatist congregation fled to Amsterdam because, as William Bradford later wrote in *Of Plymouth Plantation:*

> *But after these things they could not long continue in any peaceable condition, but were hunted & persecuted on every side, so as their former afflictions were but as flea-bitings in comparison of these which now came upon them. For some were taken & clapt up in prison, others had their houses besett & watcht*

> *night and day, & hardly escaped their hands; and ye most were faine to flie & leave their howses & habitations, and the means of their livelehood.*[4]

Remember, that "their former afflictions" which now seemed "as flea-bitings in comparison of these which now came upon them" saw two of their pastors executed.

The Separatists had problems from the beginning in Amsterdam, but two of the most important reasons for leaving for the New World were the well-founded fears both of the loss of their children to worldliness and also fear for their future safety. The Dutch had passed new laws somewhat like the English Acts of Uniformity. There were physical assaults such as the stoning of James Chilton and his daughter just before the family left for New World. In 1619, James Chilton (aged 63) and his oldest daughter Isabella were caught in the middle of an anti-Arminian riot in Leiden. When the rioters learned of their beliefs, they were considered fair targets for violence. Chilton was hit in the head with a stone, requiring the services of the town surgeon Jacob Hey.[1] But their greatest concern was potential war with Spain when a Dutch treaty would expire in 1621.

Though a few English Separatists prospered in Amsterdam, most were unable to find work. The Pilgrims gladly accepted the risks in sailing to the New World for freedom of religion.

In 1620 a small ship named the *Mayflower* brought these believers to Cape Cod, Massachusetts. Even though many died that winter, more Separatists, or Pilgrims, came. The reason for this journey is highly censored by the 20th Century American Establishment of Religion. Teachers might be permitted to mention that these English Separatists came to America for religious freedom. But America's Established Church will not permit anyone to say what religious freedom meant to the pilgrims.[5]

These pilgrims were not a group of wild-eyed fanatics, as many claim.[6] One of the major charges against them of being irresponsible was the time of year they left. William Brewster, one of their members, had written numerous pamphlets condemning the Church of England, and the Dutch government had made arrangements to hand him over to the English authorities. If they had waited until the following spring, William Brewster would certainly have been handed over to the English authorities and executed. The travelers did, however, wait until they thought the hurricane season had ended. It is also possible that they misunderstood the climate difference at Plymouth since it was the same latitude they came from. They might not have known about the much harsher weather. It is also possible that they were blown off course. If they had followed their charter, they would have landed further south. Their preparations for the voyage can be seen in the possessions of one man who died during the voyage. His belongings were inventoried for division and included 13 pairs of boots and 13 pairs of shoes. These people were prepared for an extended period living in primitive conditions. They brought a boat called a *shallope* for exploring and for transporting goods. The supplies they brought even included manufactured goods sufficient to repair the *Mayflower* when it was damaged in the unseasonable storm at sea.

Another common misunderstanding is the *Mayflower* itself. She was registered as a boat of 180 tunnes. Tunnes, however, are not tons (2000 lbs). A tunne was a 256-gallon wine cask. The total weight was slightly more than one ton but each cask took up considerably more space than sacks of similar weight. The ship was definitely larger than modern models depict it. It could have been as much as one-third larger. The *Mayflower* made regular runs from England to the Netherlands and the pilgrims were probably already familiar with it. Sailors of that time designated ships as "sweet" and "sour." A sweet ship was relatively clean and free from disease. Sour ships were looked upon as unsafe to sail on. Because the *Mayflower* was normally a wine ship it was considered "sweet." The spillage of wine actually had a certain cleansing effect because of the antiseptic properties of the alcohol.

Complaints are often made against the ship's crew as well. Many sources say the ship's chief officer was only a master and therefore not as qualified as a "true" captain would have been. At that time, however, the term Captain was used only for officers of the British navy. The title Master is the only correct title for what we would think of as a Captain of a commercial ship. The Master of the *Mayflower* is sometimes portrayed as inexperienced for sailing at this time. A man of the same name, however, and probably the same man, is recorded as designing a ship for royal navy. The storm at sea was unusual for that time of year and was probably a hurricane. The *Mayflower* would have sunk if a crew as inexperienced as some claim had manned it. Also, relationships between the seamen and the Separatists were friendly. Upon arrival, the Separatists used their boat to help re-supply the *Mayflower* with fresh water for the return voyage. The length of time recorded for the Atlantic crossing meant that the *Mayflower* was a fast ship for that time period.

Only two animals, dogs which were to aid with hunting in the new world, were carried along. One separatist lamented that their new home would have been a paradise indeed if they had been able to bring livestock, but they were unable to bring cattle because of the number of passengers. As it was, conditions were so crowded single men had to sleep on the shallope on deck.[7]

These are not actions or equipment of fanatics but well-prepared well-thought-out actions of desperate but realistic people. One of their leaders throughout this time, William Bradford wrote of their experiences in his Of Plymouth Plantation. It is now known as their official log as well as his diary.

> *... They were encountered many times with cross winds, and met with many fierce storms, ... and her upper works made very leaky; and one of the main beams in the mid ships was bowed and cracked, ... and rather to return then to cast themselves into a desperate and inevitable peril. ... The master and others affirmed they knew the ship to be strong and firm under water; and for the buckling of the main beam, there was a great iron screw the passengers brought out of Holland, which would raise the beam into his place... So they committed themselves to the will of God, and resolved to proceed. In sundry of these storms the winds were so fierce, and the seas so high, as they could not bear a knot of sail ... in a mighty storm, a lusty young man (called John Howland)... was ... thrown into the sea; but it pleased God that he caught hold ... till he was hauled up ... with a boat hook ... yet he lived many years after, and became a profitable member both in church and commonwealth. In all this voyage there died but one of the passengers ... After long beating at sea they fell with that land which is called Cape Cod; ... they got into the Cape-harbor where they rid in safety.*
>
> *Being thus arrived in a good harbor, and brought safe to land, they fell upon their knees and blessed the God of Heaven who had brought them over the fast and furious ocean,*

> *and delivered them from all the perils and miseries thereof, again to set their feet on the firm and stable earth, their proper element.*[4]

Freedom of religion meant far more to them than it does to us today. It included the ability to earn a living without being turned away from a job because of what they believed. They could keep what little food they had instead of watching the government take it from them. The government could neither take their children from them nor forcibly indoctrinate them against their parents' beliefs. The government would no longer have the power to confiscate their property because they believed the Bible. They would be able to protect themselves from physical assault without being charged with a crime. They would be able to band together to protect themselves from outside enemies. No one would be able to seize their title, rank, or livelihoods because of their beliefs.

These fears of the English government were valid. The Established Church of England was given the power of enforcement, but its methods of doing so violated already existing laws, laws which went back to the *Magna Carta.*

> *In the first place we grant to God and confirm by this our present charter for ourselves and our heirs in perpetuity that the English Church is to be free and to have all its rights fully and its liberties entirely.*[8]

Signed by King John of England, this opening to the *Magna Carta* originally meant that the English Church would be free from the English Crown in perpetuity, that is, forever. King John would no longer appoint his own Archbishop of Canterbury and make the English Church an arm of the English government. The pope in Rome sided with the English Church, which was Roman Catholic in name at that time, though many of its churches, such as those in Ireland, were among the most biblical in the world.

Innocent III interdicted England and forced King John into relinquishing his control over the English Church. These Acts of Uniformity actually helped to split England. The first group included those who opposed the Crown's control of the Church and remained loyal to Rome. Though there is no consensus of belief from this time period, this seems to be the smallest group because anyone who favored Rome usually left the country. The Spanish attempted to invade England to force Catholicism on them and the average Englishman viewed anyone who supported Rome as a traitor.

Second were people loyal to the English Church. The vast majority of Englishmen fell into this group. These Englishmen supporting the English Church fell into two groups, those who more or less wanted things left alone and those who wanted to continue to reform or purify the English Church. These people who wanted continued reform were also known as Puritans.

The third and last group was known as Separatists. Like those who supported Rome, they were just a small group. They believed that the English Church was too corrupt to salvage, so they separated from it and formed their own congregations. They would have passed into obscurity, except for the fact that they sailed to the New World and became Americans.

John Winthrop, governor of the Massachusetts Bay Colony, was not a Separatist, but a Puritan. He set out for the New World, intending to help establish a colony founded as an establishment of the Church of England, yet far enough away from the conflicts in England that his fellow Puritans could indeed attempt to "purify" the church that already existed. Founder of the Colony of Massachusetts Bay, John Winthrop was a preacher first and a skilled statesman next. The main founding document of his colony is a sermon, "A Model of Christian Charity," written as he crossed the Atlantic.

> *Thus stands the cause between God and us. We are entered into covenant ... The Lord hath given us leave to draw our own articles. ... We have hereupon besought Him of favor and blessing. Now if the Lord shall ... bring us in peace to the place ... He ratified this covenant and sealed our commission, and will expect a strict performance ... but if we shall neglect the observation ... and, dissembling with our God, ... the Lord will surely break out in wrath against us ... and make us know the price of the breach of such a covenant.*
>
> *Now the only way to avoid this shipwreck, ... is to follow the counsel of Micah, to do justly, to love mercy, to walk humbly with our God. For this end, we must be knit together, in this work, as one man. ... We must be willing to abridge ourselves of our superfluities, for the supply of others' necessities. We must uphold a familiar commerce together in all meekness, gentleness, patience and liberality. We must ... make others' conditions our own; rejoice together, mourn together, labor and suffer together, ... as members of the same body. So shall we keep the unity of the spirit in the bond of peace. The Lord will be our God, and delight to dwell among us, as His own people, and will command a blessing upon us in all our ways, so that we shall see much more of His wisdom, power, goodness and truth, than formerly we have been acquainted with. ... He shall make us a praise and glory that men shall say of succeeding plantations, "may the Lord make it like that of New England." For we must consider that we shall be as a city upon a hill.*

> *The eyes of all people are upon us. So that if we shall deal falsely with our God ... we shall be made a story and a by-word through the world. We shall open the mouths of enemies to speak evil of the ways of God ... We shall shame ... God's worthy servants,... their prayers [will] be turned into curses ... till we be consumed out of the good land whither we are going.*
>
> *... "Beloved, there is now set before us life and death, good and evil," ... love the Lord our God, and to love one another, to walk in his ways and to keep his Commandments and ... our Covenant with Him, that we may live and be multiplied, and that the Lord our God may bless us ... But if our hearts shall turn away, ... it is propounded unto us this day, we shall surely perish...*
>
> *Therefore let us choose life,*
> *that we and our seed may live,*
> *by obeying His voice and cleaving to Him,*
> *for He is our life and our prosperity.*[9]

The phrase "A City On a Hill," has been used to describe America as a whole as a model of liberty and justice. Yet the phrase originates in Scripture and application is made here to the founding of Massachusetts Bay Colony. This seems an odd founding document, yet John Winthrop used "A Model of Christian Charity" to establish the government of the Massachusetts Bay Colony. Don't dismiss it as a mere sermon. It explains that the colonists could make any conditions of government they wished, draw their own articles. God in turn would hear their prayers and give them safety and success on one condition. The Puritans had to fulfill what they had promised, what every man in his right mind would pray his government would do. ... "To do justly, to love mercy, to walk humbly with our God."

If they strayed from that path, consequences would surely follow. ...

> *For we must consider that we shall be as a city upon a hill. The eyes of all people are upon us. So that if we shall deal falsely with our God in this work we have undertaken, and so cause Him to withdraw His present help from us, we shall be made a story and a by-word through the world.*[9]

Consider that the eyes of all the world were on America at the time of its forming, and that many still believe America should be the best and brightest nation on Earth. But we have not kept our covenant, the founding principles. By allowing Secular Humanism to overrun true faith, we must fear the withdrawal of God's help. Has it already happened?

Roger Williams originally came to the New World to serve in the pastorate in Massachusetts but decided to found his own colony after contending with various congregations over the issue of worldliness in the church. He was a preacher and founder of the colony of Rhode Island. He befriended the Indians and tried to treat them humanely, protecting them from forced conversion and paying them for their lands. He believed civil authorities should have no power over churches, an unpopular view in the established church. His beliefs were Calvinistic and often associated with Baptists.

> *First the faithful labors of many Witnesses of Jesus Christ, ... proving, that the ... Jews ... and the Church of the Christians ... were both separate from the world; ... when they have opened a gap in the ... wall of Separation between the Garden of the Church and the Wilderness of the world, God ... broke down the wall itself, removed the Candlestick, and made his Garden a Wilderness, ... if he will ever*

> *please to restore his Garden and Paradise again, it must ... be walled in peculiarly unto Himself from the world, and that all ... saved out of the world are to be transplanted out ... and added unto His Church or Garden.*[10]

This is the origin of Thomas Jefferson's "wall of separation" principle. Roger Williams warned the church against breaking a hole through God's surrounding wall and polluting itself by worldly compromise. God had created the wall to protect the church, to help it thrive in the garden He had prepared. When the church violated His protection, God withdrew it and left the church to be overwhelmed by the world. Jefferson envisioned the government as protecting the church and helping it to thrive, not walling it off. Ironically, the wall has once again been penetrated by the church's worldliness. Believers have invited humanism into their churches and now Secular Humanism is free to wall true belief off from the protection of government and starve it to death. Roger Williams also said:

> *The civil state is bound before God to take off that ... yoke of soul oppression, and to proclaim ... liberty ... to choose and maintain what worship and ministry their ... consciences are persuaded of; ... to preserve the common freedom and peace; ... most suiting with the piety and Christianity of the Holy Testament of Christ Jesus.*
>
> *The civil state is ... to provide ... for the security of all ... consciences, in their respective ... worshipings... and that civil peace ... be maintained among the chief opposers and dissenters.*[10]

Roger Williams believed the state had only two legitimate functions with regard to religious or "soul liberty." It must remove any restrictions against that freedom, and it must provide protection for that liberty. These were the two ideas in the minds of the framers when they set up the federal government. Remove restrictions, provide protection. Nothing else.

This dream of Roger Williams was impossible in England. But it had more than one root in the New World. The Englishman William Penn was given land in the new world by the English Crown to pay off old world debts. As a wealthy proprietor of the province of Pennsylvania, William Penn was believed to be immune from persecution. However, William Penn was a Quaker, against the wishes of his family and class. He was put on trial while still in England. This trial gave good cause to all who were not part of England's Established Religion to fear and dread the intolerance of England toward religions not part of the Establishment. The following lengthy excerpts from Penn's personal transcript of that trial show the state of British "justice" at the time of the settlement of the new world. Please compare this trial to the excerpts from American trials in section two and those in Appendix One, Court Cases. Also note the oath the jurors were sworn to and the irony of the later behavior of the court in light of its wording.

The Form of the OATH.
"You shall well and truly Try, and true
Deliverance make betwixt our Sovereign
Lord the King, and the Prisoners at the Bar, according
to your Evidence.
So help you God."

> *That William Penn, Gent. and William Mead, late of London, ... with divers other Persons to the Jurors unknown, to the Number of 300, the 14th Day of August, in the 22d Year of the King, about Eleven of the Clock in the Forenoon, the same Day, with Force and Arms, ... in the Street called Gracechurch-Street, unlawfully*

> *and tumultuously did Assemble and Congregate themselves together ... did take upon himself to Preach and Speak, ... unto the aforesaid William Mead, and other Persons there, ... by Reason whereof a great Concourse and Tumult of People ... did remain and continue, in contempt of the said Lord the King, and of his Law, to the great Disturbance of his Peace; to the great Terror and Disturbance of many of his Liege People and Subjects....*
>
> *What say you, William Penn and William Mead, are you Guilty, as you stand indicted, in Manner and Form, as aforesaid, or Not Guilty?*[11]

William Penn and William Mead were charged with conspiracy to use force of arms to create a disturbance of the peace. The authorities closed his church and he was forced to deliver his sermon outside the building in the street. The accusation was read aloud and Penn compelled to plead guilty or not guilty. It was a lengthy charge and he asked for a copy, but was denied this until he had pleaded. He asked for reassurance that pleading before reading the charge would not result in any denial of rights.

> *COURT. No Advantage shall be taken against you; you shall have Liberty; you shall be heard.*
>
> *PEN. Then I plead Not guilty ... We confess our selves to be so far from recanting, or declining to vindicate the Assembling of our selves to Preach, Pray, or Worship the Eternal, Holy, Just God, that we declare to all the World, that we do believe it to be our indispensable Duty, to meet incessantly upon so good an Account; nor shall all the Powers upon Earth be able to*

divert us from reverencing and adoring our God who made it.

BROWN. You are not here for worshipping God, but for breaking the Law; you do yourselves a great deal of Wrong in going on in that Discourse.

PEN. I affirm I have broken no Law, nor am I guilty of the Indictment that is laid to my Charge; and to the End the Bench, the Jury, and my self, with these that hear us, ... I desire you would let me know by what Law it is you prosecute me, ... Shall I plead to an Indictment that hath no Foundation in Law? ... Why should you decline to produce that Law, since it will be impossible for the Jury to ... bring in their Verdict, who have not the Law produced, by which they should measure the Truth of this Indictment, and [my] Guilt ...?

REC. You are a sawcy Fellow, speak to the Indictment.

[Sidenote: Obser. At this time several upon the Bench urged hard upon the Prisoner to bear him down.] (Men grabbed him and forced him, possibly onto his knees, possibly flat on the floor.)

PEN. ... It is my place to speak to Matter of Law; I am arraign'd a Prisoner; my Liberty, ... is now concerned:

You are many Mouths and Ears against me... I say again, unless you shew me, and the People, the Law you ground your Indictment upon, I shall take it for granted your Proceedings are meerly Arbitrary.

REC. Upon the Common Law.

> *PEN. Where is that Common Law? ... Must I therefore be taken away because I plead for the Fundamental Laws of _England_? However, this I leave upon your Consciences, who are of the Jury (and my sole Judges) that if these Ancient Fundamental Laws, which relate to Liberty and Property, and (are not limited to particular Persuasions in Matters of Religion) must not be indispensably maintained and observed.*[11]

The court refuses to quote a specific law, claiming that many years of oral tradition must be studied, and states that it is impossible to pull out the one charge. Penn argues that it is not common law if it is so difficult to come up with. He is accused of wasting the court's time, ordered to plead, and he is finally placed in bail-dock, some form of imprisonment out of sight of the proceedings. Mead protests this and is sent to join Penn. The jury is charged to render a verdict.

> *MEAD. Are these according to the Rights and Privileges of Englishmen, that we should not be heard, but turned into the Bale-dock, for making our Defence, and the Jury to have their Charge given them in our Absence; I say these are barbarous and unjust Proceedings.*
>
> *REC. Take them away into the Hole: To hear them talk all Night, as they would, that I think doth not become the Honour of the Court, and I think you (i. e. the Jury) your selves would be tired out, and not have Patience to hear them.*
>
> *OBSER. The Jury were commanded up to agree upon their Verdict, the Prisoners remaining in the stinking Hole.*[11]

Eventually the jurors agree to a verdict for William Penn of "Guilty of speaking in Gracechurch," and not guilty for Mead, which the court calls no verdict at all. They are sent back repeatedly, threatened, insulted, but still return the same verdict.

> *REC. Gentlemen, you shall not be dismist till we have a Verdict, that the Court will accept; and you shall be lock'd up, without Meat, Drink, Fire, and Tobacco; you shall not think thus to abuse the Court; we will have a Verdict, by the help of God, or you shall starve for it.*

> *OBSER. The Court swore several Persons, to keep the Jury all Night without Meat, Drink, Fire, or any other Accommodation; they had not so much as a Chamberpot, tho' desired.*[11]

Violent threats of punishment, including nose-cutting and chaining to the floor were made against the jury and Penn many times while this verdict held. One official wished they had the power of the Spanish Inquisition to torture the jurors into obedience. The jury was imprisoned without food or facilities a second night but did not give in to the coercion. In fact, since Mead could not be proven to the jury's satisfaction to have been at the meeting, he was found not guilty. This acquitted Penn as well, since it was a charge of conspiracy. The court proceeded to fine Mead, Penn and each of the jury members for contempt and to jail them until the fines were paid.

Note that William Penn points out that the "tumult" or disturbance they were charged with did not begin until armed officers were sent to break up the meeting. Even the witnesses, who testified to seeing the officers about to arrest Penn, admitted that there was so much noise and commotion they could not hear what Penn was saying or even see whether Mead was actually present. Clearly the English government had no intention of living up to its promises of freedom of speech or the rule of law for Englishmen, even in England. Penn was given his land grant in the New World as settlement of a debt the king owed to his family. Ironically the King's court, which denied Penn justice at his trial, helped furnish the means for his establishment of freedom of religion in the colonies.

While the English struggled with the attempt to shake off the corruptions of Roman Catholicism and the persecutions of its own government, the European Continent was going through the full-blown Reformation. Martin Luther wanted to remain in Church of Rome, but was thrown out of it. Luther, however, did not back down. He continued to preach against Rome and won the support of some the German princes. This support cost Rome a great deal of tax money; so much that Rome incited a war against the German princes who supported Martin Luther and what he taught. Rome started the war because these German princes stopped sending the tithes they collected (a tax) to Rome. Instead, they used the money to support local German schools and welfare agencies. The Schmalkaldic League, an alliance of German princes, forced the Roman Catholics to sign the Peace of Augsburg in 1555. Under the terms of this peace, the German princes were allowed to have their own Establishment of Religion in their own province or state *(cuius regio, eius religio).* The German people were allowed to move to a state which had an Establishment of Religion the same as the one they practiced. All still had to support the Establishment of Religion where they lived. The Peace of Augsburg only included Roman Catholicism and Lutheranism.

Ninety-three years later, the Peace of Westphalia was signed in 1648 to end the Thirty Years War. The Peace of Westphalia expanded the permissible religions to include Calvinism and permitted, in some circumstances, other religious practices besides the Established Religion. But even after the Peace of Westphalia, everyone still had to pay taxes to the Established Religion where they lived. These two peace treaties, the Peace of Augsburg and the Peace of Westphalia both define and form the basis of the modern state and an Establishment of Religion. An Establishment of Religion was defined as the state appointing the members of the Establishment of Religion, at least the upper members, and collecting taxes to pay for it. In return, the Establishment of Religion was to support the state through its sermons and to provide education and welfare.

Both Germans (Anabaptists and Mennonites) and French (Huguenots) were left out of the two peace agreements. To avoid severe persecution, they migrated to America in great numbers. These people, as well as the English Separatists, lived with an Establishment of Religion every day. The Establishment of Religion was a branch of the local government which collected taxes, provided poorly paid clergy, places to worship, education and welfare.

Members of Established Churches also came to America in large numbers. So many Puritans came (as with the Massachusetts Bay Colony) that historians call their movement to the New World “the great migration.” Roman Catholics also came, though in smaller numbers. The English Separatists, however, left the written document which we call the *Mayflower* Compact. These Separatists, better known to us as Pilgrims, made the greatest impact on the first two amendments to the U.S. Constitution. The Puritans, Roman Catholics and members of the Established Church of England all made their contributions. But the severely persecuted Anabaptists, Mennonites, Huguenots and Pilgrims laid the real foundation for America’s religious freedom. It is therefore easy to understand how the Separatists and the others who came to America, by the time they came to form their own government, were anxious to create a system where the Establishment of Religion would no longer be able to enslave them.

---

1 Foxe, John, *Foxe's Book of Martyrs,* Chapter Seven, "An Account of the Life and Persecutions of John Wickliffe." and Chapter Twelve, "The Life and Story of the true Servant and Martyr of God, William Tyndale." c. 1560, revised in the 1700s, edited by William Byron Forbush.

2 Chaucer, Geoffrey, *The Canterbury Tales,* "The Prologue," *http://www.msgr.ca/msgr-3/canterbury_tales_parson.htm.* (Note that a more complete excerpt is contained in the Chaucer Appendix in the Section One Appendices, as well as a version close to Chaucer's original. Both are from the same source.)

3 Schaff, Dr. Phillip, *History of the Christian Church,* Volume 6, Chapter 5, quoting Thomas Fuller, British Theologian, Charles Scribner's Sons, New York, 1910.

4 Bradford, William, *History of Plymouth Plantation.* c. 1650. Chapter One.

5 Laurel Lundstrom, "Students Free to Thank Anybody Except God," Monday, November 22, 2004, *Fox News.com.*

> *ANNAPOLIS, Md. — Maryland public school students are free to thank anyone they want while learning about the 17th century celebration of Thanksgiving — as long as it's not God. And that is how it should be, administrators say. Young students across the state read stories about the Pilgrims and Native Americans, simulate Mayflower voyages, hold mock feasts and learn about the famous meal that temporarily allied two very different groups. But what teachers don't mention when they describe the feast is that the Pilgrims not only thanked the Native Americans for their peaceful three-day*

indulgence, but repeatedly thanked God. 'We teach about Thanksgiving from a purely historical perspective, not from a religious perspective,' said Charles Ridgell, St. Mary's County Public Schools curriculum and instruction director. School administrators statewide agree, saying religion never coincides with how they teach Thanksgiving to students.

6 One popular example is *Mayflower: A Story of Courage, Community and War* by Nathaniel Philbrick, 2007, Penguin. There is also a children's version: The *Mayflower and the Pilgrims' New World.* "What *Mayflower* [the Nathaniel Philbrick book] makes plain is how unorganized, unprepared and unlucky those first settlers in the New World could be.

Pickens County Progress, Staff Review, "Thanksgiving Ain't No Holiday for Wimps," 11/27.2008. "[The book]...Rethinks ... a national mythology about Pilgrims ... Philbrick tells a story of ethnic cleansing, bloody wars, environmental ruin ... recasts well-known characters ... well-researched, unbiased revisionist history." Bookmarks Magazine review Phillips & Nelson Media, Inc. from Amazon.com.

7 The paragraphs describing the *Mayflower* and its preparations are adapted from *www.Mayflower1620.com.*

8 *Magna Carta,* 1215 AD, from *The Avalon Project. Documents in Law, History and Diplomacy. Yale Law Library. avalon.law.yale.edu.*

9 From "A Model of Christian Charity," 1630. *The Avalon Project. Documents in Law, History and Diplomacy. Yale Law Library. avalon.law.yale.edu*

10 From "Mr. Cotton's Letter Lately Printed, Examined and Answered," (1644), and "The Hireling Ministry, None of Christ's" (1652) The Complete Writings of Roger Williams, by the Narragansett Club.

11 From "*THE TRYAL of WILLIAM PENN and WILLIAM MEAD*, at the Sessions held at the Old Baily in London, the 1st, 3rd, 4th, and 5th of September, 1670. Done by themselves."

2. What Do America's Founding Documents Really Say?

First. The right of conscience shall be held inviolable and neither the legislative, executive nor judicial powers of the United States, shall have the authority to alter, abrogate or infringe any part of the constitution of the several states which provide for the preservation of liberty in matters of religion.1

Pennsylvania delegation dissent to the Constitution

Though the Pilgrims came to North America to escape this tyranny, almost two hundred years later their descendants had to fight this same war again. Before freedom was secure or even certain, Samuel Adams kept records for the Committees of Correspondence. These men felt the need to set down what they intended to secure for their future in straightforward terms.

> *The Rights of the Colonists The Report of the Committee of Correspondence to the Boston Town Meeting, Nov. 20, 1772*
>
> *I. Natural Rights of the Colonists as Men.*
>
> *Among the natural rights of the Colonists are these: First, a right to life; Secondly, to liberty; Thirdly, to property; together with the right to support and defend them in the best manner they can. These are evident branches of, rather than deductions from, the duty of self-preservation, commonly called the first law of nature.*

All men have a right to remain in a state of nature... and in case of intolerable oppression, civil or religious, to leave the society... and enter into another. ...

Every natural right not expressly given up, or, from the nature of a social compact, necessarily ceded, remains.

All positive and civil laws should conform, as far as possible, to the law of natural reason and equity.

As neither reason requires nor religion permits the contrary, every man living in or out of a state of civil society has a right peaceably ... to worship God according to the dictates of his conscience.

"Just and true liberty, equal and impartial liberty," in matters spiritual and temporal, ... all men are clearly entitled to [it] by the eternal and immutable laws of God and nature, as well as by the law of nations and all well-grounded municipal laws....

"In regard to religion, mutual toleration ... is what all good ... minds in all ages have ever practised, and ... inculcated on mankind. ... This spirit of toleration, ... consistent with ... civil society, is the chief ... mark of the Church. Insomuch that Mr. Locke has ... proved, ... that such toleration ... extend to all whose doctrines are not subversive of society. The only sects ... to be... excluded ... are those ... subversive of the civil government.... Roman Catholics ... [teach] that princes excommunicated may be deposed, and ... heretics may be destroyed without mercy; ... recognizing the Pope ... in subversion of government ... into the states under whose protection they enjoy life, liberty,

and property ... leading directly to the worst anarchy and confusion, civil discord, war, and bloodshed.

The natural liberty of man, by entering into society, is abridged ... only as is necessary for the ... best good of the whole.

In the state of nature every man is, under God, judge ... of his own rights and of the injuries done him. By entering into society he agrees to an arbiter ... but he ... [does not] renounce his original right....

... He should ... pay his just quota for the support of government, the law, and the constitution; ... to furnish indifferent and impartial judges ... whether civil, ecclesiastical, marine, or military.

The natural liberty of man is to be free from any superior power on earth, and not to be under the will or legislative authority of man, but only to have the law of nature for his rule.

... It [is not] in the power of one, or any number of men, ... entering into society, to renounce their essential natural rights, or the means of preserving those rights; when the grand end of civil government, from the very nature of it ... is for the support, protection, and defence of those very rights; the principal of which, ... are Life, Liberty, and Property. If men, through fear, fraud, or mistake, should in terms renounce ... natural right, the eternal law of reason ... would absolutely vacate such renunciation. The right to freedom being the gift of God Almighty, it is not in the power of man to ... voluntarily become a slave.

II. The Rights of the Colonists as Christians.

> *... Best understood by ... carefully studying the institutes of the great Law Giver and Head of the Christian Church, ... found clearly written ... in the New Testament.*
>
> *By the ...Toleration Act, every subject in England, except Papists, &c, was restored to, and re-established in, his natural right to worship God according to the dictates of his own conscience. And... it is ... established ... that there shall be liberty of conscience allowed in the worship of God to all Christians,... Magna Charta itself is...a ... proclamation ... of ... original, inherent, indefeasible natural rights, ... Mr. Justice Blackstone, holds that this recognition was justly obtained of King John, sword in hand. And peradventure it must be one day, sword in hand, again rescued and preserved from total destruction and oblivion...*[2]

These men feared that their own new government would take away their freedoms as the English crown had. They believed in Lord Acton's yet unwritten statement, Power tends to corrupt and absolute power corrupts absolutely. Though they differed as to the best way to prevent this corruption, the various factions each put their remedies in writing. The Antifederalist George Mason crafted, and the Commonwealth of Virginia passed, a declaration of rights.

Adopted unanimously June 12, 1776, Virginia Convention of Delegates, drafted by Mr. George Mason.

> *The Virginia Declaration of Rights*
>
> *... The freedom of the press is one of the greatest bulwarks of liberty and can never be restrained but by despotic governments.*

> *... A well regulated militia, composed of the body of the people, trained to arms, is the proper, natural, and safe defense of a free state; that standing armies, in time of peace, should be avoided as dangerous to liberty; and that, in all cases, the military should be under strict subordination to, and be governed by, the civil power.*
>
> *XVI That religion, or the duty which we owe to our Creator and the manner of discharging it, can be directed by reason and conviction, not by force or violence; and therefore, all men are equally entitled to the free exercise of religion, according to the dictates of conscience; and that it is the mutual duty of all to practice Christian forbearance, love, and charity towards each other.*[1]

When the new Constitution failed to include these rights, George Mason, Patrick Henry, John Adams, John Hancock and other Antifederalists opposed it. Federalists supported the Constitution as it was written. The famous Federalists, Alexander Hamilton, James Madison and John Jay, supported the Constitution with a series of papers that we call the *Federalist Papers.* Hamilton wrote in *Federalist 84:*

> *... A bill of rights ...[is] not only unnecessary in the proposed Constitution but would even be dangerous. They would contain various exceptions to powers which are not granted; ... would afford a colorable pretext to claim more than were granted. For why declare that things shall not be done which there is no power to do? Why, ... [say] that the liberty of the press shall not be restrained, when no power is given by which restrictions may be imposed? I will not contend that such a*

> *provision would confer a regulating power, but it ... would furnish ... a plausible pretense for claiming that power. They might urge ... that the Constitution ought not to be ... providing against the abuse of an authority which was not given, and that the provision against restraining the liberty of the press afforded a clear implication that a power to ... regulate ... was intended to be vested in the national government.*[3]

For Alexander Hamilton, this is concise. He says that the Constitution only gives the Federal government the powers clearly spelled out in the body of the Constitution. The mere mention of other powers in a Bill of Rights gives dishonest men a "plausible pretense" or a "semblance of reason" to take for themselves powers which the Constitution does not give the Federal government.

Eventually, Alexander Hamilton and the Federalists lost this argument to the Antifederalists. Unlike those who were completely opposed to any federal government, the Antifederalists realized the need for a central government. The Antifederalists simply wanted a Bill of Rights because of their great fear of a central government. Their various positions were put in writing by the various state bodies. The Federalists and Antifederalists agreed that they did not want the Federal Government to have any power to do any of the things listed here. The only disagreement was over the best way to restrain the federal government. When states began voting on ratification of the Constitution, a few of those positions were put in writing by state ratification conventions.

Ratification of the Constitution, by the Convention of the State of **New York**

> *We the delegates of the State of New York, ... agreed to on the seventeenth day of September, in the year one thousand seven hundred and eighty-seven, ... and having also seriously and deliberately considered the present situation of the United States, DO declare and make known, ...That the people have an equal, natural and unalienable right, freely and peaceably to exercise their religion, according to the dictates of conscience; and that no religious sect or society ought to be favored or established by law in preference to others.*
>
> *That the people have a right to keep and bear arms; that a well regulated militia, including the people capable of bearing arms, is the proper and natural and safe defence of a free state.*[1]

All six of the **Pennsylvania** delegates on December 12, 1787 wrote objections to the entire Constitution in the following amendments:

> *The Address and reasons of dissent of the minority of the convention, of the state of Pennsylvania, to their constituents.*
>
> *The right of conscience shall be held inviolable and neither the legislative, executive nor judicial powers of the United States, shall have the authority to alter, abrogate or infringe any part of the constitution of the several states, which provide for the preservation of liberty in matters of religion.*
>
> *... The people have a right to the freedom of speech, of writing and publishing their sentiments, therefore, the freedom of the press shall not be restrained by any law of the United States.*

... The people have a right to bear arms for the defence of themselves and their own state, or the United States, or for the purpose of killing game, and no law shall be passed for disarming the people or any of them, unless for crimes committed or real danger of public injury from individuals.[1]

State of North Carolina

IN CONVENTION, AUGUST 1, 1788

... That a declaration of Rights, asserting and securing from encroachment the great Principles of civil and religious Liberty, and the unalienable Rights of the People, together with Amendments ... ought to be laid before Congress, and the convention of the States ... called for the purpose of Amending the said Constitution...

DECLARATION OF RIGHTS

16th. That the people have a right to freedom of speech, and of writing and publishing their sentiments; that the freedom of the press is one of the greatest bulwarks of Liberty, and ought not be violated.

17th. That the people have a right to keep and bear arms; that a well regulated militia composed of the body of the people, trained to arms, is the proper, natural and safe defence of a free state. That standing armies in time of peace are dangerous to Liberty, and therefore ought to be avoided, as far as the circumstances and protection of the community will admit; and that in all cases, the military should be under strict subordination to, and governed by the civil power.

> *19th. That any person religiously scrupulous of bearing arms ought to be exempt upon payment of an equivalent to employ another to bear arms in his stead.*
>
> *20th. That religion, or the duty which we owe to our Creator, and the manner of discharging it, can only be directed by reason and conviction, not by force or violence, and therefore all men have an equal, natural and unalienable right to the free exercise of religion according to the dictates of conscience, and that no particular religious sect or society ought to be favored or established by law in preference to others.*[1]

Maryland

Convention ratifying the constitution, then voting on individual amendments

> *... the freedom of the press be inviolably preserved. In prosecutions in the federal courts for libels, the constitutional preservation of this great and fundamental right, may prove invaluable. ... There be no national religion established by law, but that all persons be equally entitled to protection in their religious liberty.*[1]

The first ten amendments to the Constitution, the Bill of Rights, were based on these Antifederalist objections to the Constitution. George Mason's Virginia Declaration of Rights were rearranged and rewritten to put the amendments in what these men perceived to be the correct order beginning with the most important. The first amendment combined freedom of speech, the press, peaceable assembly and petitioning the Government for a redress of grievances after and subservient to forbidding an establishment of religion. This means that freedom of speech, the press, and peaceable assembly are rights derived from freedom of religion. It also means that these are individual or personal rights, not corporate or business rights. A newspaper or media outlet has no more rights than an individual.

> *1st Amendment: Congress shall make no law respecting an establishment of religion, or prohibiting the free exercise thereof; or abridging the freedom of speech, or of the press; or the right of the people peaceably to assemble, and to petition the Government for a redress of grievances.1*

Every 18th century American citizen, and most non-citizens, knew exactly what an Establishment of Religion was. In England it was the Church of England. In France and Spain it was the Roman Catholic Church, headed in each country by a Cardinal. In Switzerland and the Germanies (Germany was not yet a unified country) each city, state or province had its own Establishment of Religion as set down by the Peace of Augsburg and Peace of Westphalia. The Peace of Augsburg on September 25, 1555 allowed Lutherans to exist in Lutheran states with the phrase *Cuius regio, eius religio* which roughly translated means “to the prince, the religion.” Common free people were given the opportunity to move to a state or province that practiced either Roman Catholicism or Lutheranism.

Other religions had to wait until the Peace of Westphalia in 1648. Serfs still had no choice, though serfdom was dying out. The Peace of Westphalia is the treaty that founded the concept of the modern nation/state. It allowed for sovereignty of individual nations without the interference of outside forces. Other religions besides Catholicism and Lutheranism were permitted, such as Anabaptists and Calvinists. Since every country in Europe had its own Establishment of Religion, allowing people to practice a religion other than the Established

Religion was a revolutionary concept. As part of their colonization efforts, each of these countries had representatives of their Established Churches in the New World. An Established Church was funded through taxation and was responsible for taking care of the poor (welfare) and education. Public worship was a small part of the responsibilities of the Established Religion. The only large universities in England, Oxford and Cambridge, were funded and staffed by the Established Church.

In America, most people were familiar with the Congregational model of the Established Religion in the North or the Episcopal model in the South. Originally founded in Massachusetts, the Congregational model was established by the Puritans, though few followed the Puritan faith. Some model of an Established Church was carried through in all the colonies and later states.

The Congregational model was simple. When there were enough settlers in a wilderness area, they built one public building. On Sunday it was a church, and every school age child was required to attend. Monday through Friday it became a schoolhouse, with the first lesson on Monday being the Sunday sermon. In the evening this same building was the government building, or town hall. If, as was frequently the case, there were different denominations, arrangements had to be made for sharing the building.

Usually the different denominations simply used the same building at different times. Since there were severe shortages of teachers and textbooks, they used whatever was available. Though there were frequent and often-heated disagreements over these arrangements, the purpose of the first amendment was to keep the Federal Government, including the Federal Courts, out of these disagreements. John Wesley primarily influenced the Episcopal model in America. The Methodist denomination believed that Church property, including schools, publishing facilities and headquarters should be owned by the denomination. The denominational leadership controlled the appointment of teachers, pastors and leaders. In the Congregational model the local Congregations owned their own church properties. Both models, however, relied on the ancient English tradition of keeping the government out of religion.[4]

This English tradition of keeping the crown out of welfare, education and worship dates back to at least the *Magna Charta*, which opens with:

> *1. In the first place we have granted to God, and by this our present charter confirmed for us and our heirs forever that the English Church shall be free, and shall have her rights entire, and her liberties inviolate; and we will that it be thus observed...*[1]

This is what makes Henry VIII's tampering with the meaning so reprehensible. The wording was meant to keep the English government, as well as foreign governments, out of the church.

Thomas Paine despised monarchy and defended the common man. He was among the first to push for a break with England, to speak eloquently on the corrupted relationship of established church and state. His writings are still used today to inspire freedom of speech and thought and attack tyranny and corruption in organized religion.

On the 19th of April 1783 Paine printed a little pamphlet entitled "Thoughts on Peace and the Probable Advantages Thereof." In this pamphlet he pleads for "a supreme Nationality absorbing all cherished sovereignties." He also believed in the concept of a "universal republic." "Supreme Nationality" and "universal republic," should raise red flags to people who fear government control, and it may be that they did.

Paine clearly had a vision of obliterating what he believed were the hopelessly corrupt local governments in favor of a central government, the only way, he believed, to equalize everyone.

"There is scarcely any part of science, or anything in nature, which those imposters and blasphemers of science, called priests, as well Christians as Jews, have not, at some time or other, perverted, or sought to pervert to the purpose of superstition and falsehood."[5] Paine believed organized religion was another form of tyranny. The founding fathers agreed to an extent and so sought to free the church from government control and corruption. But Paine simply did not believe that the Bible was the Word of God.

> *Yet this is trash that the Church imposes upon the world as the Word of God; this is the collection of lies and contradictions called the Holy Bible! This is the rubbish called Revealed Religion!*[6]
>
> *... The continually progressive change to which the meaning of words is subject, the want of a universal language which renders translation necessary, the errors to which translations are again subject, the mistakes of copyists and printers, together with the possibility of willful alteration, are of themselves evidences that the human language, whether in speech or in print, cannot be the vehicle of the Word of God. The Word of God exists in something else.*[5]

Thomas Paine was a humanist first, an American patriot second. Paine claimed to believe in freedom of religion, but here is what he meant by that: "Time and reason must cooperate with each other to the final establishment of any principle; and therefore those who may happen to be first convinced have not a right to persecute others, on whom conviction operates more slowly. The moral principle of revolutions is to instruct, not to destroy."[7]

In many respects, Paine is the direct ancestor of the new established religion. Thomas Paine claimed to believe in a god but his god was only a god of reason. His god left man supreme with no one to temper man's judgment or get in the way of his "freedom." For a more detailed study of Thomas Paine, see Chapter Five.

The new established religion has used Henry VIII's reinterpretation principle and Paine's disdain of anything that named itself a religion to attack all other religions. As Fascism used the Big Lie, so the new established religion uses the Big Lie to first of all claim not to be a religion.

Next, the new established religion erected a "high wall of separation" between itself (the government) and all other religions. The phrase "high wall of separation" originated with Roger Williams. Over one hundred fifty years later President Thomas Jefferson used it the same way. Each of these men meant that the state was not to interfere in any way with religion.

Modern courts fabricated a "separation dogma" from the statement of President Thomas Jefferson. The acceptance of this blatant falsehood effectively shuts other religions away from the protection the Constitution is supposed to afford them. This freed the new established religion to wage war against all other religions by taxing them and using those taxes to strengthen itself. Repeatedly the high priests of the established religion point to Jefferson's "separation principle" to support their "high wall of separation."

Thomas Jefferson is frequently credited with having established the "Separation Principle," giving rise to the unconstitutional Doctrine of the Separation of Church and State. Though many think that this concept is a part of the constitution, it is actually part of a letter President

Jefferson wrote to the Danbury Baptists. Jefferson first expressed these ideas in another document called Draft for a Bill for Establishing Religious Freedom, in 1779. The Virginia General Assembly enacted it into the state's law (1786). This helps us understand what Thomas Jefferson actually believed about the relationship of religion to the state. (Emphasis added, see Chapter Four for a more complete text and commentary.)

> *... All attempts to influence it (the mind to follow a certain belief) by temporal punishments, or burthens, or by civil incapacitations, tend only to beget habits of hypocrisy and meanness, and are a departure from the plan of the holy author of our religion, who being lord both of body and mind, yet chose not to propagate it by coercions on either ...*
>
> *... That the impious presumption of legislators and rulers ... who, being themselves but fallible ... men, have assumed dominion over the faith of others, setting up their own opinions and modes of thinking as the only true and infallible, ... hath established and maintained false religions over the greatest part of the world and through all time ...*
>
> *... That our civil rights have no dependence on our religious opinions, any more than our opinions in physics or geometry; that therefore the proscribing any citizen as unworthy the public confidence, ... unless he profess or renounce this or that religious opinion, ... tends also to corrupt the principles of that very religion it is meant to encourage, by bribing, with a monopoly of worldly honours and emoluments, those who will externally profess and conform to it...*

> *... That it is time enough for the rightful purposes of civil government for its officers to interfere when principles break out into overt acts against peace and good order; ... Truth is great and will prevail if left to herself; that she is the proper and sufficient antagonist to error, and has nothing to fear from the conflict unless by human interposition disarmed of her natural weapons, free argument and debate; errors ceasing to be dangerous when it is permitted freely to contradict them.*
>
> *... All men shall be free to profess, and by argument to maintain, their opinions in matters of religion, and that the same shall in no wise diminish, enlarge, or affect their civil capacities.*
>
> *...We are free to declare, and do declare, that the rights hereby asserted are of the natural rights of mankind, and that if any act shall be hereafter passed to repeal the present or to narrow its operation, such act will be an infringement of natural right.*[1]

Jefferson was the far-left believer in reason's power to triumph during his time, yet he uses "fighting words" to express his thoughts: "antagonist," "conflict," "disarmed of her natural weapons." He could not help but acknowledge the possibility that truth might be disarmed. Other constitutional framers had an even more realistic view of how their new nation might be treated and how its rights might need to be protected. The Second Amendment is placed second because it was understood to be a necessary support to all the elements of the First. They had just fought a war against, among other things, the "divine right" of a king, believed to be god-given, to do whatever he wished with a possession, in this case his colonies. Without men who possessed with great skill at arms, abilities honed in the French and

Indian War, they would have been ill prepared to defend themselves against the injustices heaped on them by British disregard of their status as citizens of the Empire.

Peaceful means to redress grievances were tried over and over. But it was clear that England had no intention of allowing the colonists to live under laws they understood and might have been able to agree to. And since the British Government was inexorably tied to the Anglican church by the Establishment of Religion, the colonists no doubt had to consider that their religious freedoms, the very reason most of them had come to America, would receive no greater consideration than had their civil rights.

2nd Amendment: "A well-regulated Militia, being necessary to the security of a free State, the right of the People to keep and bear Arms, shall not be infringed."[1]

Samuel Adams, founder of the Sons of Liberty, was very clear that the real issue was individual, personal responsibility and the freedom to carry out that responsibility. The Constitution was to be kept out of the way, as it were, so that people would be able to act if necessary.

"The Constitution shall never be construed... to prevent the people of the United States who are peaceable citizens from keeping their own arms." "The liberties of our country, the freedom of our civil constitution, are worth defending against all hazards: And it is our duty to defend them against all attacks."[2]

North Carolina, New York and Pennsylvania voted that the people have a right to keep and bear arms. These are minor changes to Virginia's Declaration of Rights: a well-regulated militia, composed of the body of the people, trained to arms. According to the body of the ratified U.S. Constitution, Article 1 Section 8, the purpose of the militia, which is the body of the people, trained to arms, is to execute the Laws of the Union. In other words, "the body of the people, trained to arms," is to be the police force. This is why the uniformed police are called officers. "The body of the people, trained to arms," is intended to be the beat cops. Every citizen should be trained to arms, except those who by court order (such as convicted felons) cannot carry arms.

The 2nd Amendment immediately follows the 1st Amendment because arms are necessary to protect God-given rights from tyrants.

There is no freedom of religion without its pillars: freedom of speech, of the press, of peaceable assembly, and the right of the people to keep and bear arms. Freedom of speech and of the press meant the personal freedom of an individual to publish, such as Benjamin Franklin producing Poor Richard's Almanac. It also included the idea of bulk mailing rates, which were not designed to bury us in junk mail but to facilitate the inexpensive distribution of ideas on a larger scale. Today we have bloggers on the Internet. This does not mean just a corporation or business like a newspaper. The freedom of the press is for individuals.

Peaceable assembly should mean any group with no intention to commit or promote acts of violence, presenting no threat to public safety or private property, must be allowed to assemble. There should not be any punitive or prohibitive fees for permits and there should not be consideration of whether there is likely to be public agreement or happiness with the message of the group.

Keeping and bearing arms meant that individuals should have and use weapons to hunt and to defend themselves, their state, and their country. A militia was to be made of ordinary people, not professional soldiers. They could be called upon as a posse to pursue an outlaw, extra police if needed, and constituted a form of tax. In fact, the government expected that it could depend on its trained citizens to be ready in time of need. This is the only right which can be taken away by the government in connection with criminal activity as spelled out in the Pennsylvania objections to the Constitution without a Bill of Rights.

"... And no law shall be passed for disarming the people or any of them, unless for crimes committed or real danger of public injury from individuals ..."[1] This document was first written around the time when most states were creating their own constitutions. The break with England had already occurred, and it was necessary for the thirteen colonies to become thirteen states, to write down the causes of their declaration of independence and set up their own governments. Almost all felt the necessity of creating new governing documents, and in almost every case a strong statement of how the state was to treat the matter of religion was included. These documents provide a view into the minds of the men who revisionist history says wanted no part of religion in government. The facts show otherwise.

---

1 All state and constitution-related documents taken from one of two sources: *The Avalon Project. Documents in Law, History and Diplomacy. Yale Law Library. avalon.law.yale.edu.* or *National Archives, archives.gov.*

2 Samuel Adams, *The Rights of the Colonists: The Report of the Committee of Correspondence to the Boston Town Meeting, Nov. 20, 1772 Old South Leaflets* no. 173 (Boston: Directors of the Old South Work, 1906) 7: 417-428. *Hanover Historical Texts Project, http//history.hanover.edu /texts/adamss.html*

3 Alexander Hamilton and James Madison. *Federalist 84, The Federalist Papers.* Signet Classics, Penguin, Putnam: New York, NY, 2003.

4 Three reference sources for readers who wish to know more about the early organization of colonial towns are: Sydney E. Ahlstrom, *A Religious History of the American People,* Yale University, printed by Vail-Ballou Press, Inc., Binghamton, NY, 1972: William Warren Sweet, *The Story of Religion in America,* Harper, New York: NY, 1950; Ray Allen Billington, *Westward Expansion: A History of the American Frontier,* Macmillan, New York: NY, 1974.

5 Thomas Paine, "Answer to the Bishop of Lladaff," (Concerning The Age of Reason) published in the *Theophilanthropist,* New York, NY, 1810. [Submitted posthumously by the widow of Elihu Palmer, who attended Paine during his illness in 1806, in the house of William Carver.]

6 Thomas Paine, "Essay on Dream," published in New York in 1807 with the following title: "An Examination of the Passages in the New Testament, quoted from the Old and called Prophecies concerning Jesus Christ. To which is prefixed an Essay on Dream, showing by what operation of the mind a Dream is produced in sleep, and applying the same to the account of Dreams in the New Testament. With an Appendix containing my private thoughts of a Future State. And Remarks on the Contradictory Doctrine in the Books of Matthew and Mark." By Thomas Paine, New York: Printed for the Author.

7 Thomas Paine, *First Principles of Government* (1795).

3. What Were the Established Religions of the Colonies?

It is a perversion of terms to say that a charter gives rights. It operates by a contrary effect- that of taking rights away. Rights are inherently in all the inhabitants; but charters, by annulling those rights, in the majority, leave the right, by exclusion, in the hands of a few.[1]
Thomas Paine

The new Constitutions of the thirteen states were pacts between equals, not pacts between an all powerful sovereign and subjects. As Thomas Paine said, each state had to decide which rights to give up to make a government work. Knowing that the goal was to take away as few rights as possible and still have a workable government, all of the state constitutions were failures. They all took away too many rights.

The task of converting from charters to constitutions was difficult. For example, the new state of Connecticut did not write a new constitution until the 1800s. And since these men viewed the relationship between the state and church as the foundation of government, they would view what has happened to this relationship in modern America as a complete failure. It was never the intention of the men who wrote these documents to have the state persecute the church as the modern state does. The Colonial state was designed to make religion thrive. The mechanism was neutrality on the part of the Federal government, while each of the states protected and advanced the cause of religion.

At the time the original thirteen colonies became states, their state constitutions or charters were intended to be the highest authority for the average person. The federal government had limited powers. Apart from national events such as war, the federal government would not affect the daily lives of the average person. The Section One Appendix on Founding Documents lists important documents and suggestions for locating them online.

Two very important points guided the framers of the state constitutions. First, persecuted religious minorities founded all of the colonies. They feared, rightfully so, that their persecutors would follow them to America and become the majority in their new states and so renew their persecution. They had no intention of becoming persecutors. Each of the new states had the same goal: protect the little that they had. They had different ideas, however, of how to accomplish that goal. Second, the fear of the Roman Catholic Church was not some vague prejudice. In English and American documents of this time period, Roman Catholics were often referred to as Papists, that is, followers of the Papacy. Americans, Englishmen and Protestants in general viewed the Papacy as a foreign government. The Papacy had ordered a Spanish invasion of England, had started two long European wars against Protestants, sanctioned the Spanish Inquisition, interdicted England, sanctioned the wholesale confiscation of English property, sanctioned the Saint Bartholomew's Day Massacre in France, sanctioned murder and confiscation of property on the high seas. The Papacy demanded tax revenues and control of education and welfare. It also claimed to control the eternal destinies of individuals. It claimed to be the only spokesman for God on earth. Knowing full well the privations of the wilderness of New England, the English Separatists chose that harsh life in preference to living through another war in Europe instigated by Rome.

The original constitutions of the thirteen original states often included some form of an established religion. The states with an established religion usually continued to follow a modified version of the Established Church of England.

Connecticut

People who left Massachusetts founded Connecticut as a Church of England colony with one major change. It was founded on Congregational principles. An Oath of Fidelity was required of all Freemen residing in the colony.

Only church members could hold offices, vote, or make any decisions at first. Others were allowed to own land and live in the colony. Persons of other faiths could under various laws at various times get permission to avoid paying taxes to the established religion but they were expected to belong to and pay for their own church.

> *Church members only shall be free burgesses (citizens with political rights), and that they only shall choose magistrates and officers among themselves, to have power of transacting all the public civil affairs of this plantation; of making and repealing laws, dividing of inheritances, deciding of differences that may arise, and doing all things and businesses of like nature.* Fundamental Agreement, or Original Constitution of the Colony of New Haven, June 4, 1639.[2]

Massachusetts

Before the constitution of 1780, Massachusetts dealt harshly with dissenters. By the time of its 1780 constitution, however, Massachusetts followed the lead of other states in at least tolerating other faiths, though only Protestant teachers of piety were supported by the legislature. The local people had the right to choose their ministers and support the faith they practiced. If they lived in a place where their belief was not practiced, their money was to be paid to the parish where they lived. While a person was free to practice a different faith from his neighbors he might still be required to support the neighborhood church or minister.

> *Art. II. It is the right as well as the duty of all men in society, publicly ... to worship the Supreme Being, the great Creator and Preserver of the universe. And no subject shall be ... restrained... for worshipping God [according] to the dictates of his own conscience, or for his religious profession or sentiments, provided he doth not disturb the public peace or obstruct others in their religious worship.*
>
> *Art. III. As the happiness of a people and ... civil government essentially depend upon piety, religion, and morality, and ... the institution of the public worship of God and of the public instructions ... the people of this commonwealth have a right to invest their legislature with power to authorize ... towns... and other bodies-politic or religious societies to make suitable provision, at their own expense, for ... worship of God and for the support and maintenance of public Protestant teachers ... in all cases where such provision shall not be made voluntarily.*
>
> *And the people of this commonwealth ... invest their legislature with authority to enjoin ... attendance upon the instructions of the public teachers ... if there be any on whose instructions they can conscientiously and conveniently attend.*

> *... the several towns...and other bodies-politic, or religious societies, shall ... have the exclusive right and electing their public teachers and ... for their support and maintenance.*
>
> *And all moneys ... to the support of public worship and of public teachers ... be uniformly applied to ... his own religious sect or denomination, provided there be any on whose instructions he attends; otherwise it may be paid toward ... the parish or precinct in which the said moneys are raised.*
>
> *And every denomination of Christians, demeaning themselves peaceably and as good subjects of the commonwealth, shall be equally under the protection of the law; and no subordination of any sect or denomination to another shall ever be established by law.*
>
> Massachusetts Constitution, 1780.[2]

Delaware

Delaware was originally given to William Penn along with Pennsylvania but later allowed to become a separate colony. Like Pennsylvania, it was founded upon principles of religious toleration. Its charter specified that an oath of allegiance be made to the king and governor and certain other loyalty statements ascribed to, plus basic beliefs in Christian principles and practices were required to hold office. The Constitution added the assertion of belief in the inspiration of the Scriptures as a requirement to hold office.

> *I, A B. do profess faith in God the Father, and in Jesus Christ His only Son, and in the Holy Ghost, one God, blessed for evermore; and I do acknowledge the holy scriptures of the Old and New Testament to be given by divine*

> *inspiration. And all officers shall also take an oath of office.*
>
> Constitution of Delaware, 1776.[2]

Georgia

Georgia's original charter allowed liberty of conscience and free exercise of religion to all but Roman Catholics. The Georgia constitution changed this to allow freedom of conscience to Roman Catholics. The constitution allowed anyone to live in the state and practice any faith, but the constitution prohibited Catholics from holding office and also prohibited clergymen of any faith from public service.

> *ART. VI. The representatives shall be ... of the Protestant religion, and of the age of twenty-one years, and shall be possessed in their own right of two hundred and fifty acres of land, or some property to the amount of two hundred and fifty pounds.*
>
> *ART. LVI. All persons whatever shall have the free exercise of their religion; provided it be not repugnant to the peace and safety of the State; and shall not, unless by consent, support any teacher or teachers except those of their own profession.*
>
> *ART. LXII. No clergyman of any denomination shall be allowed a seat in the legislature.* Constitution of Georgia, 1777.[2]

Maryland

Maryland began as a Roman Catholic colony, the only one so chartered. Being surrounded by Protestants and other faiths, however, it was early forced to practice religious toleration. In fact, it passed the Act of Toleration in 1649. This spelled out in great detail the prohibitions against compulsory belief or practice. The requirement of a belief in Christ and the Christian faith was not viewed as compulsory belief.

> *... Forcing of the conscience in matters of Religion [has] dangerous Consequence ... and for the peaceable government of this Province, and the better to preserve mutual Love and amity amongst the Inhabitants thereof ... No ... persons ... professing to believe in Jesus Christ, shall ... be ... troubled ... in respect of his or her religion nor in the free exercise ... nor any way compelled to the belief or exercise of any other Religion ... so as they be not unfaithful to the Lord Proprietary, or ... the civil Government ....*
>
> *...All ... persons that shall presume Contrary to this Act ...willfully to ... molest any person ... professing to believe in Jesus Christ for ... his or her religion or the free exercise thereof within this Province other than is provided for in this Act... shall be compelled to pay [triple] damages ... shall also forfeit 20s sterling in money if the party ... refuse or be unable to recompense... to satisfy such fine or forfeiture, then such Offender shall be ... punished by public whipping and imprisonment without bail*
>
> Maryland Toleration Act, 1649.[2]

Massachusetts and other colonies, in contrast to Maryland, passed laws to keep dissenters out, not to guarantee their protection. It was unusual to so strictly and harshly enforce the promise of protection of divergent faiths with detailed fines and punishments as this Toleration Act did. Possibly this was meant to reassure Roman Catholics, who were subjected to severe exclusions and persecutions elsewhere in the colonies.

William Blackstone, English jurist and author of a popular law commentary written in the mid-1700s, made the position of most Englishmen on Roman Catholicism clear. He was a royalist and strong believer in British sovereignty, hardly sympathetic to the American cause of religious liberty. Yet he summed up the beliefs of most of the colonists and his statement clarifies the need for Maryland to put strong protections into place for its Roman Catholic residents.

> *As to papists, what has been said of the Protestant dissenters would hold equally strong for a general toleration of them; provided their separation was founded only upon difference of opinion in religion, and their principles did not also extend to a subversion of the civil government. If once they could be brought to renounce the supremacy of the pope, they might quietly enjoy their seven sacraments, their purgatory, and auricular confession; their worship of reliques and images; nay even their transubstantiation. But while they acknowledge a foreign power, superior to the sovereignty of the kingdom, they cannot complain if the laws of that kingdom will not treat them upon the footing of good subjects.*[4]

Maryland later made provision for the growing presence of Church of England colonists. Her Constitution echoed those of other bodies respecting the property and taxes of that faith. It also allowed Legislatures to collect a general tax to support Christian work but gave individuals the right to decide how their share would be spent.

> *... It is the duty of every man to worship God ... as he thinks most acceptable ... persons professing the Christian religion, are equally entitled to protection in their religious liberty;*

> *wherefore no person ought by any law to be molested ... on account of his religious ... practice; unless, under colour of religion, any man shall disturb the ... peace or safety of the State, or shall infringe the laws of morality, or injure others... nor ought any person to be compelled to frequent or ... maintain any particular place of worship, or any particular ministry; yet the Legislature may, ... lay a general and equal tax for the support of the Christian religion; leaving to each individual the power of appointing the payment ... to the support of any particular place of worship or minister, or for the benefit of the poor of his own denomination, or the poor in general of any particular county: but the churches ... belonging to the church of England, ought to remain to the church of England forever.*
>
> *...That no other test ... ought to be required, on admission to any office ... than such oath of support and fidelity to this State, ... and a declaration of a belief in the Christian religion.*
>
> Maryland Constitution, 1776.[2]

Maryland, like other states, required an oath of loyalty and swearing belief in the Christian faith to hold office. It specified that those whose religions forbade swearing could affirm, as did Pennsylvania and Delaware.

New Hampshire

New Hampshire, like Connecticut and Rhode Island, was founded by people who left Massachusetts, unable to live either in the Boston area or Plymouth colonies either because of too much or too little separation from worldliness in religious practice. The New Hampshire Constitution has the unusual provision of forbidding an establishment of religion (no subordination of any one sect, denomination or persuasion to another shall ever be established) while in the same article expecting everyone in New Hampshire to support a school of their own choosing. ("... parishes... shall ... have the right of electing their own teachers, and of contracting with them for their support ...") The New Hampshire constitution states that taxes collected for education must be used for the school the person paying the taxes chooses to support. Since the modern federally run public school system is Secular Humanist, and Secular Humanism is a religion, public schools are in violation of the state constitution. ("But no person shall ever be compelled to pay towards the support of the schools of any sect or denomination.")

> *[Art.] 5. Every individual has a natural ... right to worship God according to ... his own conscience ... no subject shall be ... restrained ... for worshipping God in the manner ... most agreeable to ... his own conscience; or for his religious profession ... provided he doth not disturb the public peace or disturb others in their religious worship.*
>
> *[Art.] 6. As morality and piety ... will give the best and greatest security to government, ... the several parishes ... shall ... have the right of electing their own teachers, and of contracting with them for their support ... no person shall ever be compelled to pay towards the support of the schools of any sect ... And every person, denomination or sect shall be equally under the protection of the law; and no subordination of any one sect ... to another shall ever be established.*
>
> New Hampshire Constitution, 1784.[2]

New Jersey

Since all education and all welfare programs are religious, the phrase "nor shall any ... ever be obliged to pay tithes, taxes, ... for the purpose of building or repairing any other church ... places of worship, or for the maintenance of any minister ... contrary to what he believes ... or voluntarily engaged himself to perform" means that taxes for welfare and education should not be collected.

> *That no person shall ... be deprived of ... worshipping Almighty God [according to]... conscience; nor ... be compelled to attend any place of worship, contrary to his own faith ... nor ... ever be obliged to pay tithes, taxes, ... for ... building or repairing any other church ... or places of worship, or for the maintenance of any minister ... contrary to what he believes ... or voluntarily engaged himself to perform.*
>
> *That there shall be no establishment of any one religious sect ... in preference to another; and that no Protestant ... shall be denied ... any civil right, merely on account of his religious principles ... persons, professing a belief in ... any Protestant sect. ... peaceably under the government ... shall be capable of being elected into any office ... or being a member of ... the Legislature, and shall ... enjoy every privilege and immunity*
>
> Constitution of New Jersey, 1776. [2]

New York

New York, like other states, excluded clergymen from holding office or serving in the military. New York also excluded Quakers or other conscientious objectors from military service but required them to pay a sum of money to be excused. New York does not specify Christian faith in its wording, unlike many other

Constitutions. New York warned that "liberty of conscience ... shall not ... excuse acts of licentiousness, or justify practices inconsistent with the peace or safety of this State."

> *... We are required, by the ... rational liberty, ... to expel civil tyranny ... to guard against that spiritual oppression ... wherewith the bigotry and ambition of weak and wicked priests and princes have scourged mankind, [we] ... declare, that the free exercise ... of ... worship, without discrimination ... shall forever hereafter be allowed, ... Provided, That the liberty of conscience, ... shall not ... excuse acts of licentiousness, or justify practices inconsistent with the peace or safety of this State.*
>
> *... Ministers of the gospel are ... dedicated to the service of God and the care of souls, and ought not to be diverted ... therefore, no minister of the gospel... shall, at any time hereafter ... be eligible to ... holding ... civil or military office*

Constitution of New York, 1777.[2]

North Carolina

Like New Jersey, North Carolina clearly spelled out "... no establishment of any one ... church or denomination ... in preference to any other; ... any person ... be compelled to attend any place of worship contrary to his own faith or judgment, nor be obliged to pay, for the purchase ... of any house of worship, or for the maintenance of any minister or ministry, contrary to what he believes right." Since education and welfare are religious, the state of North Carolina, like New Hampshire and New Jersey forbids collecting taxes for a school or welfare agency the taxpayer does not believe in.

> *... No clergyman, ... shall be capable of being a member of either the Senate, House of Commons, or Council of State, while ... in the exercise of the pastoral function.*
>
> *... No person, who shall deny the being of God or the truth of the Protestant religion, or the divine authority either of the Old or New Testaments, or who shall hold religious principles incompatible with the freedom and safety of the State, shall ... hold ... any office ... in the civil department within this State.*
>
> *... There shall be no establishment of any one ... church or denomination ... in preference to any other; neither shall any ... be compelled to attend any place of worship contrary to his own faith ... nor ... pay, for ... the building of any house of worship, or for the maintenance of any minister ... contrary to what he ... engaged to perform; but all persons shall ... exercise their own mode of worship: -- Provided, That nothing ... shall ... exempt preachers of treasonable or seditious discourses, from legal trial and punishment*
>
> *North Carolina Constitution, 1776.*[2]

North Carolina prohibited clergymen from holding state-level office but did not specifically prohibit any lower civil service. The state also demanded accord with basic Protestant beliefs to hold office, thereby excluding Catholics. No one could compel taxes or tithes and freedom of worship was guaranteed.

Pennsylvania

> *... All men have a natural ... right to worship Almighty God according to ... their own consciences ... no man ... can be compelled to attend any religious worship, or ... support any*

> *place of worship, or maintain any ministry, ... against, his own free will ... Nor can any man, who acknowledges the being of a God, be justly deprived ... of any civil right ... on account of his religious sentiments or ... worship: And that no authority can ... interfere with, or in any manner control, the right of conscience in the free exercise of religious worship.*
>
> Constitution of Pennsylvania, 1776.[2]

William Penn said, "Force makes hypocrites; 'tis persuasion only that makes converts."[5] Many persecuted sects made their homes there, including Jews and Roman Catholics. This constitution prohibited excluding Catholics or any others from holding office by guaranteeing the same civil rights to all.

Rhode Island

(Note that this is excerpted from the original wording of the royal charter, as if the King himself is personally speaking and granting these permissions. This makes it sound very different from most of the state constitutions and early documents.)

> *"The ... colony of Providence Plantations, ... [with] peaceable and loyal ... sober, serious and religious intentions, of godly edifying themselves, and one another, in the holy Christian faith and worship as they were persuaded; ... with the ... conversion of the ... Indian natives, ... to the sincere profession and obedience of the same faith and worship ... they have freely declared, ... to hold forth a lively experiment, that a ... civil state may stand ... among our English subjects with a full liberty in religious concernments; ... grounded upon gospel principles, will give the ... greatest security to sovereignty, and will lay [on] men the strongest obligations to true loyalty: We ...*

> *encourage the hopeful undertaking ... and to secure them in the free exercise and enjoyment of all their civil and religious rights, ... and to preserve unto them that liberty, in the true Christian faith and worship of God, which they have sought with so much travail, and with peaceable minds, and loyal subjection ... and because some of the ... inhabitants of the same colony cannot, ... conform to the public exercise of religion, according to the ... ceremonies of the Church of England ... Do hereby ... declare, That our royal will and pleasure is, that no person ... shall be ... punished, ... for any differences in opinion in matters of religion ... every person ... [may] have and enjoy his ... own judgments and conscience, in matters of religious concerns, ... not using this liberty to licentiousness and profaneness, nor to the civil injury or outward disturbance of others... And that they may ... defend themselves, in their just rights and liberties against all the enemies of the Christian faith*
>
> *Charter of Rhode Island and Providence Plantations 1663*[2]

The founder of Rhode Island, Roger Williams, is the man who originated the phrase "wall of separation" concerning church and state. But as Thomas Jefferson realized when he voiced the same concept, he had no idea of divorcing religion and government. It is clear from the charter that King Charles understood him to be forming a government based on godly principles, instead of a government-controlled church. Roger Williams wanted believers to be free of civil persecution and the king gave him permission to try his "lively experiment." He also originated the phrase "soul liberty," which was another inspiration to the framers of the Constitution and the First Amendment.

South Carolina

> *... All persons ... who acknowledge that there is one God, and a future state of rewards and punishments, and that God is publicly to be worshipped, shall be freely tolerated. The Christian Protestant religion ... is ... declared to be, the established religion of this State. That all denominations of Christian Protestants in this State, ... shall enjoy equal religious and civil privileges. ... the respective societies of the Church of England that are already formed in this State for the purpose of religious worship shall still continue incorporate and hold the religious property now in their possession. ... in order to entitle [other denominations or faiths to provision and property] each society so petitioning shall have agreed to ... the following five articles, without which no agreement for union of men upon presence of religion shall entitle them to be incorporated and esteemed as a church of the established religion of this State:*
> *1st. That there is one eternal God, and a future state of rewards and punishments.*
> *2d. That God is publicly to be worshipped.*
> *3d. That the Christian religion is the true religion*
> *4th. That the holy scriptures of the Old and New Testaments are of divine inspiration, and are the rule of faith and practice.*
> *5th. That it is lawful and the duty of every man ... to bear witness to the truth.*
> *... when called to make an appeal to God as a witness to truth, shall ... do it in that way ... most agreeable to ... his own conscience. ... the people ... may forever ... elect their own pastors or clergy, ... no person shall officiate as minister of any established church ... not ...*

> *chosen by a majority of the society ... nor until the minister so chosen and appointed shall have made ... the following declaration, over and above the aforesaid five articles: "... by God's grace out of the holy scriptures, ... to teach nothing ... of necessity to eternal salvation but that which ... may be concluded and proved from the scripture; that he will use both public and private admonitions, as well to the sick as to the whole ... and that he will be diligent in prayers, ... that he will ... fashion his own self and his family according to the doctrine of Christ, ... wholesome examples and patterns to the flock of Christ; that he will maintain ... quietness, peace, and love among all people ... No person shall disturb or molest any religious assembly ... [no]abusive language ..., that being the certain way of disturbing the peace, and of hindering the conversion of any to the truth... No person shall ... be obliged to ... support of a religious worship that he ... has not voluntarily engaged to support. ... All other property ... of the Church of England, or any other religious societies, shall remain and be secured to them forever. The poor shall be supported, and elections managed in the accustomed manner, until laws shall be provided to adjust those matters in the most equitable way."*
>
> An Act for establishing the constitution of the State of South Carolina, 1778.[2]

South Carolina established the Protestant Church as its official state church. Belief in a future state of rewards and punishments is specified for inclusion in the State's policy of religious toleration. This would include most Jews who believed in the Messiah's future rule on Earth, if not in Heaven, and even Muslims of the time period, though it would exclude animists and those who believe in Reincarnation.

Acknowledging that there are a number of Protestant denominations, it clarifies by saying that all of them will enjoy equal religious and civil privileges. The Constitution specifically excludes the Church of England from this designation, though it guarantees the retention of its properties and clergy. The Constitution also guarantees the right of Protestant churches to form anywhere and petition for denominational recognition as part of the Established Church as long as they meet specific conditions of belief and practice spelled out very clearly. Their ministers could be chosen by them but also had strict guidelines to adhere to.

All groups were free to worship as they chose in the state. Only those who wished recognition in the Established Religion had to conform to the guidelines of the Constitution. The job of caring for the poor and seeing to elections historically fell to the parish or geographic designation where the church met, and the Constitution stipulated that this was to continue as it had before until any needed adjustments could be made. It seems to indicate that the privileges of the Established Church included control of these matters.

Virginia

> *That no free government, or the blessings of liberty, can be preserved to any people, but by a firm adherence to justice, moderation, temperance, frugality, and virtue, and by frequent recurrence to fundamental principles.*
>
> *That religion, or the duty which we owe to our Creator, ... can be directed only by reason and conviction, not by force or violence; and therefore all men are equally entitled to the free exercise of religion, according to the dictates of conscience; and that it is the mutual*

> *duty of all to practice Christian forbearance, love, and charity towards each other.*[2]

The Virginia Constitution makes specific reference to universal freedom of religion and puts no real conditions of any kind on worship. It is interesting to note that the section preceding the free exercise statement deals with moral principles and says they are necessary to the preservation of freedom and liberty. Most people would acknowledge these to be Christian virtues, yet Thomas Jefferson was proud of the non-sectarian wording of his state's Constitution.[3] He used Christian as a term whose meaning everyone understood, an example of behavior, not a specific preferred belief. These universal principles are also a key element of what the founding fathers believed constituted true Natural Law. If men could practice these virtues then there would be no need to stipulate conditions of religion. The Rationalists of this time period believed they could and must practice these virtues or liberty would not survive.

The influence of seventeenth-century preachers like Roger Williams and John Winthrop, as well as eighteenth-century preachers George Whitfield and Jonathan Edwards, can be seen in examples of their all of the various state constitutions. More of Blackstone's ideas of government and law are also included for study and comparison.

When we understand the phrase "establishment of religion" was part of the daily fabric of life of the colonists, it is easy to see what the founding fathers meant. The model, though imperfect, was the Church of England. To a Colonial, an establishment of religion provided buildings, teachers, preachers, poorhouses, food, clothing, orphanages, and retirement homes for the indigent. New York and Rhode Island wrote that the state governments should not even collect taxes for an establishment of religion. Most states permitted some form of tax collection for an establishment of religion, but the funds so collected were to go where the taxpayer thought best.

---

1 Thomas Paine, *The Rights of Man, Part the Second: Combining Principle And Practice,* Chapter V, "Ways And Means Of Improving The Condition Of Europe Interspersed With Miscellaneous Observations," 1792.

2 All documents not otherwise sourced are from the Yale University *Avalon Project website, http://avalon.law.yale.edu/* or *from National Archives.gov.*

3 Thomas Jefferson, *Autobiography.* 1821. "Where the preamble [of the Statute of Virginia for Religious Freedom] declares, that coercion is a departure from the plan of the holy author of our religion, an amendment was proposed by inserting the words 'Jesus Christ,' so that it should read, 'A departure from the plan of Jesus Christ, the holy author of our religion;' the insertion was rejected by a great majority, in proof that they meant to comprehend, within the mantle of its protection, the Jew and the Gentile, the Christian and Mohammedan, the Hindoo and Infidel of every denomination."

4 William Blackstone, *Commentaries on the Law of England,* 1765–1769.

5 Quoted in *Divining America: Religion in American History,* "Religious Pluralism in the Middle Colonies," Patricia U. Bonomi, Professor Emeritus, New York University, National Humanities Center, from the center's website, viewed May 6, 2010.

4. What is an Establishment of Religion?

The people have an equal, natural and unalienable right, freely and peaceably to exercise their religion, according to the dictates of conscience; and that no religious sect or society ought to be favored or established by law in preference to others.[1]

Ratification of the Constitution, by the Convention of the State of New York

The Constitution of the United States is founded on English law and to a lesser extent, various European laws, especially German and Dutch. In each of these countries, an Establishment of Religion was the collection of taxes to support education, welfare and public worship. The various governments appointed the teachers, welfare workers and pastors and expected these people to support the government in turn.

The first amendment of the United States Constitution is the moral foundation the entire US Constitution.

> *Congress shall make no law respecting an establishment of religion, or prohibiting the free exercise thereof; or abridging the freedom of speech, or of the press; or the right of the people peaceably to assemble, and to petition the Government for a redress of grievances.*[1]

Congress is named because neither the courts nor the Executive branch have the authority to make laws. An Establishment of Religion includes public worship, education and taking care of the poor. At the time of the writing of the US Constitution, Christianity permeated the American culture. To these writers, an Establishment of Religion is the favoring of one denomination to the exclusion of other denominations by law.

While the federal government is prohibited from establishing a religion, there are no laws separating the federal government from religion. To create an artificial separation where none exists, modern secular humanist judges have resorted to a phrase in a letter of President Thomas Jefferson. Roger Williams first used this phrase, "the wall of separation" between church and state (see Chapter One). Both Roger Williams and Thomas Jefferson used the phrase "wall of separation" between religion and government the same way. They meant that government was not to interfere with or influence religion. They did not mean that religion was to have no influence on government. To the men who wrote the phrase "wall of separation," it was meant only as a restraint on the federal government. It was to have absolutely no effect on religion.

Shortly after Thomas Jefferson became president he received a letter from the Danbury, Connecticut Baptist Association. The association expressed its concern that certain men might be able to make laws to twist religious practice in their favor, to control it and make it profitable for them. These men urged Thomas Jefferson to keep holding fast to what they knew to be his views on religion and government, views expressed quite clearly in the *Draft for a Bill for Establishing Religious Freedom*, by Jefferson 1779. In Jefferson's response to the Danbury Baptists he introduces the phrase "building a wall of separation between Church & State."[2]

Ever afterward legislators, judges, politicians and so-called historians have twisted and misinterpreted the meaning of this simple statement. Look at the context. Jefferson was replying to men who feared that laws would be made trying to profit from abuse of religious freedom, from restricting it, ridiculing it, and so weaken and perhaps eventually destroy it.

Jefferson tried to reassure them that the Constitution made them safe from that fear. "... The whole American people ... declared that their legislature should 'make no law respecting an establishment of religion, or prohibiting the free exercise thereof,' thus building a wall of separation between Church & State."[2]

He meant that the Constitution protects religion from judicial and legislative corruption, not that it throws religion out or isolates it. By latching on to that "Wall of Separation" phrase and lying about what Jefferson meant, secularists have managed to convince people it said the opposite of what Jefferson meant. Jefferson wanted religion to be strong, thriving, influencing every man in every possible good way. Yet activists have abused his words to drive religion out of schools and government agencies.

From the Danbury Baptists:

> *... Our Sentiments are uniformly on the side of Religious Liberty. That Religion is at all times and places a Matter between God and Individuals. That no man ought to suffer in Name, person or effects on account of his religious Opinions. That the legitimate Power of civil Government extends no further than to punish the man who works ill to his neighbour: But Sir ... those who seek after power & gain under the pretence of government & Religion ... reproach their fellow men ... as [enemies] of religion Law & good order because [they dare] not assume the prerogative of Jehovah and make Laws to govern the Kingdom of Christ. Sir, we are sensible that the President of the United States is not the national Legislator & also sensible that the national government cannot destroy the Laws of each State; ... May God strengthen you ... against all the*

> *predetermined opposition of those who wish to rise to wealth & importance on the poverty and subjection of the people.*[3]

President Jefferson responded:

> *... Believing with you that religion is a matter which lies solely between Man & his God, that he owes account to none other for his faith or his worship, that the legitimate powers of government reach actions only, & not opinions, I contemplate with sovereign reverence that act of the whole American people which declared that their legislature should "make no law respecting an establishment of religion, or prohibiting the free exercise thereof," thus building a wall of separation between Church & State. ... I shall see with sincere satisfaction the progress of those sentiments which tend to restore to man all his natural rights, convinced he has no natural right in opposition to his social duties."*[2]

Draft for a Bill for Establishing Religious Freedom, by Jefferson 1779

SECTION I.

> *Almighty God hath created the mind free, and manifested his supreme will that free it shall remain ... all attempts to influence it ... tend only to beget habits of hypocrisy ... and are a departure from the plan of the holy author of our religion, ... [who] chose not to propagate it by coercions ... but to extend it by its influence on reason alone;*[4]

Jefferson was a believer in Rationalism, the ability of man's intellect to reason out truth, yet he coupled this belief with an acknowledgement of God's power. He believed that since God had not chosen to force man into belief, it was hardly the place of human government, flawed where God was perfect, corrupt where God was incorruptible, to impose belief on man. He detailed some of the attempts at coerced religion which he, his contemporaries, and those who founded his country, had seen firsthand in the Established Religions of Europe.

> *... rulers, civil as well as ecclesiastical, ... fallible and uninspired men... setting up their own opinions and modes of thinking as the only true and infallible ... established and maintained false religions over the greatest part of the world and through all time ... to compel a man to furnish contributions of money for the propagation of opinions which he disbelieves and abhors, is sinful and tyrannical;*[4]

Jefferson says that these men are doing the opposite of serving God. They force on others laws polluted with their wrong beliefs, just as governments have held wrong beliefs and imposed wrong laws on the people for millennia. He also condemns forcing men to support beliefs they know are wrong, which was the case even under Augsburg and Westphalia. These accords allowed the practice of some other religions but still demanded that the established religion be supported by tax money.

> *[Man should have] ... the comfortable liberty of giving his contributions to the particular pastor whose morals he would make his pattern, and whose powers he feels most persuasive to righteousness ... [one who he believes is best performing] earnest and unremitting labours for the instruction of mankind;*[4]

Jefferson believed that even if a man might belong to a denomination, he should not even be compelled to support it as a whole, but only the man or men he personally decided were most worthy of support. This was a radical idea, seldom practiced even today, as most denominations take the money of individual churches and choose their ministers or their missionaries for them. Independent churches supporting their own minister and missions causes of their choice are and have always been rare.

> *That our civil rights have no dependence on our religious opinions ... that therefore the proscribing any citizen [from] ... offices of trust and emolument, unless he profess or renounce this or that religious opinion, is depriving him injuriously of those privileges ... to which ... he has a natural right;*[4]

Another radical concept was that a man did not have to profess a certain belief to have the same rights as other men, or to hold public office. Jefferson held freedom of belief to be a natural right, part of the natural law, but a law he and the founding fathers defined very differently from Natural Law proponents who insisted on leaving God out of it. As stated at the beginning of this document, Jefferson believed man could arrive at truth through reason, that God did indeed exist and should be worshiped, and, as he will state later, that truth can be arrived at if unencumbered by man's wicked attempts to control it. This was Jefferson's idea of Natural Law, and that of these men who lived around him and created our country and our government.

> *... it tends also to corrupt ... religion it is meant to encourage, by bribing, with ... worldly honours ... those who will externally profess ... these are criminal who [yield to] temptation, yet neither are those innocent who lay the bait in their way; ... that to suffer the civil magistrate to ... restrain the profession or propagation of principles on supposition of their ill tendency is a dangerous fallacy, which*

> *at once destroys all religious liberty, because he ... will make his opinions the rule of judgment...*[4]

Jefferson lays blame on both those who would use force to compel religious conformity and those who submit to it. It breeds corruption by promising worldly rewards. It also gives rulers the power to dictate belief.

> *... time enough for ... civil government ... to interfere when [there are] ... acts against peace and good order; ... truth is great and will prevail ... and has nothing to fear ... unless ... disarmed of ... free argument and debate; errors ceasing to be dangerous when it is permitted freely to contradict them.*[4]

Government should only interfere in religion if there is danger to peace and order. Also, truth can rise to the top unless government steals her tools of warfare, including free speech, which gives truth the power to overpower error.

> *... No man shall be compelled to ... support any religious worship ... nor shall ... suffer, on account of his religious opinions or belief; ... all men shall be free to profess, and by argument to maintain, their ... religion, and that the same shall in no wise ... affect their civil capacities.*[4]

Jefferson believed a man should be able to freely profess and even argue for his beliefs. He clearly said that doing so should not affect any civil position he holds.

> *... This Assembly [has] ... no power to restrain [future] Assemblies ... to declare this act irrevocable would be of no effect in law; yet ... if any act shall be hereafter passed to repeal [it] ,,, such act will be an infringement of natural right.*[4]

The good intentions of the men of the past cannot force the men of the future to do right. They can only admonish them by setting down clearly what they believe and stating that these are part of the natural rights of man. This is Jefferson's Natural Law. It should never be infringed upon, he warns.

James Madison is sometimes called the Father of the US Constitution, since he wrote most of the document. He is also known as the Father of the Bill of Rights along with George Mason, and authored over a third of the *Federalist Papers.*

> *"... The Century preceding the last [believed] ... that Civil Govt. could not stand without ... Religious establishment; & that the Xn. [Christian] religion itself, would perish if not supported by the legal provision for its Clergy. ... Virginia conspicuously corroborates the disproof .... The Civil Govt. ... performs its functions with complete success; ... the number, the industry, and the morality of the Priesthood, & the devotion of the people ... increased by the total separation of the Church from the State."*[5]

Madison, of course, meant the same thing by separation of church and state that Jefferson and all the others had reiterated. Protect the church, be a wall to it, not wall it away from the power to do good.

As pointed out previously, most of the original state constitutions permitted state establishments of religion, in contrast to the Federal Government. Some of the original state constitutions, such New Jersey and New Hampshire, collected taxes for a state establishment of religion, but allowed the person paying the taxes to choose which school their tax money would go to. Other states, such as Massachusetts, simply collected money for an establishment of religion. North Carolina clearly banned any establishment of religion.

In every instance a generalized form of Christianity was permitted, encouraged or in some instances required. For example, public office holders in North Carolina had to believe as a Protestant. The modern liberal antagonism towards religion in general and Christianity in particular were unheard of except in the case of one man whose writings fanned the flames of patriotism and the desire for freedom like no one else's. Thomas Paine's influence on the founding of America cannot be ignored. Yet his later writings shaped a different kind of freethinking and, whatever his intentions were, they led to a new kind of establishment of religion.

---

1 All state and constitution-related documents taken from one of two sources: *The Avalon Project. Documents in Law, History and Diplomacy. Yale Law Library. avalon.law.yale.edu.* or *National Archives, archives.gov*

2 *The Writings of Thomas Jefferson,* Albert E. Bergh, ed. (Washington, D. C.: The Thomas Jefferson Memorial Association of the United States, 1904), Vol. XVI, pp. 281-282.

3 Letter of Oct. 7, 1801 from Danbury (CT) Baptist Assoc. to Thomas Jefferson, *Thomas Jefferson Papers,* Manuscript Division, Library of Congress, Wash. D.C.

4 Jefferson, Thomas. *Draft for a Bill for Establishing Religious Freedom.* Proposed to the Virginia Assembly, 1779.

5 Letter to Robert Walsh, March 2, 1819.

5. Was Thomas Paine the Founding Father of Secular Humanism in America?

"I would advise you, therefore, not to attempt unchaining the tiger, but to burn this piece before it is seen by any other person. ... If men are so wicked with religion, what would they be if without it? I intend this letter itself as a proof of my friendship."[1]
Benjamin Franklin

Thomas Paine stands out among the founding fathers in sharp contrast to their acknowledgements of faith and reliance upon God and Christianity for their work to free and found our country.

Paine was an English political writer and activist who claimed American citizenship (see end of chapter for an explanation of how the United States viewed his claim) and was given French citizenship. He wrote the three best-selling books of the 18th Century: Common Sense, The Rights of Man and The Age of Reason. His works were widely read but his influence on what eventually became the United States was surprisingly limited. He roused people to action, stated simply and passionately many necessary arguments for independence, and was respected by many of the Founding Fathers and later great men for his persuasive style of writing.

"I never tire of reading Tom Paine." Abraham Lincoln[2]

"I consider Paine our greatest political thinker. As we have not advanced, and perhaps never shall advance, beyond the Declaration and Constitution, so Paine has had no successors who extended his principles." Thomas Alva Edison[3]

"Thomas Paine needs no monument made with hands; he has erected a monument in the hearts of all lovers of liberty." Andrew Jackson.[4]

> *When Bonaparte returned from Italy he ... invited him [Paine] to dinner: in ... his rapturous address ... he declared that a statue of gold ought to be erected to him in every city in the universe, assuring him that he always slept with his book Rights of Man under his pillow and conjured him to honor him with his correspondence and advice. This anecdote is only related as a fact. Of the sincerity of the compliment, those may judge who know Bonaparte's principles best.*[5]

John Adams gave Paine full credit for his positive influence on the cause of fighting for independence. Yet he looked back on the effect of Paine's writings on the men of his time with a less than complimentary eye.

> *I am willing you should call this the Age of Frivolity ... would not object if you had named it the Age of Folly, Vice, Frenzy, Brutality, Daemons, Buonaparte, Tom Paine, or the Age of the Burning Brand from the Bottomless Pit, or anything but the Age of Reason. I know not whether any man in the world has had more influence on its inhabitants or affairs for the last thirty years than Tom Paine. ...Never before in any age of the world was [anyone] suffered by the poltroonery of mankind, to run through such a career of mischief. Call it then the Age of Paine.6*

Thomas Paine promoted women's rights, the abolition of slavery, an end to the practice of dueling, even sought laws against cruelty to animals. He urged the revolutionary French not to execute their king, to be the first nation in the world to abolish the death penalty, and was imprisoned and almost executed himself as a result. Biographer Robert Ingersoll insists, "The good people of this world agree with Thomas Paine."[4]

But when he died none of the great names of the revolution, the Constitutional Convention, or any of the other founding fathers came to his funeral. He was buried on his farm, though "He wished to be buried in the Quaker burying ground. ... The committee of the Quakers refused to receive his body, at which he seemed deeply moved."[7]

Benjamin Franklin might have remained his friend, yet he said concerning the publication of works like *The Age of Reason,*

> *I have read your manuscript with some attention. By the argument it contains against a particular Providence, though you allow a general Providence, you strike at the foundation of all religion. For without the belief of a Providence that takes cognizance of, guards, and guides, and may favor particular persons, there is no motive to worship a Deity, to fear his displeasure, or to pray for his protection. I will not enter into any discussion of your principles though you seem to desire it. At present I shall only give you my opinion that ... the consequence of printing this piece will be a great deal of odium [hate] drawn upon yourself, mischief to you, and no benefit to others. He that spits into the wind, spits in his own face. But were you to succeed, do you imagine any good would be done by it? ...*

> *Think how great a portion of mankind consists of weak and ignorant men and women and of inexperienced, inconsiderate youth of both sexes who have need of the motives of religion to restrain them from vice, to support their virtue. ... I would advise you, therefore, not to attempt unchaining the tiger, but to burn this piece before it is seen by any other person. ... If men are so wicked with religion, what would they be if without it? I intend this letter itself as a proof of my friendship.*[1]

Thomas Paine was a bitter, caustic critic of Christianity and organized religion of any kind. He clearly saw the corruption of the Established Religion but he rejected truth and the Scriptures as coming from God himself. He saw the Bible as concocted by the organized church. He denounced many state constitutions for claiming to be tolerant but being tolerant only of Christianity, and attacked the authority of Scriptures repeatedly. Although his ideas have existed for centuries, Thomas Paine was the founding father to whom Secular Humanists look back to justify most of their beliefs and ideas. Secularists today loudly echo Thomas Paine's views on Christianity.

> *"No falsehood is so fatal as that which is made an article of faith."*[8]

> *"Of all the tyrannies that afflict mankind, tyranny in religion is the worst. Every other species of tyranny is limited to the world we live in, but this attempts a stride beyond the grave and seeks to pursue us into eternity."*[9]

> *"What is it the New Testament teaches us? To believe that the Almighty committed debauchery with a woman engaged to be married; and the belief of this debauchery is called faith."*[10]

"The Bible: a history of wickedness that has served to corrupt and brutalize mankind."[11]

"The Christian system of religion is an outrage on common sense."[12]

"It has been the scheme of the Christian church, and of all the other invented systems of religion, to hold man in ignorance of the Creator, as it is of government to hold him in ignorance of his rights. The systems of the one are as false as those of the other, and are calculated for mutual support."[10]

"Priests and conjurors are of the same trade."[12]

"Jesus Christ, ... at once both God and man, and also the Son of God, celestially begotten, on purpose to be sacrificed, because they say that Eve in her longing ... had eaten an apple."[13]

"The Church was resolved to have a New Testament, and as, after the lapse of more than three hundred years, no handwriting could be proved or disproved, the Church, which like former impostors had then gotten possession of the State, had everything its own way. It invented creeds... and out of the loads of rubbish that were presented it voted four to be Gospels, and others to be Epistles, as we now find them arranged."[14]

"Whenever we read the obscene stories, the voluptuous debaucheries, the cruel and torturous executions, the unrelenting vindictiveness, with which more than half the Bible is filled, it would be more consistent that we called it the word of a demon that the Word of God. It is a history of wickedness that has served to corrupt and brutalize mankind; and

for my own part, I sincerely detest it, as I detest everything that is cruel."[11]

"As to the Christian system of faith, it appears to me as a species of atheism -- a sort of religious denial of God. It professed to believe in man rather than in God. It is as near to atheism as twilight to darkness. It introduces between man and his Maker an opaque body, which it calls a Redeemer, as the moon introduces her opaque self between the earth and the sun, and it produces by this means a religious or irreligious eclipse of the light. It has put the whole orbit of reason into shade."[15]

"The most detestable wickedness, the most horrid cruelties, and the greatest miseries that have afflicted the human race have had their origin in this thing called revelation, or revealed religion."[10]

"Yet this is the trash that the Church imposes upon the world as the Word of God; this is the collection of lies and contradictions called the Holy Bible! this is the rubbish called Revealed Religion!"[16]

"The continually progressive change to which the meaning of words is subject, the want of a universal language which renders translation necessary, the errors to which translations are again subject, the mistakes of copyists and printers, together with the possibility of willful alteration, are of themselves evidences that the human language, whether in speech or in print, cannot be the vehicle of the Word of God. The Word of God exists in something else."[11]

"The fable of Christ and his twelve apostles, which is a parody on the Sun and the twelve signs of the Zodiac, copied from the ancient

> *religions of the Eastern world, is the least hurtful part."*[17]

John Calvin agreed with Paine's assessment that man had faults, follies and prejudices, but disagreed that reason was sufficient to overcome them.

> *...In order to our being properly qualified for becoming his disciples, we must lay aside all confidence in our own abilities, and seek light from heaven; and, abandoning the foolish opinion of free-will, must give ourselves up to be governed by God.*[18]

Samuel Adams also had a sage observation for those who claimed to be governed by reason. It is clear from the passion and the venom with which Thomas Paine frequently speaks that Adams' words apply to him. "Mankind are governed more by their feelings than by reason."[19]

Apart from the topic of religion, Thomas Paine writes as if he were a humble servant of man. The quotation below is a thinly disguised arrogance, as is the last quote in the previous section. Men like John Jay were not deceived. " ... As to The Age of Reason, it never appeared to me to have been written from a disinterested love of truth or of mankind,"[20] Jay said. Paine explains below that he needs no organized religion like the rest of the founding fathers.

> *I speak an open and disinterested language, dictated by no passion but that of humanity. To me, who have not only refused offers, because I thought them improper, but have declined rewards I might with reputation have accepted, it is no wonder that meanness and imposition appear disgustful. Independence is my happiness, and I view things as they are,*

> *without regard to place or person; my country is the world, and my religion is to do good.*[21]

John Calvin had a ready response to a man who claimed to be disinterested, that is, to seek only others' good, and to want no rewards himself, yet refuse to allow a place for the truth of God's Word in his or anyone else's life.

> *"Mingled vanity and pride appear ... when miserable men do seek after God, ... they measure him by their own carnal stupidity, and neglecting solid inquiry, fly off to indulge their curiosity in vain speculation. Hence, they ... imagine him to be whatever their own rashness has devised.*[22]

It was a common practice in that time period to write anonymously. The authors of the *Federalist Papers* did not reveal their identities. Many pamphleteers were seeking support for specific religious or political views. But Paine takes extra care to disassociate himself from parties or religions, and claims to be governed only by reason and principle. Again this seems to be arrogant. It was the age of reason for everyone, not just Paine, and principle was paramount to the cause of American liberty, but not principle without belief.

> *[Knowing] Who the Author of this Production is, is wholly unnecessary to the Public, as the Object for Attention is the DOCTRINE ITSELF, not the MAN. Yet it may not be unnecessary to say, That he is unconnected with any Party, and under no sort of Influence public or private, but the influence of reason and principle.*[23]

Paine was right about the restrictions government places on society and the dangers that could lead to. He planned to train men to be perfectly governed by reason, without the need for politics or religion.

> *Some writers have so confounded society with government, as to leave little or no distinction between them; whereas they are not only different, but have different origins. Society is produced by our wants, and government by our wickedness; the former promotes our happiness POSITIVELY by uniting our affections, the latter NEGATIVELY by restraining our vices. The one encourages intercourse, the other creates distinctions. The first a patron, the last a punisher.*
>
> *Society in every state is a blessing, but government even in its best state is but a necessary evil; in its worst state an intolerable one; for when we suffer, or are exposed to the same miseries BY A GOVERNMENT, which we might expect in a country WITHOUT GOVERNMENT, our calamity is heightened by reflecting that we furnish the means by which we suffer.*[24]

The quote below is a rallying call few could resist or disagree with. This was Thomas Paine's specialty, firing up people's emotions to a cause, in spite of his claim to be speaking only out of reason and principle. The quote following seems ironic, considering Thomas Paine had no source for his concept of virtue except his own mind. This is a common idea among humanists, however, that virtue is attainable by reason. The majority of the founding fathers disagreed.

> *O! ye that love mankind! Ye that dare oppose not only tyranny but the tyrant, stand forth! Every spot of the Old World is overrun with oppression. Freedom hath been hunted round the globe. Asia and Africa have long expelled her. Europe regards her like a stranger and England hath given her warning to depart. O!*

> *Receive the fugitive and prepare in time an asylum for mankind.*[25]

> *When we are planning for posterity, we ought to remember that virtue is not hereditary.*[26]

Below Paine voices another common humanist concept, that the cause is universal, and complete unity is necessary. He talks about freedom but actually wants universal control. Anybody who disagrees has to be put up with until Paine can convince them he is right. He believed that religion could be divorced from politics. “I bid you farewell, sincerely wishing, that as men and Christians, ye may always fully and uninterruptedly enjoy every civil and religious right.”[27] Presumably he wished religious rights to extend only to completely private practice, out of sight, out of mind, influencing no one, seen and heard nowhere, as humanists today wish.

> *The sun never shined on a cause of greater worth. 'Tis not the affair of a city, a country, a province, or a kingdom, but of a continent—of at least one eighth part of the habitable globe. 'Tis not the concern of a day, a year, or an age; posterity are virtually involved in the contest, and will be more or less affected, even to the end of time, by the proceedings now. Now is the seed time of continental union, faith and honor. The least fracture now will be like a name engraved with the point of a pin on the tender rind of a young oak; The wound will enlarge with the tree, and posterity read it in full grown characters.*[25]

> *It is of the utmost danger to society to make it [religion] a party in political disputes.*[28]

> *Mingling religion with politics may be disavowed and reprobated by every inhabitant of America.*[28]

George Washington had Thomas Paine's *Crisis* publications read to the troops to rally them. No one could motivate men like Paine. "Without the pen of Paine, the sword of Washington would have been wielded in vain,"[29] was a legendary saying even in Paine's own lifetime. Clearly Paine assigned different meanings to familiar words than conservative, Bible-believers would. He acknowledged a god, but it was purely of his own making. He speaks of hell but would never acknowledge that the Bible correctly describes it. He even mentions Heaven, using it in the sense of a supreme being and a place from which goodness and wisdom come, as was common for deists and others in that day. But keep in mind that Thomas Paine's "god" did not even satisfy a "man of the world" like Benjamin Franklin.

> *THESE are the times that try men's souls. The summer soldier and the sunshine patriot will, in this crisis, shrink from the service of their country; but he that stands it now, deserves the love and thanks of man and woman. Tyranny, like hell, is not easily conquered; yet we have this consolation with us, that the harder the conflict, the more glorious the triumph. What we obtain too cheap, we esteem too lightly: it is dearness only that gives every thing its value. Heaven knows how to put a proper price upon its goods; and it would be strange indeed if so celestial an article as FREEDOM should not be highly rated.*[30]

> *If there must be trouble, let it be in my day, that my child may have peace.*[30]

> *Those who expect to reap the blessings of freedom must, like men, undergo the fatigue of supporting it.*[31]

> *But when the country, into which I had just set my foot, was set on fire about my ears, it was time to stir. It was time for every man to stir.*[32]

Thomas Paine seems to be the best of men, ready to fight, though he considers killing in battle to be murder. It seems a noble cause until he begins to describe the aristocratic enemy. His low insults inflame the class envy of common against nobles. He says it doesn't matter if your enemy has "noble blood." And yet he has to mention it, has to insult it in gross terms.

> *It matters not where you live, or what rank of life you hold, the evil or the blessing will reach you all. The far and the near, the home counties and the back, the rich and the poor, will suffer or rejoice alike. The heart that feels not now is dead; the blood of his children will curse his cowardice, who shrinks back at a time when a little might have saved the whole, and made them happy. I love the man that can smile in trouble, that can gather strength from distress, and grow brave by reflection. 'Tis the business of little minds to shrink; but he whose heart is firm, and whose conscience approves his conduct, will pursue his principles unto death.*

> *My own line of reasoning is to myself as straight and clear as a ray of light. Not all the treasures of the world, so far as I believe, could have induced me to support an offensive war, for I think it murder; but if a thief breaks into my house, burns and destroys my property, and kills or threatens to kill me, or those that are in it, and to "bind me in all cases whatsoever" to his absolute will, am I to suffer it? What signifies it to me, whether he who does it is a king or a common man; my countryman or not my countryman; whether it*

be done by an individual villain, or an army of them? If we reason to the root of things we shall find no difference; neither can any just cause be assigned why we should punish in the one case and pardon in the other. Let them call me rebel and welcome, I feel no concern from it; but I should suffer the misery of devils, were I to make a whore of my soul by swearing allegiance to one whose character is that of a sottish, stupid, stubborn, worthless, brutish man.[30]

Thomas Paine claimed it was essential to protect enemies in order to protect everyone. Yet he insisted that those who disagreed must change, and that it would simply take time to change them. This is sometimes interpreted as a need for "re-education" in socialist totalitarian regimes, and resulted in confinement in the Gulag Archipelago for Aleksandr Solzhenitzyn.

He that would make his own liberty secure must guard even his enemy from oppression; for if he violates this duty he establishes a precedent that will reach to himself.

It is never to be expected in a revolution that every man is to change his opinion at the same moment. There never yet was any truth or any principle so irresistibly obvious that all men believed it at once. Time and reason must cooperate with each other to the final establishment of any principle; and therefore those who may happen to be first convinced have not a right to persecute others, on whom conviction operates more slowly. The moral principle of revolutions is to instruct, not to destroy.

An avidity to punish is always dangerous to liberty. It leads men to stretch, to misinterpret,

> *and to misapply even the best of laws. He that would make his own liberty secure must guard even his enemy from oppression; for if he violates this duty he establishes a precedent that will reach to himself.*[23]

The preceding quote seems to reassure the readers that Paine would never stoop to treating enemies as England treated the American colonists. Secular Humanist newscasters claim it's not oppression to mock or refuse to report on conservative events. Politicians must "protect" their constituents from a "violation of the establishment clause" when they forbid a nativity scene at a firehouse. Judges must "protect" schoolchildren from "religious indoctrination " by permitting only "Science," that is, evolution, to be taught in classrooms. The tree Paine planted, home-grown from the words of a founding father, has borne the bitter fruit of a uniquely American breed of Secular Humanism.

Did Paine intend this? Would he, like the other founding fathers, have cried out in horror at how people have interpreted his words? It's hard to imagine he could make the claim of never having had any such intention when he tried to undermine the very foundation upon which the freedom we have was built. He "reasoned" out his own god, his own heaven and hell, his own virtue. He blasphemed the Christ who sealed our faith with the reality of His life, death, and resurrection.

Paine had more thoughts on the subject of religion. Some seem innocuous, and some actually good and right sentiments. But remember that he is creating his own religion, forged from his own reason.

> *I believe in one God, and no more; and I hope for happiness beyond this life.*[34]

> *The word of god is the creation we behold and it is in this word, which no human invention*

> *can counterfeit or alter, that God speaketh universally to man.*[34]
>
> *What more does man want to know than that the hand or power that made these things is divine, is omnipotent? Let him believe this with the force it is impossible to repel, if he permits his reason to act, and his rule of moral life will follow of course.*[35]
>
> *It is necessary to the happiness of man, that he be mentally faithful to himself. Infidelity does not consist in believing, or in disbelieving; it consists in professing to believe what he does not believe.*[36]
>
> *Men did not make the earth... It is the value of the improvements only, and not the earth itself, that is individual property... Every proprietor owes to the community a ground rent for the land which he holds.*[37]

Sometimes Paine spoke the truth about genuinely hypocritical and apostate practices he saw around him. Sometimes he used the "fruit of the poisoned tree" argument to conclude that because a bad "Christian" church (or Jewish synagogue, or Islamic mosque) did something clearly wrong, all religions had to be bad.

> *Each of those churches show certain books, which they call revelation, or the word of God. The Jews say, that their word of God was given by God to Moses, face to face; the Christians say, that their word of God came by divine inspiration: and the Turks say, that their word of God (the Koran) was brought by an angel from Heaven. Each of those churches accuse the other of unbelief; and for my own part, I disbelieve them all.*[38]

All national institutions of churches, whether Jewish, Christian, or Turkish, appear to me no other than human inventions set up to terrify and enslave mankind, and monopolize power and profit.[34]

It is impossible to calculate the moral mischief, if I may so express it, that mental lying has produced in society. When a man has so far corrupted and prostituted the chastity of his mind, as to subscribe his professional belief to things he does not believe, he has prepared himself for the commission of every other crime.[34]

The following quote could be called a basis for the whole of modern belief system of Secular Humanism. The humanist will say that he was not given the revelation, therefore it is no revelation. He has a choice about whether to believe the Bible, because he has only a believer's word that God spoke them to some prophet a long time ago. Remember that to a humanist belief means opinion, not conclusions based on evidence.

It is a contradiction in terms and ideas to call anything a revelation that comes to us at second hand, either verbally or in writing. Revelation is necessarily limited to the first communication. After this, it is only an account of something which that person says was a revelation made to him; and though he may find himself obliged to believe it, it cannot be incumbent on me to believe it in the same manner, for it was not a revelation made to me, and I have only his word for it that it was made to him.[38]

Christians often say that the greatest gift of God was the sacrifice of His Son, a source of great joy and cause for humble thanksgiving to the believer. Paine claims that

Christians ignore the beauty and perfection of creation and God's freely giving that gift to us. He claims we are proud, because we must have our maker die for us.

> *But if objects for gratitude and admiration are our desire, do they not present themselves every hour to our eyes? Do we not see a fair creation prepared to receive us the instant we are born – a world furnished to our hands, that cost us nothing? Is it we that light up the sun, that pour down the rain, and fill the earth with abundance? Whether we sleep or wake, the vast machinery of the universe still goes on. Are these things, and the blessings they indicate in future, nothing to us? Can our gross feelings be excited by no other subjects than tragedy and suicide? Or is the gloomy pride of man become so intolerable, that nothing can flatter it but a sacrifice of the Creator?*[39]

> *If Jesus Christ was the being which those Mythologists tell us he was, and that he came into this world to suffer, which is a word they sometimes use instead of to die, the only real suffering he could have endured, would have been to live. His existence here was a state of exilement or transportation from Heaven, and the way back to his original country was to die. In fine, everything in this strange system is the reverse of what it pretends to be.*[11]

Paine had seen the Roman Catholic Church corruptly claim that people had to pay money to have their sins pardoned, even have the living pay for the sins of the dead to help them escape purgatory. This clear heresy was already dealt with by men like Martin Luther, John Calvin and John Wycliffe, but it is a common thing for humanists to ignore an answer to an argument and keep blaming those who have any remote connection (called by the name of a Christian religion is close enough for Paine) for a past wrong. So he reasons his way to a discounting of the doctrine of original sin, clearly taught in the Scriptures, explaining that man does not need a Savior, because he never fell from grace or separated himself from God.

> *The doctrine of redemption is founded on a mere pecuniary idea corresponding to that of a debt which another person might pay; and as this pecuniary idea corresponds again with the system of second redemption, obtained through the means of money given to the Church for pardons, the probability is that the same persons fabricated both the one and the other of those theories; and that, in truth there is no such thing as redemption — that it is fabulous, and that man stands in the same relative condition with his Maker as he ever did stand since man existed, and that it is his greatest consolation to think so.*[40]

> *For what is the amount of all his prayers but an attempt to make the Almighty change his mind, and act otherwise than he does? It is as if he were to say: Thou knowest not so well as I.*[40]

Paine wants to appear humble here, so in the previous quote he claims that it is pride for Christians to believe that God wishes them to pray and honors what they say. But he casts off that pretense as he speaks in the next quote, and shows that he is superior to pathetic believers in prayer, whatever god they pray to. His religion is science, the study and appreciation of nature, the only practice by which man may worship. Today, Secular Humanism still holds "Science" as its worship. Devotees have taken Paine's teachings to their logical conclusion, that nature generated life apart from any divinity, out of the non-living, over billions of uniformitarianism years, and evolution was the mechanism of the new "creation."

> *I do not believe in the creed professed by the Jewish church, by the Roman church, by the Greek church, by the Turkish church, by the Protestant church, nor by any church that I know of. My own mind is my own church.*[4]
>
> *It is only by the exercise of reason that man can discover God.*[36]
>
> *That which is now called natural philosophy, embracing the whole circle of science, of which astronomy occupies the chief place, is the study of the works of God, and of the power and wisdom of God in his works, and is the true theology.*[14]

Paine calls Job and Psalm 19 older works than the rest of the Bible. Humanists claim respect for the ancient, the proto-philosophies where man's reason might have been purer than the religiously corrupted mind of today. He doesn't give credit to the writers or authors for having the truth revealed to them by God, but seems to think they mechanically, accidentally, arrived at it through a primitive form of rationalism.

> *The Book of Job and the 19th Psalm, which even the Church admits to be more ancient than the chronological order in which they stand in the book called the Bible, are theological orations conformable to the original system of theology. The internal evidence of those orations proves to a demonstration that the study and contemplation of the works of creation, and of the power and wisdom of God, revealed and manifested in those works, made a great part in the religious devotion of the times in which they were written; and it was this devotional study and contemplation that led to the discovery of the principles upon which what*

> *are now called sciences are established; and it is to the discovery of these principles that almost all the arts that contribute to the convenience of human life owe their existence. Every principal art has some science for its parent, though the person who mechanically performs the work does not always, and but very seldom, perceive the connection.*
>
> *It is a fraud of the Christian system to call the sciences human invention; it is only the application of them that is human. Every science has for its basis a system of principles as fixed and unalterable as those by which the universe is regulated and governed. Man cannot make principles, he can only discover them.*
>
> *The Almighty Lecturer, by displaying the principles of science in the structure of the universe, has invited man to study and to imitation. It is as if He had said to the inhabitants of this globe that we call ours, "I have made an earth for man to dwell upon, and I have rendered the starry heavens visible, to teach him science and the arts. He can now provide for his own comfort, and learn from my munificence to all to be kind to each other."*[14]

John Calvin had a name for men who tried to elevate Nature to the role of godhood, even those like Paine who still claimed they only wanted a God revealed by the study of Nature. Calvin was not fooled.

> *At this day... the earth sustains on her bosom many monster minds, minds which are not afraid to employ the seed of Deity deposited in human nature as a means of suppressing the name of God. Can anything be more detestable*

> *than this madness in man, who, finding God a hundred times both in his body and his soul, makes his excellence in this respect a pretext for denying that there is a God? He will not say that chance has made him different from the brutes; ... but, substituting Nature as the architect of the universe, he suppresses the name of God.*[41]

We must cast aside all previous belief. Worship God through the study of His creation, and learn that as He was kind and generous to make all this for us, we should be kind and generous to our fellow-man. We will automatically be right and do right. Christianity is an impediment to our progress as men.

> *The age of ignorance commenced with the Christian system.*[15]

> *People in general do not know what wickedness there is in this pretended word of God. Brought up in habits of superstition, they take it for granted that the Bible is true, and that it is good; they permit themselves not to doubt of it, and they carry the ideas they form of the benevolence of the Almighty to the book which they have been taught to believe was written by his authority. Good heavens! it is quite another thing; it is a book of lies, wickedness, and blasphemy; for what can be greater blasphemy than to ascribe the wickedness of man to the orders of the Almighty?*[42]

> *Of all the systems of religion that ever were invented, there is none more derogatory to the Almighty, more unedifying to man, more repugnant to reason, and more contradictory in itself, than this thing called Christianity. Too absurd for belief, too impossible to convince,*

> *and too inconsistent for practice, it renders the heart torpid, or produces only atheists and fanatics.*[10]

> *The study of theology as it stands in Christian churches, is the study of nothing; it is founded on nothing; it rests on no principles; it proceeds by no authorities; it has no data; it can demonstrate nothing; and admits of no conclusion. Not any thing can be studied as a science without our being in possession of the principles upon which it is founded; and as this is not the case with Christian theology, it is therefore the study of nothing.*[10]

John Calvin had a different belief about Christian Theology, and he clearly understood why men like Thomas Paine could arrogantly speak as if it was a thing to be despised. Clearly Thomas Paine had never sought the true God as had the men of the Scriptures. Moses, Isaiah, Daniel, Paul; men who knew the true God, demonstrated true humility toward His Word and teachings.

> *Hence that dread and amazement with which as Scripture uniformly relates, holy men were struck and overwhelmed whenever they beheld the presence of God. When we see those who previously stood firm and secure so quaking with terror, that the fear of death takes hold of them, no, they are, in a manner swallowed up and annihilated, the inference to be drawn is that men are never duly touched and impressed with a conviction of their insignificance, until they have contrasted themselves with the majesty of God.*[43]

Thomas Paine left America for England after the revolution was won, escaped England just ahead of arrest for treason, and fled to France, where he was feted by the new Republic, though he spoke no French, and made a citizen of France. He was even elected to a post in their revolutionary government. However, when he interceded against the king's execution, he was thrown in prison and threatened with the guillotine himself. Paine wrote for help to his former American co-patriots and received this reply.

> *"Mr. [James] Monroe [Minister to the French Republic from the United States] has told me, that he has no orders [meaning from the American Government] respecting you; but I am sure he will leave nothing undone to liberate you; but, from what I can learn, from all the late Americans, you are not considered, either by the Government, or by the individuals, as an American citizen. You have been made a French citizen, which you have accepted, and you have further made yourself a servant of the French Republic; and, therefore, it would be out of character for an American Minister to interfere in their internal concerns. You must therefore either be liberated out of compliment to America, or stand your trial, which you have a right to demand."*[44]

Thomas Paine was shocked by this response. America, however, had received significant aid from France in the fight against England. Paine had collaborated with those who had imprisoned and threatened to execute America's ally, the King of France. Also, Paine had made himself a Frenchman and accepted a French government position. He shouldn't ask for deliverance from his own country's laws, however far into madness that country and its laws had descended. After all, he had helped hurry them into that descent.

Eventually Paine was freed and did return to America, only to find himself an outcast. He may very well have died wondering why, but the answer was simple enough. His fellow founding fathers did not believe that, because they had guaranteed Thomas Paine the constitutional right to believe as he would, they had to disobey the God they still worshiped and dishonor and the Scriptures they still reverenced to be his friend.

"A man that is an heretic after the first and second admonition reject; Knowing that he that is such is subverted [perverted or warped], and sinneth, being condemned of himself" (Titus 3:10, KJV).

By the end of the Nineteen-century unbelief demanded and received equal standing with Christianity. The twentieth century saw unbelief organize under the name of Secular Humanism into a religion and become the established religion of US federal government.

---

1 From a letter by Benjamin Franklin, possibly written to Thomas Paine in 1785. There is some critical dispute as to whether it was written to Paine, but there is no question that the letter is commenting specifically on those like Paine who claim to believe in God while excluding belief in God's personal interest in man's morality or provision of salvation.

2 William Herndon, Lincoln law partner and biographer documented this in notes from Herndon to Jesse W. Weik, a Lincoln admirer, between 1 October 1881 and 27 February 1891, containing reminiscences of Lincoln's life, research material used in their joint Lincoln biography, *Herndon's Lincoln: The True Story of a Great Life,* a three volume edition published by Belford, Clarke & Company beginning in 1889.

3 Thomas A. Edison, "The Philosophy of Paine," a June 7, 1925 essay from the book, *The Diary and Sundry Observations,* edited by Dagobert D. Runes (1948).

4 Robert Green Ingersoll, "Thomas Paine," *North American Review,* August, 1892.

5 Thomas Clio Rickman, *Life of Thomas Paine,* 1819.

6 John Adams, in a letter to Benjamin Waterhouse, 29 October 1805.

7 Testimony of Madame Bonneville, friend and caregiver to Paine at the time of his death, reported in the biography by Robert Green Ingersoll, "Thomas Paine," *North American Review,* August, 1892.

8 Thomas Paine, *Examination of the Prophecies,* pamphlet published in 1807.

9 Thomas Paine, "A letter to the Hon. Thomas Erskine, on the Prosecution of Thomas Williams for publishing the *Age of Reason.* With his discourse at the Society of the Theophilanthropists. Paris: Printed for the Author. This pamphlet was carried through Barrois' English press in Paris, September 1797.10 Thomas Paine, *The Age of Reason,* Part II, Chapter 3, "Conclusion," 1794.

11 Thomas Paine, *The Age of Reason,* Part I, Chapter 7, "Examination of the Old Testament," 1794

12 Thomas Paine, *The Age of Reason,* Part II, Chapter 2, "The New Testament," 1794.

13 Thomas Paine, *The Age of Reason,* Part I, Chapter 4, "Of the Bases of Christianity," 1794.

14 Thomas Paine, "Of The Books Of The New Testament: Address To The Believers In The Book Called The Scriptures," *Prospect Papers Magazine* (also titled "A View of the Moral World,"), 1804, published monthly by Elihu Palmer in New York.

15 Thomas Paine, *The Age of Reason,* Part I, Chapter 11, "Of the Theology of Christians and the True Theology," 1794.

16 Thomas Paine, "Essay on Dream," published with the following title: "An Examination of the Passages in the New Testament, quoted from the Old and called Prophecies concerning Jesus Christ. To which is prefixed an Essay on Dream, showing by what operation of the mind a Dream is produced in sleep, and applying the same to the account of Dreams in the New Testament. With an Appendix containing my private thoughts of a Future State. And Remarks on the Contradictory Doctrine in the Books of Matthew and Mark." By Thomas Paine, New York: Printed for the Author. New York, 1807.

17 Thomas Paine, "Letter to Andrew Dean," New York, August 15, 1806.

18 John Calvin, Commentary on Luke 24:45. from *Commentary On A Harmony of the Evangelists, Matthew, Mark, and Luke,* translator from Latin and collator with the French version Rev. William Pringle, Volume 3, Edinburgh, Calvin Translation Society, 1847-1850, *Calvin's Commentaries, Vol. 33: Matthew, Mark and Luke, Part III,* translated by John King, 1847-50.

19 Samuel Adams, "Letter to John Pitts," 21 January 1776.

20 William Jay, *The Life of John Jay* (NY: J. & J. Harper, 1833) p. 80, from his "Charge to the Grand Jury of Ulster County" on Sept. 9, 1777

21 Thomas Paine, *The Rights of Man,* Part II, Chapter 5, "Ways and Means of Improving the Conditions of Europe Interspersed With Miscellaneous Observations," 1791.

22 John Calvin, *Institutes of the Christian Religion,* Thomas Norton, Translator, Part 1, Chapter 4, "The

Knowledge of God Stifled or Corrupted Ignorantly or Maliciously," Section 4, 1581.

23 Thomas Paine, *Common Sense,* "Introduction," January 10, 1776.

24 Thomas Paine, *Common Sense,* "Of the Origin and Design of Government in General, with Concise Remarks on the English Constitution," January 10, 1776.

25 Thomas Paine, *Common Sense,* "Thoughts on the Present State of American Affairs," January 10, 1776.

26 Thomas Paine, *Common Sense,* "Of the Present Ability of America, with Some Miscellaneous Reflections," January 10, 1776.

27 Thomas Paine, *Common Sense,* "Epistle to the Quakers," January 10, 1776.

28 Thomas Paine, *Common Sense,* "Appendix," January 10, 1776.

29 Attributed to John Adams in the Annual Report of the Attorney General (1957) by New York Department of Law.

30 Thomas Paine, *The American Crisis*, I, December 23, 1776.

31 Thomas Paine, *The American Crisis,* IV, September 11, 1777.

32 Thomas Paine, *The American Crisis*, VII, November 21, 1778.

33 Thomas Paine, *Dissertation on First Principles of Government,* July 1795.

34 Thomas Paine, *The Age of Reason,* Part I, Chapter 1, "The Author's Profession of Faith." 1794.

35 Thomas Paine, *The Age of Reason,* Part I, Chapter 9, "In What the True Revelation Consists," 1794.

36 Thomas Paine, *The Age of Reason,* Part I, Chapter 9, "Concerning God, and the Lights Cast on His Existence and Attributes by the Bible," 1794.

37 Thomas Paine, *Agrarian Justice,* printed in English by W. Adlard in Paris, and in London for T. Williams, No. 8 Little Turnstile, Holborn, 1797.

38 Thomas Paine, *The Age of Reason*, Part I, Chapter 2, "Of Missions and Revelations," 1794.

39 Thomas Paine, *The Age of Reason,* Part I, Chapter 6, "Of the True Theology," 1794.

40 Thomas Paine, *The Age of Reason*, Part I, Chapter 8, "Of the New Testament," 1794.

41 John Calvin, *Institutes of the Christian Religion,* Thomas Norton, Translator, Part I, Of the Knowledge of God As Creator, Chapter 5, "The Knowledge of God Conspicuous in the Creation, and Continual Government of the World," Section 4, 1581.

42 Thomas Paine, *The Age of Reason,* Part II, Chapter 1, "The Old Testament," 1794.

43 John Calvin, *Institutes of the Christian Religion,* Thomas Norton, Translator, Part I, Of the Knowledge of God As Creator, Chapter 1, "The Knowledge of God and Ourselves Mutually Connected – The Nature of that Connection," Section 3, 1581.

44 Thomas Paine, "Memorial to James Monroe," 10 Sept. 1794, (a letter to Monroe in which he quotes from this letter received from a friend while Paine was in France).

Appendixes

Appendix One: Court Cases

Church of the Holy Trinity v. United States 1892 U.S. Supreme Court Church of the Holy Trinity v. United States, 143 U.S. 457 (1892) No. 143

Argued and submitted January 7, 1892 Decided February 29, 1892 143 U.S. 457

ERROR TO THE CIRCUIT COURT OF THE UNITED

STATES FOR THE SOUTHERN DISTRICT OF NEW YORK

Syllabus

The Act of February 26, 1880, "to prohibit the importation and migration of foreigners and aliens under contract or agreement to perform labor in the United States, its Territories, and the District of Columbia," 23 Stat. 332, c. 164, does not apply to a contract between an alien, residing out of the United States, and a religious society incorporated under the laws of a state, whereby he engages to remove to the United States and to enter into the service of the society as its rector or minister.

THE case is stated in the opinion.

MR. JUSTICE BREWER delivered the opinion of the Court.

Plaintiff in error is a corporation duly organized and incorporated as a religious society under the laws of the State of New York. E. Walpole Warren was, prior to

September, 1887, an alien residing in England. In that month the plaintiff in error made a contract with him by which he was to remove to the City of New York and enter into its service as rector and pastor, and in pursuance of such contract, Warren did so remove and enter upon such service. It is claimed by the United States that this contract on the part of the plaintiff in error was forbidden by 23 Stat. 332, c. 164, and an action was commenced to recover the penalty prescribed by that act. The circuit court held that the contract was within the prohibition of the statute, and rendered judgment accordingly, 36 F.3d 3, and the single question presented for our determination is whether it erred in that conclusion.

The first section describes the act forbidden, and is in these words:

"Be it enacted by the Senate and House of Representatives of the United States of America in Congress assembled, that from and after the passage of this act it shall be unlawful for any person, company, partnership, or corporation, in any manner whatsoever, to prepay the transportation, or in any way assist or encourage the importation or migration, of any alien or aliens, any foreigner or foreigners, into the United States, its territories, or the District of Columbia under contract or agreement, parol or special, express or implied, made previous to the importation or migration of such alien or aliens, foreigner or foreigners, to perform labor or service of any kind in the United States, its territories, or the District of Columbia."

We find, therefore, that the title of the act, the evil which was intended to be remedied, the circumstances surrounding the appeal to Congress, the reports of the committee of each house, all concur in affirming that the intent of Congress was simply to stay the influx of this cheap unskilled labor.

But, beyond all these matters, no purpose of action against religion can be imputed to any legislation, state or national, because this is a religious people. This is historically true. From the discovery of this continent to the present hour, there is a single voice making this affirmation.

The commission to Christopher Columbus, prior to his sail westward, is from “Ferdinand and Isabella, by the grace of God, King and Queen of Castile,” etc., and recites that “it is hoped that by God’s assistance some of the continents and islands in the ocean will be discovered,” etc. The first colonial grant, that made to Sir Walter Raleigh in 1584, was from “Elizabeth, by the grace of God, of England, Fraunce and Ireland, Queene, defender of the faith,” etc., and the grant authorizing him to enact statutes of the government of the proposed colony provided that “they be not against the true Christian faith nowe professed in the Church of England.” The first charter of Virginia, granted by King James I in 1606, after reciting the application of certain parties for a charter, commenced the grant in these words:

“We, greatly commending, and graciously accepting of, their Desires for the Furtherance of so noble a Work, which may, by the Providence of Almighty God, hereafter tend to the Glory of his Divine Majesty, in propagating of Christian Religion to such People, as yet live in Darkness and miserable Ignorance of the true Knowledge and Worship of God, and may in time bring the Infidels and Savages, living in those parts, to human Civility, and to a settled and quiet government; DO, by these our Letters-Patents, graciously accept of, and agree to, their humble and well intended Desires.”

Language of similar import may be found in the subsequent charters of that colony, from the same king, in 1609 and 1611, and the same is true of the various charters granted to the other colonies. In language more or less emphatic is the establishment of the Christian religion declared to be one of the purposes of the grant. The celebrated compact made by the pilgrims in the *Mayflower*, 1620, recites:

"Having undertaken for the Glory of God, and Advancement of the Christian Faith, and the Honour of our King and Country, a Voyage to plant the first Colony in the northern Parts of Virginia; Do by these Presents, solemnly and mutually, in the Presence of God and one another, covenant and combine ourselves together into a civil Body Politick, for our better Ordering and Preservation, and Furtherance of the Ends aforesaid."

The fundamental orders of Connecticut, under which a provisional government was instituted in 1638-39, commence with this declaration:

"Forasmuch as it hath pleased the Allmighty God by the wise disposition of his diuyne pruidence so to Order and dispose of things that we the Inhabitants and Residents of Windsor, Hartford, and Wethersfield are now cohabiting and dwelling in and vppon the River of Conectecotte and the Lands thereunto adioyneing; And well knowing where a people are gathered togather the word of God requires that to mayntayne the peace and vnion of such a people there should be an orderly and decent Gouerment established according to God, to order and dispose of the affayres of the people at all seasons as occation shall require; doe therefore assotiate and conioyne our selues to be as one Publike state or Comonwelth, and doe, for our selues and our Successors and such as shall be adioyned to vs att any tyme hereafter, enter into Combination and Confederation togather, to mayntayne and presearue the liberty and purity of the gospell of our Lord Jesus weh we now prfesse, as also the disciplyne of the Churches, weh according to the truth of the said gospell is now practiced amongst vs."

In the charter of privileges granted by William Penn to the province of Pennsylvania, in 1701, it is recited:

"Because no People can be truly happy, though under the greatest Enjoyment of Civil Liberties, if abridged of the Freedom of their Consciences, as to their Religious Profession and Worship; And Almighty God being the only Lord of Conscience, Father of Lights and Spirits, and the Author as well as Object of all divine Knowledge, Faith, and Worship, who only doth enlighten the Minds, and persuade and convince the Understandings of People, I do hereby grant and declare," etc.

Coming nearer to the present time, the declaration of independence recognizes the presence of the Divine in human affairs in these words:

"We hold these truths to be self-evident, that all men are created equal, that they are endowed by their Creator with certain unalienable Rights, that among these are Life, Liberty, and the pursuit of Happiness. . . . We therefore the Representatives of the United States of America, in General Congress, Assembled, appealing to the Supreme Judge of the world for the rectitude of our intentions, do, in the Name and by Authority of the good these Colonies, solemnly publish and declare," etc.; "And for the support of this Declaration, with a firm reliance on the Protection of Divine Providence, we mutually pledge to each other our Lives, our Fortunes, and our sacred Honor."

If we examine the constitutions of the various states, we find in them a constant recognition of religious obligations. Every Constitution of every one of the forty-four states contains language which, either directly or by clear implication, recognizes a profound reverence for religion, and an assumption that its influence in all human affairs is essential to the wellbeing of the community. This recognition may be in the preamble, such as is found in the Constitution of Illinois, 1870:

"We, the people of the State of Illinois, grateful to Almighty God for the civil, political, and religious liberty which He hath so long permitted us to enjoy, and looking to Him for a blessing upon our endeavors to secure and transmit the same unimpaired to succeeding generations," etc.

It may be only in the familiar requisition that all officers shall take an oath closing with the declaration, "so help me God." It may be in clauses like that of the Constitution of Indiana, 1816, Art. XI, section 4: "The manner of administering an oath or affirmation shall be such as is most consistent with the conscience of the deponent, and shall be esteemed the most solemn appeal to God." Or in provisions such as are found in Articles 36 and 37 of the declaration of rights of the Constitution of Maryland, 1867: "That, as it is the duty of every man to worship God in such manner as he thinks most acceptable to Him, all persons are equally entitled to protection in their religious liberty, wherefore no person ought, by any law, to be molested in his person or estate on account of his religious persuasion or profession, or for his religious practice, unless, under the color of religion, he shall disturb the good order, peace, or safety of the state, or shall infringe the laws of morality, or injure others in their natural, civil, or religious rights; nor ought any person to be compelled to frequent or maintain or contribute, unless on contract, to maintain any place of worship or any ministry; nor shall any person, otherwise competent, be deemed incompetent as a witness or juror on account of his religious belief, provided he believes in the existence of God, and that, under his dispensation, such person will be held morally accountable for his acts, and be rewarded or punished therefore, either in this world or the world to come. That no religious test ought ever to be required as a qualification for any office of profit or trust in this state, other than a declaration of belief in the existence of God;

nor shall the legislature prescribe any other oath of office than the oath prescribed by this constitution."

Or like that in Articles 2 and 3 of part 1st of the Constitution of Massachusetts, 1780: "It is the right as well as the duty of all men in society publicly, and at stated seasons, to worship the Supreme Being, the great Creator and Preserver of the universe. . . . As the happiness of a people and the good order and preservation of civil government essentially depend upon piety, religion, and morality, and as these cannot be generally diffused through a community but by the institution of the public worship of God and of public instructions in piety, religion, and morality, therefore, to promote their happiness, and to secure the good order and preservation of their government, the people of this commonwealth have a right to invest their legislature with power to authorize and require, and the legislature shall, from time to time, authorize and require, the several towns, parishes, precincts, and other bodies politic or religious societies to make suitable provision at their own expense, for the institution of the public worship of God and for the support and maintenance of public Protestant teachers of piety, religion, and morality, in all cases where such provision shall not be made voluntarily."

Or, as in sections 5 and 14 of Article 7 of the Constitution of Mississippi, 1832: "No person who denies the being of a God, or a future state of rewards and punishments, shall hold any office in the civil department of this state. . . . Religion morality, and knowledge being necessary to good government, the preservation of liberty, and the happiness of mankind, schools, and the means of education, shall forever be encouraged in this state."

Or by Article 22 of the Constitution of Delaware, (1776), which required all officers, besides an oath of allegiance, to make and subscribe the following declaration: "I, A.

B., do profess faith in God the Father, and in Jesus Christ His only Son, and in the Holy Ghost, one God, blessed for evermore, and I do acknowledge the Holy Scriptures of the Old and New Testament to be given by divine inspiration."

Even the Constitution of the United States, which is supposed to have little touch upon the private life of the individual, contains in the First Amendment a declaration common to the constitutions of all the states, as follows: "Congress shall make no law respecting an establishment of religion, or prohibiting the free exercise thereof," etc., and also provides in Article I, Section 7, a provision common to many constitutions, that the executive shall have ten days (Sundays excepted) within which to determine whether he will approve or veto a bill.

There is no dissonance in these declarations. There is a universal language pervading them all, having one meaning. They affirm and reaffirm that this is a religious nation. These are not individual sayings, declarations of private persons. They are organic utterances. They speak the voice of the entire people. While, because of a general recognition of this truth, the question has seldom been presented to the courts, yet we find that in Updegraph v. Commonwealth, 11 S. & R. 394, 400, it was decided that "Christianity, general Christianity, is, and always has been, a part of the common law of Pennsylvania; . . . not Christianity with an established church and tithes and spiritual courts, but Christianity with liberty of conscience to all men."

And in People v. Ruggles, 8 Johns. 290, 294-295, Chancellor Kent, the great commentator on American law, speaking as Chief Justice of the Supreme Court of New York, said: "The people of this state, in common with the people of this country, profess the general doctrines of Christianity as the rule of their faith and practice, and to scandalize the author of these doctrines is not only, in a religious point of view, extremely impious, but, even in respect to the obligations due to society, is a gross violation of decency and good order. . . . The free, equal, and undisturbed enjoyment of religious opinion, whatever it may be, and free and decent discussions on any religious subject, is granted and secured; but to revile, with malicious and blasphemous contempt, the religion professed by almost the whole community is an abuse of that right. Nor are we bound by any expressions in the Constitution, as some have strangely supposed, either not to punish at all, or to punish indiscriminately the like attacks upon the religion of Mahomet or of the Grand Lama, and for this plain reason, that the case assumes that we are a Christian people, and the morality of the country is deeply engrafted upon Christianity, and not upon the doctrines or worship of those impostors."

And in the famous case of Vidal v. Girard's Ex'rs, 2 How. 127, 198, this Court, while sustaining the will of Mr. Girard, with its provision for the creation of a college into which no minister should be permitted to enter, observed: "It is also said, and truly, that the Christian religion is a part of the common law of Pennsylvania."

If we pass beyond these matters to a view of American life, as expressed by its laws, its business, its customs, and its society, we find everywhere a clear recognition of the same truth. Among other matters, note the following: the form of oath universally prevailing, concluding with an appeal to the Almighty; the custom of opening sessions of all deliberative bodies and most conventions with prayer; the prefatory words of all wills,"In the name of God, amen;" the laws respecting the observance of the Sabbath, with the general cessation of all secular business, and the closing of courts, legislatures, and other similar public assemblies on that day; the churches and church organizations which abound in every city, town, and hamlet; the multitude of charitable organizations existing every where under Christian auspices; the gigantic missionary associations, with general support, and aiming to establish Christian missions in every quarter of the globe. These, and many other matters which might be noticed, add a volume of unofficial declarations to the mass of organic utterances that this is a Christian nation. In the face of all these, shall it be believed that a Congress of the United States intended to make it a misdemeanor for a church of this country to contract for the services of a Christian minister residing in another nation?

Suppose, in the Congress that passed this act, some member had offered a bill which in terms declared that if any Roman Catholic church in this country should contract with Cardinal Manning to come to this country and enter into its service as pastor and priest, or any Episcopal church should enter into a like contract with Canon Farrar, or any Baptist church should make similar arrangements with Rev. Mr. Spurgeon, or any Jewish synagogue with some eminent rabbi, such contract should be adjudged unlawful and void, and the church making it be subject to prosecution and punishment. Can it be believed that it would have received a minute of approving thought or a single vote? Yet it is contended that such was, in effect, the meaning of this statute. The construction invoked cannot be accepted as correct. It is a case where there was presented a definite evil, in view of which the legislature used general terms with the purpose of reaching all phases of that evil, and thereafter, unexpectedly, it is developed that the general language thus employed is broad enough to reach cases and acts which the whole history and life of the country affirm could not have been intentionally legislated against. It is the duty of the courts under those circumstances to say that, however broad the language of the statute may be, the act, although within the letter, is not within the intention of the legislature, and therefore cannot be within the statute.

The judgment will be reversed, and the case remanded for further proceedings in accordance with this opinion.

Epperson vs. Arkansas, 1968, United States Supreme Court

(Author's Note: Italicized material represents direct quotations. Material in regular type represents the author's comments.)

(The following paragraph is not part of a trial transcript, but is quoted from the website *Voices For Evolution*.)

In 1968, in Epperson v. Arkansas, the United States Supreme Court invalidated an Arkansas statute that prohibited the teaching of evolution. The Court held the statute unconstitutional on grounds that the First Amendment to the U.S. Constitution does not permit a state to require that teaching and learning must be tailored to the principles or prohibitions of any particular religious sect or doctrine.

(Epperson v. Arkansas (1968) 393 U.S. 97, 37 U.S. Law Week 4017, 89S. Ct. 266, 21 L. Ed 228)

Following are excerpts from the Supreme Court transcript of this trial, taken from the website www.bc.edu/ bc_org/avp/cas/comm/ free_speech/epperson. Background material in the transcript explains that a teacher hired in 1964 to teach High School Biology completed her first year without incident. Her second year, however, a new textbook was obtained for her class which included a chapter on Darwin's theory. The teacher was apparently aware of the state's constitutional issue and decided to protect herself from disciplinary action before any was taken by suing the state to have the statue voided. The excerpt begins by stating the position of the attorney representing the State of Arkansas explaining how the state would interpret the statute.

On the other hand, counsel for the State, in oral argument in this Court, candidly stated that, despite the State Supreme Court's equivocation, Arkansas would interpret the statute "to mean that to make a student aware of the theory . . . just to teach that there was [103] such a theory" would be grounds for dismissal and for prosecution under the statute; and he said "that the Supreme Court of Arkansas' opinion should be interpreted in that manner." He said: "If Mrs. Epperson would tell her students that 'Here is Darwin's theory, that man ascended or descended from a lower form of being,' then I think she would be under this statute liable for prosecution."

In any event, we do not rest our decision upon the asserted vagueness of the statute. On either interpretation of its language, Arkansas' statute cannot stand. It is of no moment whether the law is deemed to prohibit mention of Darwin's theory, or to forbid any or all of the infinite varieties of communication embraced within the term "teaching." Under either interpretation, the law must be stricken because of its conflict with the constitutional prohibition of state laws respecting an establishment of religion or prohibiting the free exercise thereof. The overriding fact is that Arkansas' law selects from the body of knowledge a particular segment which it proscribes for the sole reason that it is deemed to conflict with a particular religious doctrine; that is, with a particular interpretation of the Book of Genesis by a particular religious group.

The following excerpt includes the specific opinion of Justice Black on this matter.

MR. JUSTICE BLACK, concurring.

I am by no means sure that this case presents a genuinely justiciable case or controversy. Although Arkansas Initiated Act No. 1, the statute alleged to be unconstitutional, was passed by the voters of Arkansas in

1928, we are informed that there has never been even a single attempt by the State to enforce it. And the pallid, unenthusiastic, even apologetic defense of the Act presented by the State in this Court indicates that the State would make no attempt to enforce the law should it remain on the books for the next century. Now, nearly 40 years after the law has slumbered on the books as though dead, a teacher alleging fear that the State might arouse from its lethargy and try to punish her has asked for a declaratory judgment holding the law unconstitutional. She was subsequently joined by a parent who alleged his interest in seeing that his two then school-age sons "be informed of all scientific theories and hypotheses ..."

Notwithstanding my own doubts as to whether the case presents a justiciable controversy, the Court brushes aside these doubts and leaps headlong into the middle of the very broad problems involved in federal intrusion into state powers to decide what subjects and schoolbooks it may wish to use in teaching state pupils. ... But, agreeing to consider this as a genuine case or controversy, I cannot agree to thrust the Federal Government's long arm the least bit further into state school curriculums than decision of this particular case requires. And the Court, in order to invalidate the Arkansas law as a violation of the First Amendment, has been compelled to give the State's law a broader meaning than the State Supreme Court was willing to give it. The Arkansas Supreme Court's opinion, in its entirety, stated that:

"Upon the principal issue, that of constitutionality, the court holds that Initiated Measure No. 1 of 1928, Ark. Stat. Ann. § 80-1627 and § 80-1628 (Repl. 1960), is a valid exercise of the state's power to specify the curriculum in its public schools. The court expresses no opinion on the question whether the Act prohibits any explanation of the theory of evolution or merely prohibits teaching that the theory is true; the answer not being necessary to a decision in the case, and the issue not having been raised."

It is plain that a state law prohibiting all teaching of human development or biology is constitutionally quite different from a law that compels a teacher to teach as true only one theory of a given doctrine. It would be difficult to make a First Amendment case out of a state law eliminating the subject of higher mathematics, or astronomy, or biology from its curriculum. And, for all the Supreme Court of Arkansas has said, this particular Act may prohibit that and nothing else. This Court, however, treats the Arkansas Act as though it made it a misdemeanor to teach or to use a book that teaches that evolution is true. But it is not for this Court to arrogate to itself the power to determine the scope of Arkansas statutes. Since the highest court of Arkansas has deliberately refused to give its statute that meaning, we should not presume to do so.

The Supreme Court struck down this Arkansas statue partly because it believed the state was violating the first and fourteenth amendments and partly because it believed the law to be too vaguely worded. The significant fact is in Black's statement that Arkansas had a chance to deal with the issue without federal interference and failed to do so. Black did not like even the idea that a Federal hand might be reaching into a state issue. Education specifics were supposed to be up to the states in those days. Arkansas gave away its state's right, and the rights of states in the future, by allowing the Supreme Court to establish this precedent.

The important issue of this case is just what Black said. The federal government made a ruling in a state issue and that shouldn't have happened. Time after time cases like this one have whittled away autonomy and replaced it with precedent. The power of the federal courts took away, little by little, the control of states over education and transferred it to the federal government. The Supreme Court has been a powerful tool in taking away our protection, our freedom, our rights and our property.

Segraves vs. State of California, 1981

(Author's Note: Italicized material represents direct quotations. Material in regular type represents the author's comments.)

(The following paragraph is not part of a trial transcript, but is quoted from the website Voices For Evolution)

In 1981, in Segraves v. State of California the Court found that the California State Board of Education's Science Framework, as written and as qualified by its anti-dogmatism policy, gave sufficient accommodation to the views of Segraves, contrary to his contention that class discussion of evolution prohibited his and his children's free exercise of religion. The anti-dogmatism policy provided that class discussions of origins should emphasize that scientific explanations focus on "how", not "ultimate cause," and that any speculative statements concerning origins, both in texts and in classes, should be presented conditionally, not dogmatically. The court's ruling also directed the Board of Education to widely disseminate the policy, which in 1989 was expanded to cover all areas of science, not just those concerning issues of origins. (Segraves v. California (1981) Sacramento Superior Court #278978)

Following are excerpts from the oral presentation of the case. Superior Court Judge Irving Perluss adopted a very friendly and informal tone, insisting on the oral format, making light of the need for huge amounts of documentation, and so it's a bit difficult to find a clean copy of this transcript to draw from. Most of the sections are the opinion of the judge, but there is an instance where a witness, Dr. Meyer, is called upon to speak.

These excerpts come from a personal website built by Frank Fire, who says he is “a firefighter/ paramedic. (with a name like that, what else would I be?) I also built it to promote critical thinking and to promote the defense of the First Amendment.” The text contained a number of typos and formatting errors which have been corrected for ease of reading, but the basic format is that of the original transcript.

The judge’s tone seemed to imply that the case was not important enough to be recorded and everyone should just get together as friends and settle things. It established an important precedent, however, and Frank Fire performed an important service by posting a copy of the transcript.

And isn’t it truly wonderful that in our country we can seek to invoke the awesome authority of the courts to assuage the feelings of a single child, a child. And in the final analysis, I believe that is what this case is all about. The play between establishment on the one hand, in terms of accommodation, and free exercise on the other. Now, fortunately -- I say “fortunately” because I’m the fellow that has to make the decision -- the issues have been narrowed here to the point where we are not faced with such a dilemma, and thus there is on contention here that evolution should not be taught in the public schools. I think you’ve heard me say on several occasions that if there were, it would be rejected as an impermissible accommodation, for that battle was fought and resolved by the Supreme Court of the United States, in Epperson versus Arkansas. Now, moreover, the Plaintiffs have disclaimed any interest in an accommodation which would require the teaching of special creation in the public schools. And I might say, in -- and of course, this is what they call, “dicta,” this is not part of the decision in this case, but this is my -- my view -- that is was appropriate that they do so, for I have no doubt, whatever, that such an accommodation would be held to be violated with the establishment clause, and forbidden. I think this is so, as a matter of law. It was basically held to be such in the -- in the opinion of the California Attorney General in 58 Attorney General Opinions, 262. And of course, it was held in the decision of Daniels versus Waters in the Sixth Circuit, which was referred to during the course of our trial.

Now, the issue, simply stated, accordingly, is whether or not the free exercise of religion by Mr. Segraves and his children was thwarted by the instruction in science that children had received in school, and if so, has there been sufficient accommodation for their views?

The Court, in addition, is prepared to find and does find that the science framework, as written, and if qualified by the policy of the Board exemplified by Exhibit N, does provide sufficient accommodation for the views of the Plaintiff. This is so, in my judgment, even if, as was alluded to by Mr. Turner, there is some problem about whether that was ever officially adopted as a policy by the Board because the fact is now that by virtue of the statement of the representative of the Board, more than one, not only the Attorney General but the representatives of the Board, that is current Board policy and shall remain as current Board policy until a Board changes it. I think all teachers -- I hope all teachers endeavor to follow the Code of Ethics and the administrative regulation that we have read 80130 of Title Five. But nevertheless, all of us conclude, and I conclude myself, sometimes are needed -- we need to be reminded of our responsibilities. It seems to me that what has happened here has developed from a lack of communication from the Board to the school to the classroom teacher. I think it is the emphasis on tolerance and understanding that should be communicated as a fundamental policy of the State Board of Education. This is true not only in science, but it's true throughout the entire public school system. I must add that it seems to the Court, also, that persons seeking tolerance and understanding must practice it, also. Only in this way can all of us enjoy the religious liberty which is our fundamental right.

Mr. Turner has already quoted from the concurring opinion of Justice Stewart, and Sherbert versus Vernor. I think it's worth repeating because those are resounding and beautiful words where he said, "I am convinced that no liberty is more essential to the continued vitality of the free society which our constitution guarantees than is the religious liberty protected by the free exercise clause explicit in the First Amendment and embedded in the Fourteenth." I think Justice Stewart has spoken well.

In the final analysis, ladies and gentlemen, counsel, all that Plaintiffs seek, in the Court's view, presently is contained in Board policy. It appears, however, that this Board policy may not have been communicated to all who should know of it, and who should be guided by that policy. As this is a Court of equity, it seems to the Court that an appropriate remedy may be fashioned.

It will be the order of the Court that there shall be disseminated to all the publishers, institutions, school districts, schools, and persons regularly receiving the science framework a copy of the Board policy set forth in Exhibit N. By this, the Court means, insofar as possible, the policies shall -- the policy shall be sent to those who have received the framework in the past. It shall be included in the framework disseminated in the future. It follows that if there are violations of this policy when disseminated it becomes a matter of concern for students and parents to adjust with their local teachers, their local schools, and their local school boards.

"Now, when you begin to think of textbooks that talk about belief, now to me belief is not a scientific word. One knows, one accumulates data, one has a comprehension of, one understands, one does a lot of things, but to me belief always, in my situation, has been something I associate with my theology. I would not like to see my theology and my science get mixed. I have never dealt with a scientific process where somebody says, 'I believe.' I have dealt with theological processes where one believes. In short, I think at that point you begin to mix epistemologies, and that's confusing."

And then I said to him,

"But I see, as I comprehend this case, we are talking about the very kind of disclaimer that you have just told us about, that you have just told us about, that at the beginning of a science textbook should there not be a statement --because not everyone is a scientist and knows all the background of scientists -- but shouldn't there be a statement saying, 'this does not deal with theology?'"

Dr. Mayer,

"Absolutely. I would -- I would say there should be a clear explanation that perhaps should run through the entire textbook within the student's mind what it is he's dealing with. He's dealing with science. We are not making a pretense to teach him music, art, poetry, theology, or any other discipline. Science does these things, and outside of that realm, science is not only moot, but might even be harmful."

Court,

"And, moreover, science is not dogmatic in that it is open ended and there is an absence of preset conclusions?"

The witness,

"Yes sir."

Now, there is one additional statement from Justice Stewart -- forgive me if I quote from him often, but our son clerked for him as a clerk, and so I -- I think he's a great man.

Justice Stewart also said in the concurring opinion, and in the Sherbert case, and these are the words that I felt were most pertinent to our case where he said, "And I think that the guarantee of religious liberty embodied in the free exercise clause affirmatively requires government to create an atmosphere of hospitality and accommodation to individual belief or disbelief. In short, I think our constitution commands the positive protection by government of religious freedom, not only for a minority, however small, not only for the majority, however large, but for each of us." I don't think any of us could really quarrel with that.

As I view this case, accordingly, counsel, I really don't believe that either side has lost. I truly believe that both sides have won. I think that we have all won because hopefully what we have achieved in this case is understanding.

California had a policy to make sure teachers didn't make evolution a dogma. The judge made a very kind and inclusive statement that everybody won but the man and his children lost the case.

The anti-dogmatism policy provided that class discussions of origins should emphasize that scientific explanations focus on "how," not "ultimate cause," and that any speculative statements concerning origins, both in texts and in classes, should be presented conditionally, not dogmatically.

This California statute may or may not have been sufficient to protect the religious beliefs of students. The intended result seems to have been that each side is free to believe what it will about origins. A consequence that may have been unintended is that by accepting and operating under this standard, by attempting to place both sides on an equal footing, Evolutionists reveal that they really do regard Evolution as a set of beliefs, in spite of the judge's contention that Science doesn't deal with beliefs.

McLean v. Arkansas Board of Education, 1982

(Author's Note: Italicized material represents direct quotations. Material in regular type represents the author's comments.)

(The following paragraph is not part of a trial transcript, but is quoted from the website Voices For Evolution.)

In 1982, in McLean v. Arkansas Board of Education, a federal court held that a "balanced treatment" statute violated the Establishment Clause of the U.S. Constitution. The Arkansas statute required public schools to give balanced treatment to "creation-science" and "evolution-science". In a decision that gave a detailed definition of the term "science," the court declared that "creation science" is not in fact a science. The court also found that the statute did not have a secular purpose, noting that the statute used language peculiar to creationist literature in emphasizing origins of life as an aspect of the theory of evolution. While the subject of life's origins is within the province of biology, the scientific community does not consider the subject as part of evolutionary theory, which assumes the existence of life and is directed to an explanation of how life evolved after it originated. The theory of evolution does not presuppose either the absence or the presence of a creator. (McLean v. Arkansas Board of Education (1982) 529 F. Supp. 1255, 50 U.S. Law Week 2412)

Following are excerpts from the trial transcript. The source is *www.talkorigins.org/faqs/mclean-v-arkansas.*

Special attention should be paid to the notation in the preceding paragraph, however, the one that says While the subject of life's origins is within the province of biology, the scientific community does not consider the subject as part of evolutionary theory, which assumes the existence of life and is directed to an explanation of how life evolved after it originated. The theory of evolution does not presuppose either the absence or the presence of a creator. Keep this idea in mind for later consideration.

On March 19, 1981, the Governor of Arkansas signed into law Act 590 of 1981, entitled "Balanced Treatment for Creation-Science and Evolution-Science Act." The Act is codified as Ark. Stat. Ann. &80-1663, et seq., (1981 Supp.). Its essential mandate is stated in its first sentence: "Public schools within this State shall give balanced treatment to creation-science and to evolution-science." On May 27, 1981, this suit was filed challenging the constitutional validity of Act 590 on three distinct grounds.

First, it is contended that Act 590 constitutes an establishment of religion prohibited by the First Amendment to the Constitution, which is made applicable to the states by the Fourteenth Amendment. Second, the plaintiffs argue the Act violates a right to academic freedom which they say is guaranteed to students and teachers by the Free Speech Clause of the First Amendment. Third, plaintiffs allege the Act is impermissibly vague and thereby violates the Due Process Clause of the Fourteenth Amendment.

The following excerpt is significant because it tells you that the courts have taken upon themselves the right to sole and indisputable power to tell us what the Constitution says and what it means. The courts can tell you how to think about this because people let them tell you how to think about it before. Now you're stuck.

There is no controversy over the legal standards under which the Establishment Clause portion of this case must be judged. The Supreme Court has on a number of occasions expounded on the meaning of the clause, and the pronouncements are clear. Often the issue has arisen in the context of public education, as it has here. In Everson v. Board of Education, 330 U.S. 1, 15-16 (1947), Justice Black stated:

The "establishment of religion" clause of the First Amendment means at least this: Neither a state nor the Federal Government can set up a church. Neither can pass laws which aid one religion, aid all religions, or prefer one religion over another. Neither can force nor influence a person to go to or to remain away from church against his will or force him to profess a belief or disbelief in any religion. No person can be punished for entertaining or professing religious beliefs or disbeliefs, for church-attendance or non-attendance. No tax, large or small, can be levied to support any religious activities or institutions, whatever they may be called, or what ever form they may adopt to teach or practice religion. Neither a state nor the Federal Government can, openly or secretly, participate in the affairs of any religious organizations or groups and vice versa. In the words of Jefferson, the clause ... was intended to erect "a wall of separation between church and State."

The Establishment Clause thus enshrines two central values: voluntarism and pluralism. And it is in the area of the public schools that these values must be guarded most vigilantly.

Designed to serve as perhaps the most powerful agency for promoting cohesion among a heterogeneous democratic people, the public school must keep scrupulously free from entanglement in the strife of sects. The preservation of the community from divisive conflicts, of Government from irreconcilable pressures by religious groups, or religion from censorship and coercion however subtly exercised, requires strict confinement of the State to instruction other than religious, leaving to the individual's church and home, indoctrination in the faith of his choice. [McCollum v. Board of Education, 333 U.S. 203, 216-217 (1948), (Opinion of Frankfurter, J., joined by Jackson, Burton, and Rutledge, J.J.)]

What Black said was proper and correct, up to the point where he inserted Jefferson's explanation about the "wall of separation." People have gotten to think that that's actually in the Constitution because of mentions like this, but it isn't. And it's been used to promote the idea that all mention of any religion must be excised from education because education must be a state function. What Thomas Jefferson actually meant is just the opposite of what Justice Black says. Thomas Jefferson, the extreme leftist of his day, meant that the state must not interfere in the affairs of the Church; the wall was to protect the Church from the state. Thomas Jefferson meant what all of the founding fathers meant. No aspect of the federal government, including the courts, had any power, any authority to do anything at all with any aspect an establishment of religion. An Establishment of Religion is welfare, education and worship. Yet Justice Black in this case doesn't even stop there. He goes on to quote Frankfurter, and Frankfurter goes too far. He presupposes that the government must be the teacher or the people can't be cohesive.

Education wasn't originally a state function. It was usurped by the state from religious leaders and parents. In every society from ancient times to the present, where the government took over teaching the children, the seeds of that government's destruction were sown. The teaching of religion doesn't automatically mean that there will be strife or coercion or even indoctrination. Who puts up a fuss about religious instruction? People who don't want to be reminded that they are responsible to God. Look for them, and you'll see where the strife and coercion is coming from.

In the second place, no one even pretends that all religion has been excised from the public school. Yoga classes are taught in Physical Education. Teaching the Crusades in History class can't be done without bringing up religious issues, wrong ones and right ones. Teachers interweave culture and religion with Foreign Language study, and even studying Science brings up medical treatments at the Temple of Aesclipius and Egyptian pharmaceutical papyri ceremonially buried with priests.

The term "scientific creationism" first gained currency around 1965 following publication of *The Genesis Flood* in 1961 by Whitcomb and Morris. There is undoubtedly some connection between the appearance of the BSCS texts emphasizing evolutionary thought and efforts of Fundamentalist to attach the theory. (Mayer)

In the 1960's and early 1970's, several Fundamentalist organizations were formed to promote the idea that the Book of Genesis was supported by scientific data. The terms "creation science" and "scientific creationism" have been adopted by these Fundamentalists as descriptive of their study of creation and the origins of man. Perhaps the leading creationist organization is the Institute for Creation Research (ICR), which is affiliated with the Christian heritage College and supported by the Scott Memorial Baptist Church in San Diego, California. The ICR, through the Creation-Life Publishing Company, is the leading publisher of creation science material. other creation science organizations include the Creation Science Research Center (CSRC) of San Diego and the Bible Science Association of Minneapolis, Minnesota. In 1963, the Creation Research Society (CRS) was formed from a schism in the American Scientific Affiliation (ASA). It is an organization of literal Fundamentalists who have the equivalent of a master's degree in some recognized area of science. A purpose of the organization is "to reach all people with the vital message of the scientific and historical truth about creation." Nelkin,

The Science Textbook Controversies and the Politics of Equal Time, 66.

The preceding quote sets up the case being presented, the argument, not about whether teachers should have the freedom to teach what they believe is important and right, but whether a particular teaching must be attacked, discredited and beaten out of the schools. The court has already made itself the authority on what the state is and what religion is and how they can't be in the same room together. That includes the concept that the school is the state. A lengthy summary of the history of Fundamentalism is included in the transcript, because it's necessary for an inextricable bond to be formed between Creation Science and religious extremists. The transcript contends that proponents of this bill were on a religious crusade and that they attempted to conceal the fact to allow their bill to pass.

Senator James L. Holsted [was chosen to] introduce the act. Holsted, a self-described "born again" Christian Fundamentalist, introduced the act in the Arkansas Senate. He did not consult the State Department of Education, scientists, science educators or the Arkansas Attorney General. The Act was not referred to any Senate committee for hearing and was passed after only a few minutes' discussion on the Senate floor. In the House of Representatives, the bill was referred to the Education Committee which conducted a perfunctory fifteen minute hearing. No scientist testified at the hearing, nor was any representative from the State Department of Education called to testify.

The State failed to produce any evidence which would warrant an inference or conclusion that at any point in the process anyone considered the legitimate educational value of the Act. It was simply and purely an effort to introduce the Biblical version of creation into the public school curricula. The only inference which can be drawn from these circumstances is that the Act was passed with the specific purpose by the General Assembly of advancing religion. The Act therefore fails the first prong of the three-pronged test, that of secular legislative purpose, as articulated in Lemon v. Kurtzman, supra, and Stone v. Graham, supra.

An immediate attack is made on the bill's credentials. There were no scientists, no Department of Education input, no senate committee ruled on it, so it can't be valid. More about the issue of scientists later, but at least the last two entities can be identified as instruments of government control. The state must retain sole power here. A bill merely created and submitted by earnest, intelligent citizens is no good on its face.

A presentation of the basic tenets of Creation Science and Evolutionary Science follows in the transcript, setting the two in opposition to each other. An attack is made on this method of presentation as follows and the "true" definition of science is arrived at so that Creation Science can quickly be excluded entirely from serious consideration. The statement that "in a free society, knowledge does not require the imprimatur of legislation in order to become science" is almost laughable if it weren't such a lie. This whole case is about legislating what is and isn't Science.

In addition to the fallacious pedagogy of the two model approach, Section 4(a) lacks legitimate educational value because "creation-science" as defined in that section is simply not science. Several witnesses suggested definitions of science. A descriptive definition was said to be that science is what is "accepted by the scientific community" and is "what scientists do." The obvious implication of this description is that, in a free society, knowledge does not require the imprimatur of legislation in order to become science.

More precisely, the essential characteristics of science are:(1) It is guided by natural law;

(2) It has to be explanatory by reference to nature law;(3) It is testable against the empirical world;(4) Its conclusions are tentative, i.e. are not necessarily the final word; and (5) It is falsifiable. (Ruse and other science witnesses).

The term "Natural Law" comes from Plato and Aristotle. Aristotle acknowledged the possibility of an "unmoved mover," but Plato is famous for having thrown "the gods" (and the true God) out of his perfect society thousands of years ago. This court has taken an adversarial position carefully devised to exclude the possibility of Creation and set its own position up as the only possible fact. It's not fact, it's philosophy. The entire "definition" of Science presented here is Naturalism, a philosophy designed to exclude God, not true Science at all but a way to set up the worship of man's intellect as an extension of nature.

As many times as the transcript argues that Creation Science proofs don't prove anything, you would think that it would become clear that this premise as a definition of Science doesn't prove anything. About the only thing true about "Science" as defined here is that its conclusions certainly are tentative. Yet the position taken is that they are the final word. This is the dogma of a belief, a religion, not Science.

Note the folksy statements that Science is "what scientists do." Naturally that excludes Creationists, even though most of these proponents of Creation Science hold advanced degrees from accredited institutions in recognized scientific fields. Unless you presuppose that a Creationist can't be a scientist you would have to grant that these people really are scientists and therefore they also do what scientists do.

Creation science as described in Section 4(a) fails to meet these essential characteristics. First, the section revolves around 4(a)(1) which asserts a sudden creation "from nothing." Such a concept is not science because it depends upon a supernatural intervention which is not guided by natural law. It is not explanatory by reference to natural law, is not testable and is not falsifiable.

The same arguments are applicable to Evolution, or would be if Evolution were forced to justify its tenets by actually coming up with a viable theory to cover origins. Instead it is allowed to slide by with the explanation that it doesn't deal with origins. Actually, it does, but more along the lines of Eastern religions which allow for an endless cycle of time, progressively more billions of years. How can the statement that it presupposes the existence of life be satisfactory? It allows for all of Evolutionary theory to be based on presuppositions, and indeed that's all it is, suppositions based on the founding premise that we suppose there isn't any God who started everything.

Creation science as defined in Section 4(a), not only fails to follow the canons of dealing with scientific theory, it also fails to fit the more general descriptions of "what scientists think" and "what scientists do." The scientific community consists of individuals and groups, nationally and internationally, who work independently in such varied fields as biology, paleontology, geology, and astronomy. Their work is published and subject to review and testing by their peers. The journals for publication are both numerous and varied. There is, however, not one recognized scientific journal which has published an article espousing the creation science theory described in Section 4(a). Some of the State's witnesses suggested that the scientific community was "close-minded" on the subject of creationism and that explained the lack of acceptance of the creation science arguments. Yet no witness produced a scientific article for which publication has been refused. Perhaps some members of the scientific community are resistant to new ideas. It is, however, inconceivable that such a loose knit group of independent thinkers in all the varied fields of science could, or would, so effectively censor new scientific thought.

The reader is directed to Dr. Richard Sternberg's discussion of what happened to him when he published an article by Dr. Stephen Meyer which contained material related to Intelligent Design, not even espousing Creationism. (See the Section Three Appendix for specific examples of attacks on recognized members of the scientific community because of a connection with Intelligent Design.)

The trial transcript simply dismisses the possibility that the scientific community could be narrow minded. No doubt thousands of articles and books which have been refused publication could have been produced as evidence of this narrow-mindedness. The transcript later brings up the fact that a woman who was charged with developing curriculum materials was unable to find any that met her criteria for inclusion. In other words, her fruitless search proves one of two points, either that reputable scientists cannot get creationist material published or that her criteria is narrow-minded and exclusive of this material.

The defendants' argument would be more persuasive if, in fact, there were only two theories or idea about the origins of life and the world. That there are a number of theories was acknowledge by the State's witnesses, Dr. Wickramasinghe and Dr. Geisler. Dr. Wickramasinghe testified at length in support of a theory that life on earth was "seeded" by comets which delivered genetic material and perhaps organisms to the earth's surface from interstellar dust far outside the solar system. The "seeding" theory further hypothesizes that the earth remains under the continuing influence of genetic material from space which continues to affect life. While Wickramasinghe's theory about the origins of life on earth has not received general acceptance within the scientific community, he has, at least, used scientific methodology to produce a theory of origins which meets the essential characteristics of science.

It is a logical fallacy to create a definition and then make it the only definition anybody can use to prove anything. The preceding exposition of the theory of "genetic seeding" by Dr. Wickramasinghe is presented to prove that creation science isn't allowed to set itself off against Evolution because Evolution isn't the only theory of how things are the way they are. There's this one, which the Scientific community doesn't recognize and won't even fund further study about. Excellent choice. A theory with a completely unprovable, unexaminable and already generally discarded premise is at least good Science.

Robert Gentry's discovery of radioactive polonium haloes in granite and coalified woods is, perhaps, the most recent scientific work which the creationists use as argument for a "relatively recent inception" of the earth and a "worldwide flood." The existence of polonium haloes in granite and coalified wood is thought to be inconsistent with radiometric dating methods based upon constant radioactive decay rates. Mr. Gentry's findings were published almost ten years ago and have been the subject of some discussion in the scientific community. The discoveries have not, however, led to the formulation of any scientific hypothesis or theory which would explain a relatively recent inception of the earth or a worldwide flood. Gentry's discovery has been treated as a minor mystery which will eventually be explained. It may deserve further investigation, but the National Science Foundation has not deemed it to be of sufficient import to support further funding.

The National Science Foundation has decided not to fund this promising area of research for only one reason: It might disprove a few presuppositions Evolutionists cling to. If ever there was an example of narrow-mindedness in the scientific community, here it is. Demanding that Creationists must produce something "new" before they will get a hearing is a humorous thought coming from someone who resurrects Plato to craft a definition of Science. This is a common dismissal of Creationist evidence, that it's old so it isn't valid. How is age a worthy criteria for judging evidentiary value? If you can prove you were born in the United States thirty years ago is that evidence too old to be admitted as proof of citizenship?

In any event, if Act 590 is implemented, many teachers will be required to teach materials in support of creation science which they do not consider academically sound. Many teachers will simply forego teaching subjects which might trigger the "balanced treatment" aspects of Act 590 even though they think the subjects are important to a proper presentation of a course.

Implementation of Act 580 will have serious and untoward consequences for students, particularly those planning to attend college. Evolution is the cornerstone of modern biology, and many courses in public schools contain subject matter relating to such varied topics as the age of the earth, geology and relationships among living things. Any student who is deprived of instruction as to the prevailing scientific thought on these topics will be denied a significant part of science education. Such a deprivation through the high school level would undoubtedly have an impact upon the quality of education in the State's colleges and universities, especially including the pre-professional and professional programs in the health sciences.

"Evolution is the cornerstone of modern biology," certainly gives enormous weight to a theoretical teaching that is not supposed to be presented as dogma. While it's true that eliminating evolution from the curriculum would severely limit what can be taught, this bill did not ask for that to be done. It asked for balance, for equal time, to present the opposing viewpoint. This transcript direly predicts that instead teachers will live n fear of reprisals from wild-eyed religionists and children's education will suffer. They will be denied a full preparation and have stunted opportunities and a blighted future. Who would not fear the possibility that their children might fail to learn important things, things they need to go on in their education?

The defendants argue in their brief that evolution is, in effect, a religion, and that by teaching a religion which is contrary to some students' religious views, the State is infringing upon the student's free exercise rights under the First Amendment. Mr. Ellwanger's legislative findings, which were adopted as a finding of fact by the Arkansas Legislature in Act 590, provides:

Evolution-science is contrary to the religious convictions or moral values or philosophical beliefs of many students and parents, including individuals of many different religious faiths and with diverse moral and philosophical beliefs. Act 590, &7(d).

The defendants argue that the teaching of evolution alone presents both a free exercise problem and an establishment problem which can only be redressed by giving balanced treatment to creation science, which is admittedly consistent with some religious beliefs. This argument appears to have its genesis in a student note written by Mr. Wendell Bird, "Freedom of Religion and Science Instruction in Public Schools," 87 Yale L.J. 515 (1978). The argument has no legal merit.

If creation science is, in fact, science and not religion, as the defendants claim, it is difficult to see how the teaching of such a science could "neutralize" the religious nature of evolution.

Assuming for the purposes of argument, however, that evolution is a religion or religious tenet, the remedy is to stop the teaching of evolution, not establish another religion in opposition to it. Yet it is clearly established in the case law, and perhaps also in common sense, that evolution is not a religion and that teaching evolution does not violate the Establishment Clause, Epperson v. Arkansas, supra, Willoughby v. Stever, No. 15574-75 (D.D.C. May 18, 1973); aff'd. 504 F.2d 271 (D.C. Cir. 1974), cert. denied , 420 U.S. 924 (1975); Wright v. Houston Indep. School Dist., 366 F. Supp. 1208 (S.D. Tex 1978), aff.d. 486 F.2d 137 (5th Cir. 1973), cert. denied 417 U.S. 969 (1974).

As proof that Evolution is not a religion, the transcript cites precedent, case law. This is circular reasoning if there ever was such a thing. The court rules that Evolution is not a religion because another court has already ruled that Evolution is not a religion. Case closed.

The Court closes this opinion with a thought expressed eloquently by the great Justice Frankfurter:

We renew our conviction that "we have at stake the very existence of our country on the faith that complete separation between the state and religion is best for the state and best for religion." Everson v. Board of Education, 330 U.S. at 59. If nowhere else, in the relation between Church and State, "good fences make good neighbors." [McCollum v. Board of Education, 333 U.S. 203, 232 (1948)]

Once again Justice Frankfurter claims for the state the sole right to educate, and to dictate what shall and shall not be allowed in the scope of that education.

The quote from Robert Frost's 1914 poem "Mending Wall" is extremely significant in this context. The narrator of the poem objects to the metaphorical walls dividing people from one another. If the state is that neighbor on the other side, I feel the same as the narrator of Frost's poem:

Before I built a wall I'd ask to know
What I was walling in or walling out,
And to whom I was like to give offense.
Something there is that doesn't love a wall,
That wants it down.'
I could say 'Elves' to him,
But it's not elves exactly, and I'd rather
He said it for himself. I see him there
Bringing a stone grasped firmly by the top
In each hand, like an old-stone savage armed.
He moves in darkness as it seems to me,
Not of woods only and the shade of trees.
He will not go behind his father's saying,
And he likes having thought of it so well
He says again,
'Good fences make good neighbors.'

Edwards v. Aguillard, U.S. Supreme Court, 1987

(Author's Note: Italicized material represents direct quotations.

Material in regular type represents the author's comments.)

(The following paragraph is not part of a trial transcript, but is quoted from the website Voices For Evolution)

In 1987, in Edwards v. Aguillard, the U.S. Supreme Court held unconstitutional Louisiana's "Creationism Act." This statute prohibited the teaching of evolution in public schools, except when it was accompanied by instruction in "creation science." The Court found that, by advancing the religious belief that a supernatural being created humankind, which is embraced by the term creation science, the act impermissibly endorses religion. In addition, the Court found that the provision of a comprehensive science education is undermined when it is forbidden to teach evolution except when creation science is also taught. (Segraves v. State of California (1981) Sacramento Superior Court #278978)

Instead of excerpts from the full trial transcript, which is essentially the same issue as that treated in the case of McLean v. Arkansas Board of Education, 1982, what follows is Justice Antonin Scalia's dissenting opinion, which was shared by the Chief Justice William Rehnquist. This material is taken from www.talkorigins.org/faqs/ edwards-v-aguillard. It is lengthy and includes many notes and references but his statement is in vocabulary easy to understand and well worth reading. It is possible to get through the notes and references with patient effort. There is no inserted commentary because the justice's statements are those of a straightforward, honest man honestly frustrated by his inability to stop an injustice. They need no real explanation and would be difficult to improve upon.

Even if I agreed with the questionable premise that legislation can be invalidated under the Establishment Clause on the basis of its motivation alone, without regard to its effects, I would still find no justification for today's decision. The Louisiana legislators who passed the "Balanced Treatment for Creation-Science and Evolution-Science Act" (Balanced Treatment Act), La. Rev. Stat. Ann. 17:286.1-17:286.7 (West 1982), each of whom had sworn to support the Constitution were well aware of the potential Establishment Clause problems and considered that aspect of the legislation with great care. After seven hearings and several months of study, resulting in substantial revision of the original proposal, they approved the Act overwhelmingly and specifically articulated the secular purpose they meant it to serve.

Although the record contains abundant evidence of the sincerity of that purpose (the only issue pertinent to this case), the Court today holds, essentially on the basis of "its visceral knowledge regarding what must have motivated the legislators," 778 F.2d 225, 227 (CA5 1985)

(Gee, J., dissenting) (emphasis added), that the members of the Louisiana Legislature knowingly violated their oaths and then lied about it. I dissent. Had requirements of the Balanced Treatment Act that are not apparent on its face been clarified by an interpretation of the Louisiana Supreme Court, or by the manner of its implementation, the Act might well be found unconstitutional; but the question of its constitutionality cannot rightly be disposed of on the gallop, by impugning the motives of its supporters.

I

This case arrives here in the following posture: The Louisiana Supreme Court has never been given an opportunity to interpret the Balanced Treatment Act, State officials have never attempted to implement it, and it has never been the subject of a full evidentiary hearing. We can only guess at its meaning. We know that it forbids instruction in either "creation-science" or "evolution-science" without instruction in the other, @ 17:286.4A, but the parties are sharply divided over what creation science consists of. Appellants insist that it is a collection of educationally valuable scientific data that has been censored from classrooms by an embarrassed scientific establishment. Appellees insist it is not science at all but thinly veiled religious doctrine. Both interpretations of the intended meaning of that phrase find considerable support in the legislative history.

At least at this stage in the litigation, it is plain to me that we must accept appellants' view of what the statute means. To begin with, the statute itself defines "creation-science" as "the scientific evidences for creation and inferences from those scientific evidences." @ 17:286.3(2) (emphasis added). If, however, that definition is not thought sufficiently helpful, the means by which the Louisiana Supreme Court will give the term more precise content is quite clear -- and again, at this stage in the litigation, favors the appellants' view. "Creation science" is unquestionably a "term of art," see Brief for 72 Nobel Laureates et al. as Amici Curiae 20, and thus, under Louisiana law, is "to be interpreted according to [its] received meaning and acceptation with the learned in the art, trade or profession to which [it] refer[s]." La. Civ. Code Ann., Art. 15 (West 1952). The only evidence in the record of the "received meaning and acceptation" of "creation science" is found in five affidavits filed by appellants. In those affidavits, two scientists, a philosopher, a theologian, and an educator, all of whom claim extensive knowledge of creation science, swear that it is essentially a collection of scientific data supporting the theory that the physical universe and life within it appeared suddenly and have not changed substantially since appearing. See App. to Juris. Statement A-19 (Kenyon); id., at A-36 (Morrow); id., at A-41 (Miethe). These experts insist that creation science is a strictly scientific concept that can be presented without religious reference. See id., at A-19 -- A-20, A-35 (Kenyon); id., at A-36 -- A-38 (Morrow); id., at A-40, A-41, A-43 (Miethe); id., at A-47, A-48 (Most); id., at A-49 (Clinkert). At this point, then, we must assume that the Balanced Treatment Act does not require the presentation of religious doctrine.

Nothing in today's opinion is plainly to the contrary, but what the statute means and what it requires are of rather little concern to the Court. Like the Court of Appeals, 765 F.2d 1251, 1253, 1254 (CA5 1985), the Court finds it necessary to consider only the motives of the legislators who supported the Balanced Treatment Act, ante, at 586, 593-594, 596. After examining the statute, its legislative history, and its historical and social context, the Court holds that the Louisiana Legislature acted without "a secular legislative purpose" and that the Act therefore fails the "purpose" prong of the three-part test set forth in Lemon v. Kurtzman, 403 U.S. 602, 612 (1971). As I explain below, infra, at 636-640, I doubt whether that "purpose" requirement of Lemon is a proper interpretation of the Constitution; but even if it were, I could not agree with the Court's assessment that the requirement was not satisfied here.

This Court has said little about the first component of the Lemon test. Almost invariably, we have effortlessly discovered a secular purpose for measures challenged under the Establishment Clause, typically devoting no more than a sentence or two to the matter. See, e. g., Witters v. Washington Dept. of Services for Blind, 474 U.S. 481, 485-486 (1986); Grand Rapids School District v. Ball, 473 U.S. 373, 383 (1985); Mueller v. Allen, 463 U.S. 388, 394-395 (1983); Larkin v. Grendel's Den, Inc., 459 U.S. 116, 123-124 (1982); Widmar v. Vincent, 454 U.S. 263, 271 (1981); Committee for Public Education & Religious Liberty v. Regan, 444 U.S. 646, 654, 657 (1980); Wolman v. Walter, 433 U.S. 229, 236 (1977) (plurality opinion); Meek v. Pittenger, 421 U.S. 349, 363 (1975); Committee for Public Education & Religious Liberty v. Nyquist, 413 U.S. 756, 773 (1973); Levitt v. Committee for Public Education & Religious Liberty, 413 U.S. 472, 479-480, n. 7 (1973); Tilton v. Richardson, 403 U.S. 672, 678-679 (1971) (plurality opinion); Lemon v. Kurtzman, supra, at 613. In fact, only once before deciding Lemon, and twice since, have we invalidated a law for lack of a secular purpose. See Wallace v. Jaffree, 472 U.S. 38 (1985); Stone v. Graham, 449 U.S. 39 (1980) (per curiam); Epperson v. Arkansas, 393 U.S. 97 (1968).

Nevertheless, a few principles have emerged from our cases, principles which should, but to an unfortunately large extent do not, guide the Court's application of Lemon today. It is clear, first of all, that regardless of what "legislative purpose" may mean in other contexts, for the purpose of the Lemon test it means the "actual" motives of those responsible for the challenged action. The Court recognizes this, see ante, at 585, as it has in the past, see, e. g., Witters v. Washington Dept. of

Services for Blind, supra, at 486; Wallace v. Jaffree, supra, at 56. Thus, if those legislators who supported the Balanced Treatment Act in fact acted with a "sincere" secular purpose, ante, at 587, the Act survives the first component of the Lemon test, regardless of whether that purpose is likely to be achieved by the provisions they enacted.

Our cases have also confirmed that when the Lemon Court referred to "a secular . . . purpose," 403 U.S., at 612, it meant "a secular purpose." The author of Lemon, writing for the Court, has said that invalidation under the purpose prong is appropriate when "there [is] no question that the statute or activity was motivated wholly by religious considerations." Lynch v. Donnelly, 465 U.S. 668, 680 (1984) (Burger, C. J.) (emphasis added); see also id., at 681, n. 6; Wallace v. Jaffree, supra, at 56 ("The First Amendment requires that a statute must be invalidated if it is entirely motivated by a purpose to advance religion") (emphasis added; footnote omitted). In all three cases in which we struck down laws under the Establishment Clause for lack of a secular purpose, we found that the legislature's sole motive was to promote religion. See Wallace v. Jaffree, supra, at 56, 57, 60; Stone v. Graham, supra, at 41, 43, n. 5; Epperson v. Arkansas, supra, at 103, 107-108; see also Lynch v. Donnelly, supra, at 680 (describing Stone and Epperson as cases in which we invalidated laws "motivated wholly by religious considerations"). Thus, the majority's invalidation of the Balanced Treatment Act is defensible only if the record indicates that the Louisiana Legislature had no secular purpose.

It is important to stress that the purpose forbidden by Lemon is the purpose to "advance religion." 403 U.S., at 613; accord, ante, at 585 ("promote" religion); Witters v. Washington Dept. of Services for Blind, supra, at 486 ("endorse religion"); Wallace v. Jaffree, 472 U.S., at 56 ("advance religion"); ibid. ("endorse . . . religion");

Committee for Public Education & Religious Liberty v. Nyquist, supra, at 788 ("'advancing' . . . religion"); Levitt v. Committee for Public Education & Religious Liberty, supra, at 481 ("advancing religion"); Walz v. Tax Comm'n of New York City, 397 U.S. 664, 674 (1970) ("establishing, sponsoring, or supporting religion"); Board of Education v. Allen, 392 U.S. 236, 243 (1968) ("'advancement or inhibition of religion'") (quoting Abington School Dist. v. Schempp, 374 U.S. 203, 222 (1963)). Our cases in no way imply that the Establishment Clause forbids legislators merely to act upon their religious convictions. We surely would not strike down a law providing money to feed the hungry or shelter the homeless if it could be demonstrated that, but for the religious beliefs of the legislators, the funds would not have been approved. Also, political activism by the religiously motivated is part of our heritage. Notwithstanding the majority's implication to the contrary, ante, at 589-591, we do not presume that the sole purpose of a law is to advance religion merely because it was supported strongly by organized religions or by adherents of particular faiths. See Walz v. Tax Comm'n of New York City, supra, at 670; cf. Harris v. McRae, 448 U.S. 297, 319-320 (1980). To do so would deprive religious men and women of their right to participate in the political process. Today's religious activism may give us the Balanced Treatment Act, but yesterday's resulted in the abolition of slavery, and tomorrow's may bring relief for famine victims. Similarly, we will not presume that a law's purpose is to advance religion merely because it "'happens to coincide or harmonize with the tenets of some or all religions,'" Harris v. McRae, supra, at 319 (quoting McGowan v. Maryland, 366 U.S. 420, 442 (1961)), or because it benefits religion, even substantially. We have, for example, turned back Establishment Clause challenges to restrictions on abortion funding, Harris v. McRae, supra, and to Sunday closing laws, McGowan v.

Maryland, supra, despite the fact that both "agre[e] with the dictates of [some] Judaeo-Christian religions," id., at 442. "In many instances, the Congress or state legislatures conclude that the general welfare of society, wholly apart from any religious considerations, demands such regulation." Ibid. On many past occasions we have had no difficulty finding a secular purpose for governmental action far more likely to advance religion than the Balanced Treatment Act. See, e. g., Mueller v. Allen, 463 U.S., at 394-395 (tax deduction for expenses of religious education); Wolman v. Walter, 433 U.S., at 236 (plurality opinion) (aid to religious schools); Meek v. Pittenger, 421 U.S., at 363 (same); Committee for Public Education & Religious Liberty v. Nyquist, 413 U.S., at 773 (same); Lemon v. Kurtzman, 403 U.S., at 613 (same); Walz v. Tax Comm'n of New York City, supra, at 672 (tax exemption for church property); Board of Education v. Allen, supra, at 243 (textbook loans to students in religious schools). Thus, the fact that creation science coincides with the beliefs of certain religions, a fact upon which the majority relies heavily, does not itself justify invalidation of the Act.

Finally, our cases indicate that even certain kinds of governmental actions undertaken with the specific intention of improving the position of religion do not "advance religion" as that term is used in Lemon. 403 U.S., at 613. Rather, we have said that in at least two circumstances government must act to advance religion, and that in a third it may do so.

First, since we have consistently described the Establishment Clause as forbidding not only state action motivated by the desire to advance religion, but also that intended to "disapprove," "inhibit," or evince "hostility" toward religion, see, e. g., ante, at 585 ("'disapprove'") (quoting Lynch v. Donnelly, supra, at 690 (O'CONNOR, J., concurring)); Lynch v. Donnelly, supra, at 673 ("hostility"); Committee for Public Education & Religious

Liberty v. Nyquist, supra, at 788 ("'inhibi[t]'"); and since we have said that governmental "neutrality" toward religion is the preeminent goal of the First Amendment, see, e. g., Grand Rapids School District v. Ball, 473 U.S., at 382; Roemer v. Maryland Public Works Bd., 426 U.S. 736, 747 (1976) (plurality opinion); Committee for Public Education & Religious Liberty v. Nyquist, supra, at 792-793; a State which discovers that its employees are inhibiting religion must take steps to prevent them from doing so, even though its purpose would clearly be to advance religion. Cf. Walz v. Tax Comm'n of New York City, supra, at 673. Thus, if the Louisiana Legislature sincerely believed that the State's science teachers were being hostile to religion, our cases indicate that it could act to eliminate that hostility without running afoul of Lemon's purpose test.

Second, we have held that intentional governmental advancement of religion is sometimes required by the Free Exercise Clause. For example, in Hobbie v. Unemployment Appeals Comm'n of Fla., 480 U.S. 136 (1987); Thomas v. Review Bd., Indiana Employment Security Div., 450 U.S. 707 (1981); Wisconsin v. Yoder, 406 U.S. 205 (1972); and Sherbert v. Verner, 374 U.S. 398 (1963), we held that in some circumstances States must accommodate the beliefs of religious citizens by exempting them from generally applicable regulations. We have not yet come close to reconciling Lemon and our Free Exercise cases, and typically we do not really try. See, e. g., Hobbie v. Unemployment Appeals Comm'n of Fla., supra, at 144-145; Thomas v. Review Bd., Indiana Employment Security Div., supra, at 719-720. It is clear, however, that members of the Louisiana Legislature were not impermissibly motivated for purposes of the Lemon test if they believed that approval of the Balanced Treatment Act was required by the Free Exercise Clause.

We have also held that in some circumstances government may act to accommodate religion, even if that action is not required by the First Amendment. See Hobbie v. Unemployment Appeals Comm'n of Fla., supra, at 144-145. It is well established that "the limits of permissible state accommodation to religion are by no means co-extensive with the noninterference mandated by the Free Exercise Clause." Walz v. Tax Comm'n of New York City, supra, at 673; see also Gillette v. United States, 401 U.S. 437, 453 (1971). We have implied that voluntary governmental accommodation of religion is not only permissible, but desirable. See, e. g., ibid. Thus, few would contend that Title VII of the Civil Rights Act of 1964, which both forbids religious discrimination by private-sector employers, 78 Stat. 255, 42 U. S. C. @ 2000e-2(a)(1), and requires them reasonably to accommodate the religious practices of their employees, @ 2000e(j), violates the Establishment Clause, even though its "purpose" is, of course, to advance religion, and even though it is almost certainly not required by the Free Exercise Clause. While we have warned that at some point, accommodation may devolve into "an unlawful fostering of religion," Hobbie v. Unemployment Appeals Comm'n of Fla., supra, at 145, we have not suggested precisely (or even roughly) where that point might be. It is possible, then, that even if the sole motive of those voting for the Balanced Treatment Act was to advance religion, and its passage was not actually required, or even believed to be required, by either the Free Exercise or Establishment Clauses, the Act would nonetheless survive scrutiny under Lemon's purpose test.

One final observation about the application of that test: Although the Court's opinion gives no hint of it, in the past we have repeatedly affirmed "our reluctance to attribute unconstitutional motives to the States." Mueller v. Allen, supra, at 394; see also Lynch v. Donnelly, 465 U.S., at 699 (BRENNAN, J., dissenting). We "presume that legislatures act in a constitutional manner." Illinois v. Krull, 480 U.S. 340, 351 (1987); see also Clements v. Fashing, 457 U.S. 957, 963 (1982) (plurality opinion); Rostker v. Goldberg, 453 U.S. 57, 64

(1981); McDonald v. Board of Election Comm'rs of Chicago, 394 U.S. 802, 809 (1969). Whenever we are called upon to judge the constitutionality of an act of a state legislature, "we must have 'due regard to the fact that this Court is not exercising a primary judgment but is sitting in judgment upon those who also have taken the oath to observe the Constitution and who have the responsibility for carrying on government.'" Rostker v. Goldberg, supra, at 64 (quoting Joint Anti-Fascist Refugee Committee v. McGrath, 341 U.S. 123, 164 (1951) (Frankfurter, J., concurring)). This is particularly true, we have said, where the legislature has specifically considered the question of a law's constitutionality. Ibid.

With the foregoing in mind, I now turn to the purposes underlying adoption of the Balanced Treatment Act.

II

II A

We have relatively little information upon which to judge the motives of those who supported the Act. About the only direct evidence is the statute itself and transcripts of the seven committee hearings at which it was considered. Unfortunately, several of those hearings were sparsely attended, and the legislators who were present revealed little about their motives. We have no committee reports, no floor debates, no remarks inserted into the legislative history, no statement from the Governor, and no postenactment statements or testimony from the bill's sponsor or any other legislators. Cf. Wallace v. Jaffree, 472 U.S., at 43, 56-57. Nevertheless, there is ample evidence that the majority is wrong in holding that the Balanced Treatment Act is without secular purpose.

At the outset, it is important to note that the Balanced Treatment Act did not fly through the Louisiana Legislature on wings of fundamentalist religious fervor -- which would be unlikely, in any event, since only a small minority of the State's citizens belong to fundamentalist religious denominations. See B. Quinn, H. Anderson, M. Bradley, P. Goetting, & P. Shriver, Churches and Church Membership in the United States 16 (1982). The Act had its genesis (so to speak) in legislation introduced by Senator Bill Keith in June 1980. After two hearings before the Senate Committee on Education, Senator Keith asked that his bill be referred to a study commission composed of members of both Houses of the Louisiana Legislature. He expressed hope that the joint committee would give the bill careful consideration and determine whether his arguments were "legitimate." 1 App. E-29

-- E-30. The committee met twice during the interim, heard testimony (both for and against the bill) from several witnesses, and received staff reports. Senator Keith introduced his bill again when the legislature reconvened. The Senate Committee on Education held two more hearings and approved the bill after substantially amending it (in part over Senator Keith's objection). After approval by the full Senate, the bill was referred to the House Committee on Education. That committee conducted a lengthy hearing, adopted further amendments, and sent the bill on to the full House, where it received favorable consideration. The Senate concurred in the House amendments and on July 20, 1981, the Governor signed the bill into law.

Senator Keith's statements before the various committees that considered the bill hardly reflect the confidence of a man preaching to the converted. He asked his colleagues to "keep an open mind" and not to be "biased" by misleading characterizations of creation science. Id., at E-33. He also urged them to "look at this subject on its merits and not on some preconceived idea." Id., at E-34; see also 2 id., at E-491. Senator Keith's reception was not especially warm. Over his strenuous objection, the Senate Committee on Education voted 5-1 to amend his bill to deprive it of any force; as amended, the bill merely gave teachers permission to balance the teaching of creation science or evolution with the other. 1 id., at E-442 -- E-461. The House Committee restored the "mandatory" language to the bill by a vote of only 6-5, 2 id., at E-626 -- E-627, and both the full House (by vote of 52-35), id., at E-700 -- E-706, and full Senate (23-15), id., at E-735 -- E-738, had to repel further efforts to gut the bill.

The legislators understood that Senator Keith's bill involved a "unique" subject, 1 id., at E-106 (Rep. M. Thompson), and they were repeatedly made aware of its potential constitutional problems, see, e. g., id., at E-26 -- E-28 (McGehee); id., at E-38 -- E-39 (Sen. Keith); id., at E-241 -- E-242 (Rossman); id., at E-257 (Probst); id., at E-261 (Beck); id., at E-282 (Sen. Keith). Although the Establishment Clause, including its secular purpose requirement, was of substantial concern to the legislators, they eventually voted overwhelmingly in favor of the Balanced Treatment Act: The House approved it 71-19 (with 15 members absent), 2 id., at E-716 -- E-722; the Senate 26-12 (with all members present), id., at E-741 -- E-744. The legislators specifically designated the protection of "academic freedom" as the purpose of the Act. La. Rev. Stat. Ann. @ 17:286.2 (West 1982). We cannot accurately assess whether this purpose is a "sham," ante, at 587, until we first examine the evidence presented to the legislature far more carefully than the Court has done.

Before summarizing the testimony of Senator Keith and his supporters, I wish to make clear that I by no means intend to endorse its accuracy. But my views (and the views of this Court) about creation science and evolution are (or should be) beside the point. Our task is not to judge the debate about teaching the origins of life, but to ascertain what the members of the Louisiana Legislature believed. The vast majority of them voted to approve a bill which explicitly stated a secular purpose; what is crucial is not their wisdom in believing that purpose would be achieved by the bill, but their sincerity in believing it would be.

Most of the testimony in support of Senator Keith's bill came from the Senator himself and from scientists and educators he presented, many of whom enjoyed academic credentials that may have been regarded as quite impressive by members of the Louisiana Legislature. To a substantial extent, their testimony was devoted to lengthy, and, to the layman, seemingly expert scientific expositions on the origin of life. See, e. g., 1 App. E-11 -- E-18 (Sunderland); id., at E-50 -- E-60 (Boudreaux); id., at E-86 -- E-89 (Ward); id., at E-130 -- E-153 (Boudreaux paper); id., at E-321 -- E-326 (Boudreaux); id., at E-423 -- E-428 (Sen. Keith). These scientific lectures touched upon, inter alia, biology, paleontology, genetics, astronomy, astrophysics, probability analysis, and biochemistry. The witnesses repeatedly assured committee members that "hundreds and hundreds" of highly respected, internationally renowned scientists believed in creation science and would support their testimony. See, e. g., id., at E-5 (Sunderland); id., at E-76 (Sen. Keith); id., at E-100 -- E-101 (Reiboldt); id., at E-327 -- E-328 (Boudreaux); 2 id., at E-503 -- E-504 (Boudreaux).

Senator Keith and his witnesses testified essentially as set forth in the following numbered paragraphs:

(1) There are two and only two scientific explanations for the beginning of life -- evolution and creation science. 1 id., at E-6 (Sunderland); id., at E-34 (Sen. Keith); id., at

E-280 (Sen. Keith); id., at E-417 -- E-418 (Sen. Keith). Both are bona fide "sciences." Id., at E-6 -- E-7 (Sunderland); id., at E-12 (Sunderland); id., at E-416 (Sen. Keith); id., at E-427 (Sen. Keith); 2 id., at E-491 -- E-492 (Sen. Keith); id., at E-497 -- E-498 (Sen. Keith). Both posit a theory of the origin of life and subject that theory to empirical testing. Evolution posits that life arose out of inanimate chemical compounds and has gradually evolved over millions of years. Creation science posits that all life forms now on earth appeared suddenly and relatively recently and have changed little. Since there are only two possible explanations of the origin of life, any evidence that tends to disprove the theory of evolution necessarily tends to prove the theory of creation science, and vice versa. For example, the abrupt appearance in the fossil record of complex life, and the extreme rarity of transitional life forms in that record, are evidence for creation science. 1 id., at E-7 (Sunderland); id., at E-12 -- E-18 (Sunderland); id., at E-45 -- E-60 (Boudreaux); id., at E-67 (Harlow); id., at E-130 -- E-153 (Boudreaux paper); id., at E-423 -- E-428 (Sen. Keith).

(2) The body of scientific evidence supporting creation science is as strong as that supporting evolution. In fact, it may be stronger. Id., at E-214 (Young statement); id., at E-310 (Sen. Keith); id., at E-416 (Sen. Keith); 2 id., at E-492 (Sen. Keith). The evidence for evolution is far less compelling than we have been led to believe. Evolution is not a scientific "fact," since it cannot actually be observed in a laboratory. Rather, evolution is merely a scientific theory or "guess." 1 id., at E-20 -- E-21 (Morris); id., at E-85 (Ward); id., at E-100 (Reiboldt); id., at E-328 -- E-329 (Boudreaux); 2 id., at E-506 (Boudreaux). It is a very bad guess at that. The scientific problems with evolution are so serious that it could accurately be termed a "myth." 1 id., at E-85 (Ward); id., at E-92 -- E-93 (Kalivoda); id., at E-95 -- E-97 (Sen.

Keith); id., at E-154 (Boudreaux paper); id., at E-329 (Boudreaux); id., at E-453 (Sen. Keith); 2 id., at E-505 -- E-506 (Boudreaux); id., at E-516 (Young).

(3) Creation science is educationally valuable. Students exposed to it better understand the current state of scientific evidence about the origin of life. 1 id., at E-19 (Sunderland); id., at E-39 (Sen. Keith); id., at E-79 (Kalivoda); id., at E-308 (Sen. Keith); 2 id., at E-513 -- E-514 (Morris). Those students even have a better understanding of evolution. 1 id., at E-19 (Sunderland). Creation science can and should be presented to children without any religious content. Id., at E-12 (Sunderland); id., at E-22 (Sanderford); id., at E-35 -- E-36 (Sen. Keith); id., at E-101 (Reiboldt); id., at E-279 -- E-280 (Sen. Keith); id., at E-282 (Sen. Keith).

(4) Although creation science is educationally valuable and strictly scientific, it is now being censored from or misrepresented in the public schools. Id., at E-19 (Sunderland); id., at E-21 (Morris); id., at E-34 (Sen. Keith); id., at E-37 (Sen. Keith); id., at E-42 (Sen. Keith); id., at E-92 (Kalivoda); id., at E-97 -- E-98 (Reiboldt); id., at E-214 (Young statement); id., at E-218 (Young statement); id., at E-280 (Sen. Keith); id., at E-309 (Sen. Keith); 2 id., at E-513 (Morris). Evolution, in turn, is misrepresented as an absolute truth. 1 id., at E-63 (Harlow); id., at E-74 (Sen. Keith); id., at E-81 (Kalivoda); id., at E-214 (Young statement); 2 id., at E-507 (Harlow); id., at E-513 (Morris); id., at E-516 (Young). Teachers have been brainwashed by an entrenched scientific establishment composed almost exclusively of scientists to whom evolution is like a "religion." These scientists discriminate against creation scientists so as to prevent evolution's weaknesses from being exposed. 1 id., at E-61 (Boudreaux); id., at E-63 -- E-64 (Harlow); id., at E-78 -- E-79 (Kalivoda); id., at E-80 (Kalivoda); id., at E-95 -- E-97 (Sen. Keith); id., at E-

129 (Boudreaux paper); id., at E-218 (Young statement); id., at E-357 (Sen. Keith); id., at E-430 (Boudreaux).

(5) The censorship of creation science has at least two harmful effects. First, it deprives students of knowledge of one of the two scientific explanations for the origin of life and leads them to believe that evolution is proven fact; thus, their education suffers and they are wrongly taught that science has proved their religious beliefs false. Second, it violates the Establishment Clause. The United States Supreme Court has held that secular humanism is a religion. Id., at E-36 (Sen. Keith) (referring to Torcaso v. Watkins, 367 U.S. 488, 495, n. 11 (1961)); 1 App. E-418 (Sen. Keith); 2 id., at E-499 (Sen. Keith). Belief in evolution is a central tenet of that religion. 1 id., at E-282 (Sen. Keith); id., at E-312 -- E-313 (Sen. Keith); id., at E-317 (Sen. Keith); id., at E-418 (Sen. Keith); 2 id., at E-499 (Sen. Keith). Thus, by censoring creation science and instructing students that evolution is fact, public school teachers are now advancing religion in violation of the Establishment Clause. 1 id., at E-2 -- E-4 (Sen. Keith); id., at E-36 -- E-37, E-39 (Sen. Keith); id., at E-154 -- E-155 (Boudreaux paper); id., at E-281 -- E-282 (Sen. Keith); id., at E-313 (Sen. Keith); id., at E-315 -- E-316 (Sen. Keith); id., at E-317 (Sen. Keith); 2 id., at E-499 -- E-500 (Sen. Keith).

Senator Keith repeatedly and vehemently denied that his purpose was to advance a particular religious doctrine. At the outset of the first hearing on the legislation, he testified: "We are not going to say today that you should have some kind of religious instructions in our schools. . . . We are not talking about religion today. . . . I am not proposing that we take the Bible in each science class and read the first chapter of Genesis." 1 id., at E-35. At a later hearing, Senator Keith stressed: "To . . . teach religion and disguise it as creationism . . . is not my intent. My intent is to see to it that our textbooks are not censored." Id., at E-280. He made many similar statements throughout the hearings. See, e. g., id., at E-41; id., at E-282; id., at E-310; id., at E-417; see also id., at E-44 (Boudreaux); id., at E-80 (Kalivoda).

We have no way of knowing, of course, how many legislators believed the testimony of Senator Keith and his witnesses. But in the absence of evidence to the contrary (4), we have to assume that many of them did. Given that assumption, the Court today plainly errs in holding that the Louisiana Legislature passed the Balanced Treatment Act for exclusively religious purposes.

II B

Even with nothing more than this legislative history to go on, I think it would be extraordinary to invalidate the Balanced Treatment Act for lack of a valid secular purpose. Striking down a law approved by the democratically elected representatives of the people is no minor matter. "The cardinal principle of statutory construction is to save and not to destroy. We have repeatedly held that as between two possible interpretations of a statute, by one of which it would be unconstitutional and by the other valid, our plain duty is to adopt that which will save the act." NLRB v. Jones & Laughlin Steel Corp., 301 U.S. 1, 30 (1937). So, too, it seems to me, with discerning statutory purpose. Even if the legislative history were silent or ambiguous about the existence of a secular purpose -- and here it is not -- the statute should survive Lemon's purpose test. But even more validation than mere legislative history is present here. The Louisiana Legislature explicitly set forth its secular purpose ("protecting academic freedom") in the very text of the Act. La. Rev. Stat. @ 17:286.2 (West 1982). We have in the past repeatedly relied upon or deferred to such expressions, see, e. g., Committee for Public Education & Religious Liberty v. Regan, 444 U.S., at 654; Meek v. Pittenger, 421 U.S., at 363, 367-368; Committee for Public Education & Religious Liberty v.

Nyquist, 413 U.S., at 773; Levitt v. Committee for Public Education & Religious Liberty, 413 U.S., at 479-480, n. 7; Tilton v. Richardson, 403 U.S., at 678-679 (plurality opinion); Lemon v. Kurtzman, 403 U.S., at 613; Board of Education v. Allen, 392 U.S., at 243.

The Court seeks to evade the force of this expression of purpose by stubbornly misinterpreting it, and then finding that the provisions of the Act do not advance that misinterpreted purpose, thereby showing it to be a sham. The Court first surmises that "academic freedom" means "enhancing the freedom of teachers to teach what they will," ante, at 586 -- even though "academic freedom" in that sense has little scope in the structured elementary and secondary curriculums with which the Act is concerned. Alternatively, the Court suggests that it might mean "maximiz[ing] the comprehensiveness and effectiveness of science instruction," ante, at 588 -- though that is an exceedingly strange interpretation of the words, and one that is refuted on the very face of the statute. See @ 17:286.5. Had the Court devoted to this central question of the meaning of the legislatively expressed purpose a small fraction of the research into legislative history that produced its quotations of religiously motivated statements by individual legislators, it would have discerned quite readily what "academic freedom" meant: students' freedom from indoctrination. The legislature wanted to ensure that students would be free to decide for themselves how life began, based upon a fair and balanced presentation of the scientific evidence -- that is, to protect "the right of each [student] voluntarily to determine what to believe (and what not to believe) free of any coercive pressures from the State." Grand Rapids School District v. Ball, 473 U.S., at 385. The legislature did not care whether the topic of origins was taught; it simply wished to ensure that when the topic was taught, students would receive "'all of the evidence.'" Ante, at 586 (quoting Tr. of Oral Arg. 60).

As originally introduced, the "purpose" section of the Balanced Treatment Act read: "This Chapter is enacted for the purposes of protecting academic freedom . . . of students . . . and assisting students in their search for truth." 1 App. E-292 (emphasis added). Among the proposed findings of fact contained in the original version of the bill was the following: "Public school instruction in only evolution-science . . . violates the principle of academic freedom because it denies students a choice between scientific models and instead indoctrinates them in evolution science alone." Id., at E-295 (emphasis added). Senator Keith unquestionably understood "academic freedom" to mean "freedom from indoctrination." See id., at E-36 (purpose of bill is "to protect academic freedom by providing student choice"); id., at E-283 (purpose of bill is to protect "academic freedom" by giving students a "choice" rather than subjecting them to "indoctrination on origins")

If one adopts the obviously intended meaning of the statutory term "academic freedom," there is no basis whatever for concluding that the purpose they express is a "sham." Ante, at 587. To the contrary, the Act pursues that purpose plainly and consistently. It requires that, whenever the subject of origins is covered, evolution be "taught as a theory, rather than as proven scientific fact" and that scientific evidence inconsistent with the theory of evolution (viz., "creation science") be taught as well. La. Rev. Stat. Ann. @ 17:286.4A (West 1982). Living up to its title of "Balanced Treatment for Creation-Science and Evolution-Science Act," @ 17.286.1, it treats the teaching of creation the same way. It does not mandate instruction in creation science, @ 17:286.5; forbids teachers to present creation science "as proven scientific fact," @ 17:286.4A; and bans the teaching of creation science unless the theory is (to use the Court's terminology) "discredit[ed] '. . . at every turn'" with the teaching of evolution. Ante, at 589 (quoting 765 F.2d, at 1257). It surpasses understanding how the Court can see in this a purpose "to restructure the science curriculum to conform with a particular religious viewpoint," ante, at 593,"to provide a persuasive advantage to a particular religious doctrine," ante, at 592,"to promote the theory of creation science which embodies a particular religious tenet," ante, at 593, and "to endorse a particular religious doctrine," ante, at 594.

The Act's reference to "creation" is not convincing evidence of religious purpose. The Act defines creation science as "scientific evidenc[e]," @ 17:286.3(2) (emphasis added), and Senator Keith and his witnesses repeatedly stressed that the subject can and should be presented without religious content. See supra, at 623. We have no basis on the record to conclude that creation science need be anything other than a collection of scientific data supporting the theory that life abruptly appeared on earth. See n. 4, supra. Creation science, its proponents insist, no more must explain whence life came than evolution must explain whence came the inanimate materials from which it says life evolved. But even if that were not so, to posit a past creator is not to posit the eternal and personal God who is the object of religious veneration. Indeed, it is not even to posit the "unmoved mover" hypothesized by Aristotle and other notably nonfundamentalist philosophers. Senator Keith suggested this when he referred to "a creator however you define a creator." 1 App. E-280 (emphasis added).

The Court cites three provisions of the Act which, it argues, demonstrate a "discriminatory preference for the teaching of creation science" and no interest in "academic freedom." Ante, at 588. First, the Act prohibits discrimination only against creation scientists and those who teach creation science. @ 17:286.4C. Second, the Act requires local school boards to develop and provide to science teachers "a curriculum guide on presentation of creation-science." @ 17:286.7A. Finally, the Act requires the Governor to designate seven creation scientists who shall, upon request, assist local school boards in developing the curriculum guides. @ 17:286.7B. But none of these provisions casts doubt upon the sincerity of the legislators' articulated purpose of "academic freedom" -- unless, of course, one gives that term the obviously erroneous meanings preferred by the Court. The Louisiana legislators had been told repeatedly that creation scientists were scorned by most educators and scientists, who themselves had an almost religious faith in evolution. It is hardly surprising, then, that in seeking to achieve a balanced,"nonindoctrinating" curriculum, the legislators protected from discrimination only those teachers whom they thought were suffering from discrimination. (Also, the legislators were undoubtedly aware of Epperson v. Arkansas, 393 U.S. 97 (1968), and thus could quite reasonably have concluded that discrimination against evolutionists was already prohibited.) The two provisions respecting the development of curriculum guides are also consistent with "academic freedom" as the Louisiana Legislature understood the term. Witnesses had informed the legislators that, because of the hostility of most scientists and educators to creation science, the topic had been censored from or badly misrepresented in elementary and secondary school texts. In light of the unavailability of works on creation science suitable for classroom use (a fact appellees concede, see Brief for Appellees 27, 40) and the existence of ample materials on evolution, it was entirely reasonable for the legislature to conclude that science teachers attempting to implement the Act would need a curriculum guide on creation science, but not on evolution, and that those charged with developing the guide would need an easily accessible group of creation scientists. Thus, the provisions of the Act of so much concern to the Court support the conclusion that the legislature acted to advance "academic freedom."

The legislative history gives ample evidence of the sincerity of the Balanced Treatment Act's articulated purpose. Witness after witness urged the legislators to support the Act so that students would not be "indoctrinated" but would instead be free to decide for themselves, based upon a fair presentation of the scientific evidence, about the origin of life. See, e. g., 1 App. E-18 (Sunderland) ("all that we are advocating" is presenting "scientific data" to students and "letting [them] make up their own mind[s]"); id., at E-19 -- E-20 (Sunderland) (Students are now being "indoctrinated" in evolution through the use of "censored school books. . . . All that we are asking for is [the] open unbiased education in the classroom . . . your students deserve"); id., at E-21 (Morris) ("A student cannot [make an intelligent decision about the origin of life] unless he is well informed about both [evolution and creation science]"); id., at E-22 (Sanderford) ("We are asking very simply [that] . . . creationism [be presented] alongside . . . evolution and let people make their own mind[s] up"); id., at E-23 (Young) (the bill would require teachers to live up to their "obligation to present all theories" and thereby enable "students to make judgments themselves"); id., at E-44 (Boudreaux) ("Our intention is truth and as a scientist, I am interested in truth"); id., at E-60 -- E-61 (Boudreaux) ("We [teachers] are guilty of a lot of brainwashing. . . . We have a duty to . . . [present the] truth" to students "at all levels from gradeschool on through the college level"); id., at E-79 (Kalivoda) ("This [hearing] is being held I think to determine whether children will benefit from freedom of information or if they will be handicapped educationally by having little or no information about creation"); id., at E-80 (Kalivoda) ("I am not interested in teaching religion in schools. . . . I am interested in the truth and [students] having the opportunity to hear more than one side"); id., at E-98 (Reiboldt) ("The students have a right to know there is an alternate creationist point of view. They have a right to know the scientific evidences which suppor[t] that alternative"); id., at E-218 (Young statement) (passage of the bill will ensure that "communication of scientific ideas and discoveries may be unhindered"); 2 id., at E-514 (Morris) ("Are we going to allow [students] to look at evolution, to look at creationism, and to let one or the other stand or fall on its own merits, or will we by failing to pass this bill . . . deny students an opportunity to hear another viewpoint?"); id., at E-516 -- E-517 (Young) ("We want to give the children here in this state an equal opportunity to see both sides of the theories"). Senator Keith expressed similar views. See, e. g., 1 id., at E-36; id., at E-41; id., at E-280; id., at E-283.

Legislators other than Senator Keith made only a few statements providing insight into their motives, but those statements cast no doubt upon the sincerity of the Act's articulated purpose. The legislators were concerned primarily about the manner in which the subject of origins was presented in Louisiana schools -- specifically, about whether scientifically valuable information was being censored and students misled about evolution. Representatives Cain, Jenkins, and F. Thompson seemed impressed by the scientific evidence presented in support of creation science. See 2 id., at E-530 (Rep. F. Thompson); id., at E-533 (Rep. Cain); id., at E-613 (Rep. Jenkins). At the first study commission hearing, Senator Picard and Representative M. Thompson questioned Senator Keith about Louisiana teachers' treatment of evolution and creation science. See 1 id., at E-71 -- E-74. At the close of the hearing, Representative M. Thompson told the audience:

"We as members of the committee will also receive from the staff information of what is currently being taught in the Louisiana public schools. We really want to see [it]. I . . . have no idea in what manner [biology] is presented and in what manner the creationist theories [are] excluded in the public school[s]. We want to look at what the status of the situation is." Id., at E-104.

Legislators made other comments suggesting a concern about censorship and misrepresentation of scientific information. See, e. g., id., at E-386 (Sen. McLeod); 2 id., at E-527 (Rep. Jenkins); id., at E-528 (Rep. M. Thompson); id., at E-534 (Rep. Fair).

It is undoubtedly true that what prompted the legislature to direct its attention to the misrepresentation of evolution in the schools (rather than the inaccurate presentation of other topics) was its awareness of the tension between evolution and the religious beliefs of many children. But even appellees concede that a valid secular purpose is not rendered impermissible simply because its pursuit is prompted by concern for religious sensitivities. Tr. of Oral Arg. 43, 56. If a history teacher falsely told her students that the bones of Jesus Christ had been discovered, or a physics teacher that the Shroud of Turin had been conclusively established to be inexplicable on the basis of natural causes, I cannot believe (despite the majority's implication to the contrary, see ante, at 592-593) that legislators or school board members would be constitutionally prohibited from taking corrective action, simply because that action was prompted by concern for the religious beliefs of the misinstructed students.

In sum, even if one concedes, for the sake of argument, that a majority of the Louisiana Legislature voted for the Balanced Treatment Act partly in order to foster (rather than merely eliminate discrimination against) Christian fundamentalist beliefs, our cases establish that that alone would not suffice to invalidate the Act, so long as there was a genuine secular purpose as well. We have, moreover, no adequate basis for disbelieving the secular purpose set forth in the Act itself, or for concluding that it is a sham enacted to conceal the legislators' violation of their oaths of office. I am astonished by the Court's unprecedented readiness to reach such a conclusion, which I can only attribute to an intellectual predisposition created by the facts and the legend of Scopes v. State, 154 Tenn. 105, 289 S. W. 363 (1927) -- an instinctive reaction that any governmentally imposed requirements bearing upon the teaching of evolution must be a manifestation of Christian fundamentalist repression. In this case, however, it seems to me the Court's position is the repressive one. The people of Louisiana, including those who are Christian fundamentalists, are quite entitled, as a secular matter, to have whatever scientific evidence there may be against evolution presented in their schools, just as Mr. Scopes was entitled to present whatever scientific evidence there was for it. Perhaps what the Louisiana Legislature has done is unconstitutional because there is no such evidence, and the scheme they have established will amount to no more than a presentation of the Book of Genesis. But we cannot say that on the evidence before us in this summary judgment context, which includes ample uncontradicted testimony that "creation science" is a body of scientific knowledge rather than revealed belief. Infinitely less can we say (or should we say) that the scientific evidence for evolution is so conclusive that no one could be gullible enough to believe that there is any real scientific evidence to the contrary, so that the legislation's stated purpose must be a lie. Yet that illiberal judgment, that Scopes-in-reverse, is ultimately the basis on which the Court's facile rejection of the Louisiana Legislature's purpose must rest.

Since the existence of secular purpose is so entirely clear, and thus dispositive, I will not go on to discuss the fact that, even if the Louisiana Legislature's purpose were exclusively to advance religion, some of the well-established exceptions to the impermissibility of that purpose might be applicable -- the validating intent to eliminate a perceived discrimination against a particular religion, to facilitate its free exercise, or to accommodate it. See supra, at 617-618. I am not in any case enamored of those amorphous exceptions, since I think them no more than unpredictable correctives to what is (as the next Part of this opinion will discuss) a fundamentally unsound rule. It is surprising, however, that the Court does not address these exceptions, since the context of the legislature's action gives some reason to believe they may be applicable. (6)

Because I believe that the Balanced Treatment Act had a secular purpose, which is all the first component of the Lemon test requires, I would reverse the judgment of the Court of Appeals and remand for further consideration.

III

I have to this point assumed the validity of the Lemon "purpose" test. In fact, however, I think the pessimistic evaluation that THE CHIEF JUSTICE made of the totality of Lemon is particularly applicable to the "purpose" prong: it is "a constitutional theory [that] has no basis in the history of the amendment it seeks to interpret, is difficult to apply and yields unprincipled results ..." Wallace v. Jaffree, 472 U.S., at 112 (REHNQUIST, J., dissenting).

Our cases interpreting and applying the purpose test have made such a maze of the Establishment Clause that even the most conscientious governmental officials can only guess what motives will be held unconstitutional. We have said essentially the following: Government may not act with the purpose of advancing religion, except when forced to do so by the Free Exercise Clause (which is now and then); or when eliminating existing governmental hostility to religion (which exists sometimes); or even when merely accommodating governmentally uninhibited religious practices, except that at some point (it is unclear where) intentional accommodation results in the fostering of religion, which is of course unconstitutional. See supra, at 614-618.

But the difficulty of knowing what vitiating purpose one is looking for is as nothing compared with the difficulty of knowing how or where to find it. For while it is possible to discern the objective "purpose" of a statute (i. e., the public good at which its provisions appear to be directed), or even the formal motivation for a statute where that is explicitly set forth (as it was, to no avail, here), discerning the subjective motivation of those enacting the statute is, to be honest, almost always an impossible task. The number of possible motivations, to begin with, is not binary, or indeed even finite. In the present case, for example, a particular legislator need not have voted for the Act either because he wanted to foster religion or because he wanted to improve education. He may have thought the bill would provide jobs for his district, or may have wanted to make amends with a faction of his party he had alienated on another vote, or he may have been a close friend of the bill's sponsor, or he may have been repaying a favor he owed the Majority Leader, or he may have hoped the Governor would appreciate his vote and make a fundraising appearance for him, or he may have been pressured to vote for a bill he disliked by a wealthy contributor or by a flood of constituent mail, or he may have been seeking favorable publicity, or he may have been reluctant to hurt the feelings of a loyal staff member who worked on the bill, or he may have been settling an old score with a legislator who opposed the bill, or he may have been mad at his wife who opposed the bill, or he may have been intoxicated and utterly unmotivated when the vote was called, or he may have accidentally voted "yes" instead of "no," or, of course, he may have had (and very likely did have) a combination of some of the above and many other motivations. To look for the sole purpose of even a single legislator is probably to look for something that does not exist.

Putting that problem aside, however, where ought we to look for the individual legislator's purpose? We cannot of course assume that every member present (if, as is unlikely, we know who or even how many they were) agreed with the motivation expressed in a particular legislator's preenactment floor or committee statement. Quite obviously, "what motivates one legislator to make a speech about a statute is not necessarily what motivates scores of others to enact it." United States v. O'Brien, 391 U.S. 367, 384 (1968). Can we assume, then, that they all agree with the motivation expressed in the staff-prepared committee reports they might have read -- even though we are unwilling to assume that they agreed with the motivation expressed in the very statute that they voted for? Should we consider postenactment floor statements? Or postenactment testimony from legislators, obtained expressly for the lawsuit? Should we consider media reports on the realities of the legislative bargaining? All of these sources, of course, are eminently manipulable. Legislative histories can be contrived and sanitized, favorable media coverage orchestrated, and postenactment recollections conveniently distorted. Perhaps most valuable of all would be more objective indications -- for example, evidence regarding the individual legislators' religious affiliations. And if that, why not evidence regarding the fervor or tepidity of their beliefs?

Having achieved, through these simple means, an assessment of what individual legislators intended, we must still confront the question (yet to be addressed in any of our cases) how many of them must have the invalidating intent. If a state senate approves a bill by vote of 26 to 25, and only one of the 26 intended solely to advance religion, is the law unconstitutional? What if 13 of the 26 had that intent? What if 3 of the 26 had the impermissible intent, but 3 of the 25 voting against the bill were motivated by religious hostility or were simply attempting to "balance" the votes of their impermissibly motivated colleagues? Or is it possible that the intent of the bill's sponsor is alone enough to invalidate it -- on a theory, perhaps, that even though everyone else's intent was pure, what they produced was the fruit of a forbidden tree?

Because there are no good answers to these questions, this Court has recognized from Chief Justice Marshall, see Fletcher v. Peck, 6 Cranch 87, 130 (1810), to Chief Justice Warren, United States v. O'Brien, supra, at 383-384, that determining the subjective intent of legislators is a perilous enterprise. See also Palmer v. Thompson, 403 U.S. 217, 224-225 (1971); Epperson v. Arkansas, 393 U.S., at 113 (Black, J., concurring). It is perilous, I might note, not just for the judges who will very likely reach the wrong result, but also for the legislators who find that they must assess the validity of proposed legislation -- and risk the condemnation of having voted for an unconstitutional measure -- not on the basis of what the legislation contains, nor even on the basis of what they themselves intend, but on the basis of what others have in mind.

Given the many hazards involved in assessing the subjective intent of governmental decision makers, the first prong of Lemon is defensible, I think, only if the text of the Establishment Clause demands it. That is surely not the case. The Clause states that "Congress shall make no law respecting an establishment of religion." One could argue, I suppose, that any time Congress acts with the intent of advancing religion, it has enacted a "law respecting an establishment of religion"; but far from being an unavoidable reading, it is quite an unnatural one. I doubt, for example, that the Clayton Act, 38 Stat. 730, as amended, 15 U. S. C. @ 12 et seq., could reasonably be described as a "law respecting an establishment of religion" if bizarre new historical evidence revealed that it lacked a secular purpose, even though it has no discernible nonsecular effect. It is, in short, far from an inevitable reading of the Establishment Clause that it forbids all governmental action intended to advance religion; and if not inevitable, any reading with such untoward consequences must be wrong.

In the past we have attempted to justify our embarrassing Establishment Clause jurisprudence (7) on the ground that it "sacrifices clarity and predictability for flexibility. " Committee for Public Education & Religious Liberty v. Regan, 444 U.S., at 662. One commentator has aptly characterized this as "a euphemism . . . for . . . the absence of any principled rationale." Choper, supra n. 7, at 681. I think it time that we sacrifice some "flexibility" for "clarity and predictability." Abandoning Lemon's purpose test -- a test which exacerbates the tension between the Free Exercise and Establishment Clauses, has no basis in the language or history of the Amendment, and, as today's decision shows, has wonderfully flexible consequences -- would be a good place to start.

Notes:

1. Article VI, cl. 3, of the Constitution provides that "the Members of the several State Legislatures . . . shall be bound by Oath or Affirmation, to support this Constitution."

2. Thus the popular dictionary definitions cited by JUSTICE POWELL, ante, at 598-599 (concurring opinion), and appellees, see Brief for Appellees 25, 26; Tr. of Oral Arg. 32, 34, are utterly irrelevant, as are the views of the school superintendents cited by the majority, ante, at 595, n. 18. Three-quarters of those surveyed had "no" or "limited" knowledge of "creation-

science theory," and not a single superintendent claimed "extensive" knowledge of the subject. 2 App. E-798.

3. Although creation scientists and evolutionists also disagree about the origin of the physical universe, both proponents and opponents of Senator Keith's bill focused on the question of the beginning of life.

4. Although appellees and amici dismiss the testimony of Senator Keith and his witnesses as pure fantasy, they did not bother to submit evidence of that to the District Court, making it difficult for us to agree with them. The State, by contrast, submitted the affidavits of two scientists, a philosopher, a theologian, and an educator, whose academic credentials are rather impressive. See App. to Juris. Statement A-17 -- A-18 (Kenyon); id., at A-36 (Morrow); id., at A-39 -- A-40 (Miethe); id., at A-46 -- A-47 (Most); id., at A-49 (Clinkert). Like Senator Keith and his witnesses, the affiants swear that evolution and creation science are the only two scientific explanations for the origin of life, see id., at A-19 -- A-20 (Kenyon); id., at A-38 (Morrow); id., at A-41 (Miethe); that creation science is strictly scientific, see id., at A-18 (Kenyon); id., at A-36 (Morrow); id., at A-40 -- A-41 (Miethe); id., at A-49 (Clinkert); that creation science is simply a collection of scientific data that supports the hypothesis that life appeared on earth suddenly and has changed little, see id., at A-19 (Kenyon); id., at A-36 (Morrow); id., at A-41 (Miethe); that hundreds of respected scientists believe in creation science, see id., at A-20 (Kenyon); that evidence for creation science is as strong as evidence for evolution, see id., at A-21 (Kenyon); id., at A-34 -- A-35 (Kenyon); id., at A-37 -- A-38 (Morrow); that creation science is educationally valuable, see id., at A-19 (Kenyon); id., at A-36 (Morrow); id., at A-38 -- A-39 (Morrow); id., at A-49 (Clinkert); that creation science can be presented without religious content, see id., at A-19 (Kenyon); id., at A-35 (Kenyon); id., at A-36 (Morrow); id., at A-40 (Miethe); id., at A-43 -- A-44

(Miethe); id., at A-47 (Most); id., at A-49 (Clinkert); and that creation science is now censored from classrooms while evolution is misrepresented as proven fact, see id., at A-20 (Kenyon); id., at A-35 (Kenyon); id., at A-39 (Morrow); id., at A-50 (Clinkert). It is difficult to conclude on the basis of these affidavits -- the only substantive evidence in the record -- that the laymen serving in the Louisiana Legislature must have disbelieved Senator Keith or his witnesses.

5. The majority finds it "astonishing" that I would cite a portion of Senator Keith's original bill that was later deleted as evidence of the legislature's understanding of the phrase "academic freedom." Ante, at 589, n. 8. What is astonishing is the majority's implication that the deletion of that section deprives it of value as a clear indication of what the phrase meant -- there and in the other, retained, sections of the bill. The Senate Committee on Education deleted most of the lengthy "purpose" section of the bill (with Senator Keith's consent) because it resembled legislative "findings of fact," which, committee members felt, should generally not be incorporated in legislation. The deletion had absolutely nothing to do with the manner in which the section described "academic freedom." See 1 App. E-314 -- E-320; id., at E-440 -- E-442.

6. As the majority recognizes, ante, at 592, Senator Keith sincerely believed that "secular humanism is a bona fide religion," 1 App. E-36; see also id., at E-418; 2 id., at E-499, and that "evolution is the cornerstone of that religion," 1 id., at E-418; see also id., at E-282; id., at E-312 -- E-313; id., at E-317; 2 id., at E-499. The Senator even told his colleagues that this Court had "held" that secular humanism was a religion. See 1 id., at E-36, id., at E-418; 2 id., at E-499. (In Torcaso v. Watkins, 367 U.S. 488, 495, n. 11 (1961), we did indeed refer to "Secular Humanism" as a "religio[n].") Senator Keith and his supporters raised the "religion" of secular

humanism not, as the majority suggests, to explain the source of their "disdain for the theory of evolution," ante, at 592, but to convince the legislature that the State of Louisiana was violating the Establishment Clause because its teachers were misrepresenting evolution as fact and depriving students of the information necessary to question that theory. 1 App. E-2 -- E-4 (Sen. Keith); id., at E-36 -- E-37, E-39 (Sen. Keith); id., at E-154 -- E-155 (Boudreaux paper); id., at E-281 -- E-282 (Sen. Keith); id., at E-317 (Sen. Keith); 2 id., at E-499 -- E-500 (Sen. Keith). The Senator repeatedly urged his colleagues to pass his bill to remedy this Establishment Clause violation by ensuring state neutrality in religious matters, see, e. g., 1 id., at E-36; id., at E-39; id., at E-313, surely a permissible purpose under Lemon. Senator Keith's argument may be questionable, but nothing in the statute or its legislative history gives us reason to doubt his sincerity or that of his supporters.

7. Professor Choper summarized our school aid cases thusly:

"[A] provision for therapeutic and diagnostic health services to parochial school pupils by public employees is invalid if provided in the parochial school, but not if offered at a neutral site, even if in a mobile unit adjacent to the parochial school. Reimbursement to parochial schools for the expense of administering teacher-prepared tests required by state law is invalid, but the state may reimburse parochial schools for the expense of administering state-prepared tests. The state may lend school textbooks to parochial school pupils because, the Court has explained, the books can be checked in advance for religious content and are 'self-policing'; but the state may not lend other seemingly self-policing instructional items such as tape recorders and maps. The state may pay the cost of bus transportation to parochial schools, which the Court has ruled are 'permeated' with religion; but the state is forbidden to pay for field trip transportation visits 'to governmental, industrial, cultural, and scientific centers designed to enrich the secular studies of students.'" Choper, The Religion Clauses of the First Amendment: Reconciling the Conflict, 41 U. Pitt. L. Rev. 673, 680-681 (1980) (footnotes omitted).

Since that was written, more decisions on the subject have been rendered, but they leave the theme of chaos securely unimpaired. See, e. g., Aguilar v.Felton, 473 U.S. 402 (1985); Grand Rapids School District v. Ball, 473 U.S. 373 (1985).

Webster v. New Lenox School District, 1990, the Seventh Circuit Court of Appeals

(Author's Note: Italicized material represents direct quotations. Material in regular type represents the author's comments.)

(The following paragraph is not part of a trial transcript, but is quoted from the website Voices For Evolution)

In 1990, in Webster v. New Lenox School District, the Seventh Circuit Court of Appeals found that a school district may prohibit a teacher from teaching creation science, in fulfilling its responsibility to ensure that the First Amendment's establishment clause is not violated, and religious beliefs are not injected into the public school curriculum. The court upheld a district court finding that the school district had not violated Webster's free speech rights when it prohibited him from teaching "creation science," since it is a form of religious advocacy. (Webster v. New Lenox School District #122, 917 F. 2d 1004)

This case stands out among the others because it does not deal directly with Science teaching. The plaintiff in this case was a junior-high Social Studies teacher. As shown in the background section of the transcript, Webster's classroom textbook contained a statement that the world was more than four billion years old. It didn't propose it as a theory. It didn't say there was a possibility it might not be four billion years old. It just made a statement without qualification.

The one thing that ought to be noticed here is, in the case of Segrave vs State of California, 1981, that state had an anti-dogmatism law. This should mean, in simplest terms, that theories can't be taught as facts. Yet if you look at the thousands of textbooks and millions of even quasi-educational materials on every possible subject available to children, from post-graduate doctoral material to preschool "world explorer" cartoons, this is the way they always state their dogma. Not "studies suggest an age of four billion years for the earth," or "Scientists have said the earth may be more than four billion years old." It's stated as a fact. Our eyes run right past it now because it's so common. History books begin with Cro-Magnon and Neanderthal man, or maybe even Australopithecus Afarensis, the so-called "Lucy" fossil. Literature survey books cover "prehistory" such as cave paintings and attribute them to an earlier link to modern man. And the information is presented as factual, not theoretical.

Author's Note: The format of this transcript is somewhat unusual so the following should help to clarify its presentation here. The transcript is presented in its original format. Structure and headings (such as the Roman numeral I and the heading entitled Background) are part of the original document. All quoted material appears in italic type. Commentary by the author appears in regular type, in various places throughout. Occasionally the author picks up a quote to repeat, and this material also appears in italic type. The heading information from the very beginning of the original document, with the title of the case and various legal listings has been omitted. The transcript reproduced here begins with the name of the presiding judge and a statement of the case.

Ripple, Circuit Judge. Ray Webster sought injunctive and declaratory relief based on his claim that the New Lenox School District violated his first and fourteenth amendment rights by prohibiting him from teaching a nonevolutionary theory of creation in the classroom. He appeals the dismissal of his complaint for failure to state a claim. For the following reasons, we affirm the judgment of the district court.

I

Background

The district court dismissed Mr. Webster's suit for failure to state a claim upon which relief can be granted. See Fed. R. Civ. P. 12(b)(6). The grant of a motion to dismiss is, of course, reviewed de novo. Villegas v. Princeton Farms, Inc., 893 F.2d 919, 924 (7th Cir. 1990); Corcoran v. Chicago Park Dist., 875 F2d 609, 611 (7th Cir. 1989). It is well settled that, when reviewing the grant of a motion to dismiss, we must assume the truth of all well-pleaded factual allegations and make all possible inferences in favor of the plaintiff. Janowsky v. United States, No. 89-2219, slip op. at 4 (7th Cir. Sept. 17, 1990); Rogers v. United States, 902, F.2d 1268, 1269 (7th Cir. 1990).

A complaint should not be dismissed "unless it appears beyond doubt that the plaintiff can prove no set of facts in support of his claim which would entitle him to relief." Conley v. Gibson, 355 U. S. 41, 45-46 (1957). This obligation is especially serious when, as here, we deal with allegations involving the freedom of expression protected by the first amendment. See Stewart v. District of Columbia Armory Bd., 863 F.2d 1013, 1017-18 (D.C. Cir. 1988) ("where government action is challenged on first amendment grounds, a court should be especially 'unwilling to decide the legal questions posed by the parties without a more thoroughly developed record of proceedings in which the parties have an opportunity to prove those disputed factual assertions upon which they rely'") (quoting City of Los Angeles v. Preferred Communications, 476 U.S. 488, 494 (1986)). Courts may, however, consider exhibits attached to the complaint as part of the pleadings. Beam v. IPCO Corp., 838 F.2d 242, 244 (1988). With these constraints in mind, we set forth the pertinent facts.

A. Facts

Ray Webster teaches social studies at the Oster-Oakview Junior High School in New Lenox, Illinois. In the spring of 1987, a student in Mr. Webster's social studies class complained that Mr. Webster's teaching methods violated principles of separation between church and state. In addition to the student, both the American Civil Liberties Union and the Americans United for the Separation of Church and State objected to Mr. Webster's teaching practices. Mr. Webster denied the allegations. On July 31, 1987, the New Lenox school board (school board), through its superintendent, advised Mr. Webster by letter that he should restrict his classroom instruction to the curriculum and refrain from advocating a particular religious viewpoint.

Believing the superintendent's letter vague, Mr. Webster asked for further clarification in a letter dated September 4, 1987. In this letter, Mr. Webster also set forth his teaching methods and philosophy. Mr. Webster stated that the discussion of religious issues in his class was only for the purpose of developing an open mind in his students. For example, Mr. Webster explained that he taught nonevolutionary theories of creation to rebut a statement in the social studies textbook indicating that the world is over four billion years old. Therefore, his teaching methods in no way violated the doctrine of separation between church and state. Mr. Webster contended that, at most, he encouraged students to explore alternative viewpoints.

The superintendent responded to Mr. Webster's letter on October 13, 1987. The superintendent reiterated that advocacy of a Christian viewpoint was prohibited, although Mr. Webster could discuss objectively the historical relationship between church and state when such discussions were an appropriate part of the curriculum. Mr. Webster was specifically instructed not to teach creation science, because the teaching of this theory had been held by the federal courts to be religious advocacy.

Mr. Webster brought suit, principally arguing that the school board's prohibitions constituted censorship in violation of the first and fourteenth amendments. In particular, Mr. Webster argued that the school board should permit him to teach a nonevolutionary theory of creation in his social studies class.

Unfortunately the actual correspondence that preceded this case is not available, only summaries which in themselves seem biased in favor the school district. It would also be interesting to know exactly what the student's original complaint was and how all of this got started. It would seem necessary to know how Webster worded his letters or even how he presented his material in the classroom. But these facts are not deemed important enough to be included, apparently. We only know that Webster said he only wished to present a "nonevolutionary" theory (not a fact, not a religious belief, only a theory) to balance the statement in the textbook, which was not presented as a theory, but as a fact. The students would logically assume their textbook taught them facts, unless it told them it was presenting a theory.

B. The District Court

The district court concluded that Mr. Webster did not have a first amendment right to teach creation science in a public school. The district court began by noting that, in deciding whether to grant the school district's motion to dismiss, the court was entitled to consider the letters between the superintendent and Mr. Webster because Mr. Webster had attached these letters to his complaint as exhibits. In particular, the district court determined that the October 13, 1987 letter was critical; this letter clearly indicated exactly what conduct the school district sought to proscribe. Specifically, the October 13 letter directed that Mr. Webster was prohibited from teaching creation science and was admonished not to engage in religious advocacy. Furthermore, the superintendent's letter explicitly stated that Mr. Webster could discuss objectively the historical relationship between church and state.

The case here rests on whether Webster was denied the freedom to teach what he as an educator thought was right for his students to know. He thought it was right for his students to know that determining the age of the earth is theoretical. He taught them that there was more than one theory used to determine this information and that more than one conclusion could be reached. That is his statement of what he did and why he did it. Unless he committed perjury and lied about what he taught, it is necessary to accept his statement as fact.

In order to explain how it is possible that the factual statement in the textbook might not in fact be a fact, it was necessary to bring up an alternate theory for determining the age of the earth. It should be significant to note that it was apparently not sufficient for Webster to say, "this statement about the age of the earth is part of a theory, the theory of evolution. There are other theories about how to determine how old the earth is, but you already know all about them, so we'll just leave it at that."

He was unable to do that, because it's extremely likely that the students in his classroom had no idea that statement wasn't a fact or what any other theories that challenge it might be. We are not privy to the discussion in the classroom. It wasn't drawn out in interviews and made part of the case writings. It is possible, however, to speculate based on the modern teaching texts and quasi-educational materials available that students are not being given more than one theory to consider. They are being presented with statements of fact about things that are in reality still theories. It was therefore necessary for Webster to spell out another theory that encompasses how to determine the age of the earth. It was necessary to point out that the textbook had a fact that wasn't a fact. It was then necessary to explain why it wasn't a fact. He was a teacher. It was his job to tell students things they didn't know, even if those things weren't part of the curriculum.

The letter Webster got from the school district, the one considered critical to the disposition of the case, tells him he was prohibited from teaching creation science and was admonished not to engage in religious advocacy. Furthermore, the superintendent's letter explicitly stated that Mr. Webster could discuss objectively the historical relationship between church and state. Propping itself up on the crutch of previous court decisions, the school district considered teaching creation science teaching religion. Apparently it was not just teaching religion, but advocating it. It must not be possible to teach a concept without advocating it. Webster presented creation science as a concept in his classroom. Therefore he advocated it. Therefore he must be proscribed from it. Of course he was permitted to deal with historic church and state relationships. He was permitted to teach something, even though it really had nothing to do with correcting the error in his textbook. Because he was allowed to teach something about religion, his free speech wasn't infringed upon. Case dismissed.

The district court noted that a school board generally has wide latitude in setting the curriculum, provided the school board remains within the boundaries established by the constitution. Because the establishment clause prohibits the enactment of any law "respecting an establishment of religion," the school board could not enact a curriculum that would inject religion into the public schools. U.S. Const. amend. I. Moreover, the district court determined that the school board had the responsibility to ensure that the establishment clause was not violated.

The district court then framed the issue as whether Mr. Webster had the right to teach creation science. Relying on Edwards v. Aguillard, 482 U.S. 578 (1987), the district court determined that teaching creation science would constitute religious advocacy in violation of the first amendment and that the school board correctly prohibited Mr. Webster from teaching such material. The court further noted:

Webster has not been prohibited from teaching any nonevolutionary theories or from teaching anything regarding the historical relationship between church and state. Martino's [the superintendent] letter of October 13, 1987 makes it clear that the religious advocacy of Webster's teaching is prohibited and nothing else. Since no other constraints were placed on Webster's teaching, he had no basis for his complaint and it must fail.

Webster v. New Lenox School Dist., Mem. op, at 4-5 (N.D. Ill. May 25 1989). Accordingly, the district court dismissed the complaint.

II

Analysis

At the outset, we note that a narrow issue confronts us: Mr. Webster asserts that he has a first amendment right to determine the curriculum content of his junior high school class. He does not, however, contest the general authority of the school board, acting through its executive agent, the superintendent, to set the curriculum.

This case does not present a novel issue. We have already confirmed the right of those authorities charged by state law with curriculum development to require the obedience of subordinate employees, including the classroom teacher. Judge Wood expressed the controlling principle succinctly in Palmer v. Board of Educ., 603 F.2d 1271, 1274 (7th Cir. 1979), cert. denied, 444 U.S. 1026 (1980), when he wrote:

Parents have a vital interest in what their children are taught. Their representatives have in general prescribed a curriculum. There is a compelling state interest in the choice and adherence to a suitable curriculum for the benefit of our young citizens and society. It cannot be left to individual teachers to teach what they please.

Yet Mr. Webster, in effect, argues that the school board must permit him to teach what he pleases. The first amendment is "not a teacher license for uncontrolled expression at variance with established curricular content." Id. at 1273. See also Clard v. Holmes, 474 F.2d 928 (7th Cir.) (holding that individual teacher has no constitutional prerogative to override the judgment of his superiors as to proper course content), cert. denied, 411 U.S. 972 (1973). Clearly, the school board had the authority and the responsibility to ensure that Mr. Webster did not stray from the established curriculum by injecting religious advocacy into the classroom. "Families entrust public schools with the education of their children, but condition their trust on the understanding that the classroom will not purposely be used to advance religious views that may conflict with the private beliefs of the student and his or her family." Edwards v. Aguillard, 482 U.S. 578, 584 (1987).

There is no indication that Webster said he had a right to determine the curriculum content of his junior high school class, nor that Mr. Webster, in effect, argues that the school board must permit him to teach what he pleases. (already cited) The court acknowledges that he accepted the authority of the board. He had the required textbook and was teaching from it, or he wouldn't have run across the passage in question. He would have saved himself from a great deal of trouble if he had simply not assigned his class to read that part of the book. Yet Webster was not interested in stifling even what he considered to be a lie, or at least not a fact. He presented the statement, and then he offered an alternative. It seems extreme to state that he was guilty of "uncontrolled expression at variance with established curricular content." He also was not guilty of betraying the trust of the School District families by abusing his position to advance conflicting religious views. The key word is "advancing." It implies putting something forward as superior, similar to the idea of "advocacy." A teacher presents a concept in his class, and the board and the court assumes he is in favor of it, that he wants his students to believe it, not just listen to it. But it seems that is only the case if the teacher presents Creation Science. He can objectively present anything else. Not that.

A teacher may say, "the 'Final Solution' for dealing with the Jews was to put them in concentration camps and kill them." Is the teacher advocating death camps for Jews? Of course not. He is presenting to his class a historical position. Unless the teacher is insane, his position is quite opposite from advocating what he states. Surely other "solutions" were possible for Hitler (granting that there was a problem of the nature under discussion, which, again, no sane person would agree with) and may even have been presented to Hitler at the time of this historical event. But Hitler wanted this one. Only this one. He may even have proscribed his advisors from bringing any other theories up. He certainly would not have been interested in possible solutions that appeared to advocate or advance a religious position.

If we ever would have wanted a government to permit the presentation of an alternate theory to deal with an issue, even a religious-based theory, that would have been the time. Alternate theories were apparently stifled, because, ironically enough, survival of the fittest, one of Evolution's foundational tenets, one upon which Hitler based many of his actions, couldn't survive on its own. It had to be protected then, and it has to be protected by the American justice system now.

A junior high school student's immature stage of intellectual development imposes a heightened responsibility upon the school board to control the curriculum. See Zykan v. Warsaw Community School Corp., 631 F.2d 1300, 1304 (7th Cir. 1980). We have noted that secondary school teachers occupy a unique position for influencing secondary school students, thus creating a concomitant power in school authorities to choose the teachers and regulate their pedagogical methods. Id. "The state exerts great authority and coercive power through mandatory attendance requirements, and because of the students' emulation of teachers as role models and the children's susceptibility to peer pressure." Edwards, 482 U.S. at 584 (footnote omitted).

It is true that the discretion lodged in school boards is not completely unfettered. For example, school boards may not fire teachers for random classroom comments. Zykan, 631 F.2d at 1305. Moreover, school boards may not require instruction in a religiously inspired dogma to the exclusion of other points of view. Epperson v. Arkansas, 393 U.S. 97, 106 (1968).

Interesting that Epperson v. Arkansas is brought up to support exactly the opposite of what it accomplished. Creation Science, another point of view, was squashed and the religious dogma of Evolution was exclusively preferred.

This complaint contains no allegation that school authorities have imposed "a pall of orthodoxy" on the offerings of the entire public school curriculum, Keyishian v. Board of Regents, 385 U.S. 589, 603 (1967)," which might either implicate the state in the propagation of an identifiable religious creed or otherwise impair permanently the student's ability to investigate matters that arise in the natural course of intellectual inquiry." Zykan, 631 F2d at 1306. Therefore, this case does not present the issue of whether, or under what circumstances, a school board may completely eliminate material from the curriculum. Cf. Zykan, 631 F.2d at 1305-06 (school may not flatly prohibit teachers from mentioning relevant material). Rather, the principle that an individual teacher has no right to ignore the directives of duly appointed education authorities is dispositive of this case. Today, we decide only that, given the allegations of the complaint, the school board has successfully navigated the narrow channel between impairing intellectual inquire and propagating a religious creed.

The wording of the previous opinion implies that the school board must be guilty of promoting a religion throughout the entire curriculum before it can be said to be in violation of the separation principle or infringing upon an individual teacher's free expression right. A teacher, however, can be denied the right to express one idea, apparently. Never mind that the entire curriculum required by the state and the school board is riddled with evolutionary language. This case is a perfect example of that. Who would have thought evolution would be an issue in a social studies class?

This is a concept appearing absolutely everywhere in curriculum. It can't be repeated often enough that it exists in every subject, often in incidental but purposeful references, as a fact, not as a theory. The state and the school boards absolutely are guilty of promoting this dogma exclusive of any other, in every subject. Try to find a state-approved textbook in any academic subject that does not bring up the subject of billions of years of earth age, or discuss man as being at first entirely primitive and gradually becoming civilized, or note that the extinction of certain types of animals or plants also indicates that more adaptable types replaced them. These are evolutionary concepts.

Here, the superintendent concluded that the subject matter taught by Mr. Webster created serious establishment clause concerns. Cf. Edwards, 482 U.S. at 583-84 ("The Court has been particularly vigilant in monitoring compliance with the Establishment Clause in elementary and secondary schools."); Epperson, 393 U.S at 106 (school may not adopt programs that aid or oppose any religion). As the district court noted, the superintendent's letter is directed to this concern. "[E]ducators do not offend the First Amendment so long as their actions are reasonably related to legitimate pedagogical concerns." Hazelwood School Dist. v. Kuhlmier, 484 U.S 260, 278 (1988). Given the school board's important pedagogical interest in establishing the curriculum and legitimate concern with possible establishment clause violations, the school board's prohibition on the teaching of creation science to junior high students was appropriate. See Palmer v. Board of Educ., 603 F.2d 1274 (7th Cir. 1979) (school board has "compelling" interest in setting the curriculum). Accordingly, the district court properly dismissed Mr. Webster's complaint.

The school in this case adopted a program that both aided one religion and opposed another. The dogma of evolution was once again aided, and the truth was opposed.

Peloza v. Capistrano School District, 1994

(Author's Note: Italicized material represents direct quotations. Material in regular type represents the author's comments. This section also has material from the website Vine & Fig Tree.)

(The following paragraph is not part of a trial transcript, but is quoted from the website Voices For Evolution)

In 1994, in Peloza v. Capistrano School District, the Ninth Circuit Court of Appeals upheld a district court finding that a teacher's First Amendment right to free exercise of religion is not violated by a school district's requirement that evolution be taught in biology classes. Rejecting plaintiff Peloza's definition of a "religion" of "evolutionism", the Court found that the district had simply and appropriately required a science teacher to teach a scientific theory in biology class. (John E. Peloza v. Capistrano Unified School District, (1994) 917 F. 2d 1004)

A summary of the case follows, taken from the transcript appearing on the website *www.talkorigins.org*.

SUMMARY

High school biology teacher brought action against school district, its board of trustees, and various personnel at high school, challenging school district's requirement that he teach evolutionism, as well as school district order barring him from discussing his religious beliefs with students. The United States District Court, Central District of California, David W. Williams, J., 782 F.Supp. 1412, dismissed and awarded attorney fees to school district. Teacher appealed. The Court of Appeals held that: (1) teacher failed to state claim for violation of establishment clause of First Amendment in connection with school district's requiring him to teach evolution, i.e., that higher life forms evolved from lower ones; (2) school district's restriction on teacher's right of free speech in prohibiting teacher from talking with students about religion during school day, including times when he was not actually teaching class, was justified by school district's interest in avoiding establishment clause violation; (3) teacher's allegations of injury to his reputation as result of allegedly defamatory statements made to and about him were insufficient to support claim for deprivation of liberty interest under § 1983; but (4) teacher's complaint was not entirely frivolous, precluding award of costs and attorney fees under Rule 11 and § 1988.

The case disposition almost entirely ruled against every point the teacher Peloza brought up. One judge, Pole, offered a partial dissenting opinion, of which an excerpt follows.

I am in agreement with the majority's resolution of John Peloza's Establishment Clause and Due Process Clause claims. However, because I believe we can dismiss Peloza's free speech claims only by turning a deaf ear to the procedural posture of this case, I respectfully dissent from parts I. B and II of the majority opinion.

I

Schoolteacher John Peloza seeks a declaratory judgment permitting him to "respond to student-initiated inquiries ... regarding religion" during contract time. The majority opinion concludes that if Peloza's discussions would constitute an establishment of religion, the District may permissibly limit those discussions, even though such limitations restrict Peloza's free speech. With this I have no quarrel. But the majority's premise is that any discussions Peloza might have do constitute such an establishment, and I am unpersuaded that we may reach such a conclusion in the case's present posture.

This is an appeal from the granting of a Rule 12(b)(6) motion. As such, we are not permitted to affirm dismissal of the complaint "unless it appears beyond doubt that plaintiff can prove no set of facts in support of his claim which would entitle him to relief." Love V. United States, 915 F.2d 1242, 1245 (9th Cir.1989). At this stage, we know almost nothing about what past or future discussions might involve. I can imagine a wide range of circumstances and questions "regarding religion" which Peloza could permissibly answer without violating the Establishment Clause. For example, a student might come to a teacher during lunch and ask about Malcolm X or Martin Luther King's religious beliefs, and how and why they evolved, or about the origins of Islam, or what the seven great religions of the world were. Such questions would certainly be "regarding religion," student-initiated, and during contract time. As such, they fall within the class of discussions Peloza seeks to be permitted, yet it is hard to see how the descriptive role a teacher would have in responding to these questions would work any violation of the Establishment Clause.

The majority holding only makes sense if we presume that we know what kinds of questions are being asked and what kinds of answers Peloza would give. In the posture of this case, where we must reverse if there are any facts Peloza could conceivably prove which would entitle him to relief, this is a presumption we are forbidden from making. As a result, the majority holding means that any response to a student-initiated inquiry "regarding religion" during contract time, other than "Ask someone else," works a violation of the Establishment Clause. I cannot join in such a broad legal holding, and indeed the case law forbids it:

In each case, the inquiry calls for line-drawing; no fixed, per se rule can be framed. The Establishment Clause like the Due Process Clauses is not a precise, detailed provision in a legal code capable of ready application.... The line between permissible relationships and those barred by the Clause can no more be straight and unwavering than due process can be defined in a single stroke or phrase or test. The Clause erects a "blurred, indistinct, and variable barrier depending on all the circumstances of a particular relationship." Lemon V. Kurtzman, 403 U.S. [602, 614, 91 S.Ct. 2105, 2112, 29 L.Ed.2d 745 (1971)]. Lynch V. Donnelly, 465 U.S. 668, 678-79, 104 S.Ct. 1355,1362, 79 L.Ed.2d 604 (1984).

Roberts V. Madigan, 921 F.2d 1047 (10th Cir.1990), upon which the majority relies, is not to the contrary. There, the court had before it a host of particulars: the conduct at issue involved a teacher displaying religious books and a poster reading "You have only to open your eyes to see the hand of God" in the classroom. Id. at 1049. That court also had the benefit of a district court factual determination that the conduct "created the appearance that [the teacher] was seeking to advance his religious views." Id. As this case stands, we know far less.

The majority impermissibly attempts to narrow the scope of Peloza's complaint by relying on a written warning from the school district which Peloza has incorporated into the complaint. The letter forbids Peloza from "attempt[ing] to convert students to Christianity or initiating conversations about your religious beliefs." Complaint at 45. Were this all that the complaint said, I would have little trouble joining the majority. But the complaint alleges more; it contends that "the school district ... has directed Plaintiff not to discuss any religious matters during any of this 'instructional time,' including student-initiated conversations regarding religion during lunch, class breaks, and before and after school hours." Complaint at 3. This allegation we must take as true. If all that lies behind it is the far narrower warning the majority cites, then Peloza's case will not be long for this world. But we may not presume that this is so.

I believe that, in a broad range of cases, the majority and I could agree about what would or would not constitute a violation of the Establishment Clause. But the majority errs in presuming to know that what is at stake here is Peloza's right to "discuss his religious beliefs" with students. In doing so, it ignores the fact that this is a Rule 12(b)(6) case. More generally, it gives short shrift to the possibility that we may well be limiting free speech more broadly than the state's compelling interest in avoiding an establishment of religion would warrant.

II

I join in the majority's part II insofar as it dismisses Peloza's § 1985(3) due process and Establishment Clause claims based on his failure to properly allege a violation of these rights. However, because I conclude that Peloza's free speech claim should not have been dismissed, I would also remand, rather than dismiss, his 1985(3) claim based on alleged free speech violations.

III

Religion has been used to justify the suppression of speech for centuries. See Everson V. Board of Ed,, 330 U.S. 1, 8-10, 67 S.Ct. 504, 5074)9, 91 L.Ed. 711 (1947). With the development of a vigorous First Amendment jurisprudence, we have quelled some of the worst abuses. But points of tension remain. We must thus remain vigilant to ensure that in our rush to preserve certain fundamental rights, we do not trample others. Caution is of the essence; only through a methodical and fact-specific jurisprudence can we hope to achieve a proper accommodation.

For the reasons stated above, I respectfully dissent.

1. On appeal, Peloza abandoned his equal protection argument.

2. The Establishment Clause of the First Amendment provides that "Congress shall make no law respecting an establishment of religion..." The Fourteenth Amendment incorporates the Establishment Clause's prohibitions against offending state action as well. Board of Education v. Pico, 457 U.S. 853, 864, 102 S.Ct.2799, 2806-07, 73 L.Ed.2d 435 (1982).

3. See Webster's Third New Int'l Dictionary (G. & C. Merriam Co. Springfield, MA. 1969). p.789 ("evolutionism: 1: a theory of evolution (as in philosophy, biology, or sociology) - See Darwinism 2: adherence to or belief in evolution esp. of living beings").

4. According to Webster's, religion is the "belief in and reverence for a supernatural power accepted as the creator and governor of the universe." Webster's II New Riverside University Dictionary 993.

5. See Smith v. Board of School Com'rs of Mobile County, 827 F.2d 684, 690-95 (11th Cir.1987) (refusing to adopt district court's holding that "secular humanism" is a religion for Establishment Clause purposes; deciding case on other grounds); United States v. Allen, 760 F.2d 447, 450-51 (2d Cir.1985) (quoting Tribe, American Constitutional Law 827-28 (1987), for the proposition that, while "religion" should be broadly interpreted for Free Exercise Clause purposes, "anything 'arguably non-religious' should not be considered religious in applying the establishment clause").

6. The dissent claims this interpretation impermissibly narrows the scope of Peloza's complaint. However, the very sentence quoted by the dissent, Dissent at p.12064, focuses not on the definition of "religious matters," but on the definition of "instructional time." We agree with the dissent that a complaint must be read charitably at the Rule 12(b)(6) stage. However, a reviewing court need not go so far as to invent claims not within the reasonable intendment of the complaint.

7. As with his equal protection claim under section 1983, Peloza appears to have dropped his equal protection claim from his appeal to this court.

8. See United Brotherhood of Carpenters & Joiners of America, Local 610, AFL-CIO v. Scott, 463 U.S. 825, 830, 103 S.Ct. 3352,3357, 77 L.Ed.2d 1049 (1983) (hate speech rights protected by section 1985 so long as the State is involved in the conspiracy alleged). As to due process rights, there appears to be some confusion within this circuit. Older cases have stated that section 1985(3) provides no remedy for violation of due process rights, Cohen V. Norris, 300 F.2d 24, 28 (9th Cir. 1962) (dicta); Mitchell V. Greenough, 100 F.2d 184, 187 (9th Cir.1938) (holding), cert. denied. 306 U.S. 659, 59 S.Ct. 788, 83 L.Ed. 1056 (1939). In some more recent cases, we have allowed claims of due process violations to proceed under section 1985(3) without comment. See Judie V. Hamilton. 872 F.2d 919,924 (9th Cir.1989); Padway V. Palches. 665 F.2d 965, 969 (9th Cir. 1982). See Taylor V. Gilmartin, 686 F.2d 1346, 1358 (10th Cir.1982) (First Amendment freedom of religion protected by section 1985(3)). cert. denied, 459 U.S. 1147, 103 S.Ct. 788,74 L.Ed.2d 994 and cert. denied, 463 U.S. 1229, 103 S.Ct. 3570, 77 L.Ed.2d 1411 (1983); Action V. Gannon. 450 F.2d 1227, 1234 (8th Cir.1971) (satne); Cooper V. Molko, 512 F.Supp. 563, 570 (N.D.Cal.1981) (same); but see Africa V. Anderson, 510 F.Supp. 28, 30 (E.D.Penn.1980) (freedom of religion not protected by section 1985(3)).

The dissenting judge touches on the key point of the whole argument all of these evolution-related court case have shared. Opposition to the teaching of Evolution can only be on religious grounds and all religious talk must be stifled. Only in that way can Evolution opposition be stifled.

The judge properly questioned how a school district could make a blanket order forbidding the teacher such a wide range of activities. First, they prohibited any discussion of religion at all. Second, they forbade conversations outside the classroom and class time. Third, they forbade even student-initiated conversations.

With the development of a vigorous First Amendment jurisprudence, we have quelled some of the worst abuses. But points of tension remain. We must thus remain vigilant to ensure that in our rush to preserve certain fundamental rights, we do not trample others. Caution is of the essence; only through a methodical and fact-specific jurisprudence can we hope to achieve a proper accommodation.

This is a well-spoken statement, but it is too little, too late. The damage is done. The fundamental right to teach truth and reject error has been trampled repeatedly by court decisions designed solely to protect the State religion of Secular Humanism and its Bible of Evolution Dogma. For a judge to stop now and think of how the judicial system might have gone too far is sad. To date, judges have fervently served as the High Priests of Humanism and defended the dogma against all comers.

In an earlier court case Justice Black was quoted as having brought up Thomas Jefferson's "wall of separation" concept. That non-constitutional statement has since been solidly welded into place and given rise to a host of misinterpretations and abuses of intent and power.

A later case chose to quote Robert Frost's "Mending Wall," as if that were proof of the need for separation when its point is really the opposite. Is it possible that judges do not at all understand the intention of the founding fathers in the Constitution and documents of the same time period? And is it possible that even the United States Supreme Court had a different interpretation of the "separation principle" long after the days of the founding (see the 1844 quotation below) but before Secular Humanism became the law of the land?

The following comes from the website Vine & Fig Tree, which describes itself as Supporting: love, joy, peace, patience, gentleness, goodness, faith, meekness, sobriety [and] Opposing: Secularism, Humanism, Anti-Family Sex, Hedonism, Autonomy, Totalitarianism, and Mass Death.

In stark contrast to the myth of separation, the Founders believed that schools should positively and affirmatively teach religion. Every single person who signed the Constitution believed that religious and moral inculcation was the purpose of schools. Peloza is light-years away from the original intent of the Constitution. Consider Samuel Adams:

As piety, religion, and morality have a happy influence on the minds of men, in their public as well as private transactions, you will not think it unseasonable, although I have frequently done it, to bring to your remembrance the great importance of encouraging our University, town schools, and other seminaries of education, that our children and youth while they are engaged in the pursuit of useful science, may have their minds impressed with a strong sense of the duties they owe to God. If we continue to be a happy people, that happiness must be assured by the enacting and executing of the reasonable and wise laws expressed in the plainest language and by establishing such modes of education as tend to inculcate in the minds of youth the feelings and habits of "piety, religion and morality." (Addressing the Legislature of Mass., 1/16/1795)

Let divines and philosophers, statesmen and patriots, unite their endeavors to renovate the age, by impressing the minds of men with the importance of educating their little boys and girls, of inculcating in the minds of youth the fear and love of the Deity. . . and, in subordination to these great principles, the love of their country. . . . In short, of leading them in the study and practice of the exalted virtues of the Christian system. Letter to John Adams, 1790, who wrote back: "You and I agree." Four Letters: Being an Interesting Correspondence Between Those Eminently Distinguished Characters, John Adams, Late President of the United States; and Samuel Adams, Late Governor of Massachusetts. On the Important Subject of Government (Boston: Adams and Rhoades, 1802) pp. 9-10

It has been observed that "education has a greater influence on manners than human laws can have." [A] virtuous education is calculated to reach and influence the heart and to prevent crimes. . . . Such an education, which leads the youth beyond mere outside show, will impress their minds with a profound reverence of the Deity [and] . . . will excite in them a just regard to Divine revelation. The Life and Public Services of Samuel Adams, Wm.Wells., ed. (Boston: Little, Brown, & Co., 1865) Vol.III, p. 327.

Art. 3. Religion, morality, and knowledge, being necessary to good government and the happiness of mankind, schools and the means of education shall forever be encouraged. Northwest Ordinance, 1787

In my view, the Christian religion is the most important and one of the first things in which all children, under a free government, ought to be instructed. . . . No truth is more evident to my mind than that the Christian religion must be the basis of any government intended to secure the rights and privileges of a free people. The opinion that human reason left without the constant control of Divine laws and commands will preserve a just administration, secure freedom and other rights, restrain men from violations of laws and constitutions, and give duration to a popular government is as chimerical as the most extravagant ideas that enter the head of a maniac . .

. . Where will you find any code of laws among civilized men in which the commands and prohibitions are not founded on Christian principles? I need not specify the prohibition of murder, robbery, theft [and] trespass. Noah Webster, Letters, Harry A Warfel, ed., (NY: Library Publishers, 1953) pp. 453-454, to David McClure, Oct. 25, 1836.

Thomas Jefferson's good friend Benjamin Rush, after he signed the Declaration of Independence, was the first Founding Father to call for free public schools. He said:

[T]he only foundation for a useful education in a republic is to be laid in religion. Without this there can be no virtue, and without virtue there can be no liberty, and liberty is the object and life of all republican governments. Without religion, I believe that learning does real mischief to the morals and principles of mankind.(Benjamin Rush, Essays, Literary, Moral, and Philosophical, 1798, p.6 ["On the Mode of Education Proper in a Republic"])

Rush was clearly a Christian, but no "fundamentalist nut." In his paper entitled, "A Defense of the Use of the Bible as a Schoolbook," Rush argued,

[T]he only means of establishing and perpetuating our republican forms of government . . . is the universal education of our youth in the principles of Christianity by means of the Bible. For this Divine book, above all others, favors that equality among mankind, that respect for just laws, and those sober and frugal virtues, which constitute the soul of republicanism.

Daniel Webster reflected the views of every single Signer of the Constitution:

We regard it [public instruction] as a wise and liberal system of police by which property and life and the peace of society are secured. We seek to prevent in some measure the extension of the penal code by inspiring a salutary and conservative principle of virtue and of knowledge. [1]

[However, t]he attainment of knowledge does not comprise all which is contained in the larger term of education. The feelings are to be disciplined; the passions are to be restrained; true and worthy motives are to be inspired; a profound religious feeling is to be instilled, and pure morality inculcated. [Four years later, the U.S. Supreme Court would agree that this could only be done by having the government teach the Bible.] [2]

The cultivation of the religious sentiment represses licentiousness . . . inspires respect for law and order, and gives strength to the whole social fabric.[3]

[1] Works of Daniel Webster (Boston: Little, Brown, and Co., 1853) vol I, pp 41-42, Dec 22., 1820.[2] vol II, pp 107-108, Oct 5: 1840[3] vol II, p 615, July 4, 1851

The Father of his Country warned:

And let us with caution indulge the supposition that morality can be maintained without religion. Whatever may be conceded to the influence of refined education on minds of peculiar structure, reason and experience both forbid us to expect that national morality can prevail in exclusion of religious principle And secularists would be quick to point out that Washington was less Biblically-oriented than the most influential educators in the nation, such as Benjamin Rush and Noah Webster.

All the scholars are required to live a religious and blameless life according to the rules of God's Word, diligently reading the holy Scriptures, that fountain of Divine light and truth, and constantly attending all the duties of religion . . . . All the scholars are obliged to attend Divine worship in the College Chapel on the Lord's Day and on Days of Fasting and Thanksgiving appointed by public Authority. The Laws of Yale College in New Haven in Connecticut (New Haven: Josiah Meigs, 1787) p. 5-6, ch II, art. 1,4

William Samuel Johnson, signer of the Constitution, was appointed Columbia's first president. Under him, It is expected that all students attend public worship on Sundays. Columbia Rules (NY: Samuel Loudon, 1785) 5-8

Johnson's views on public education were similar to those of every other signer of the Constitution. In his commencement address, he told the graduates:

You this day, gentlemen, . . . have . . . received a public education, the purpose whereof hath been to qualify you the better to serve your Creator and your country . . . . Your first great duties, you are sensible, are those you owe to Heaven, to your Creator and Redeemer. Let these be ever present to your minds, and exemplified in your lives and conduct. Imprint deep upon your minds the principles of piety towards God and a reverence and fear of His holy name. The fear of God is the beginning of wisdom [Proverbs 9:10]. Remember too, that you are the redeemed of the Lord, that you are bought with a price, even the inestimable price of the precious blood of the Son of God. . . . Love, fear and serve Him as your Creator, Redeemer, and Sanctifier. Acquaint yourselves with Him in His Word and holy ordinances. Make Him your friend and protector and your felicity is secured both here and hereafter.

Early US Supreme Court decisions agreed that in a Christian nation such as America, the Bible must be taught in all government-run schools.

In 1844, the Court was asked, Can the state enforce a will which creates a government-operated school which will not teach the Bible? The Supreme Court said that the very idea of a school which will not teach the Bible is contrary to the legal foundations of this Christian nation.

It is unnecessary for us, however, to consider what would be the legal effect of a devise in Pennsylvania for the establishment of a school or college, for the propagation of . . . Deism, or any other form of infidelity. Such a case is not to be presumed to exist in a Christian country; and therefore it must be made out by clear and indisputable proof.

The government made firm assurances that the Bible would be taught in the school, and the will was approved. (Vidal v. Girard's Executors)

The Vidal Court, as it talks about Christianity and the Bible, sounds more like David Barton than anything one would hear from the post-1947 Court. The Vidal Court said that the government in its school "may, nay must impart to their youthful pupils . . . the Bible, and especially the New Testament," which must "be read and taught as a divine revelation in the college -- its general precepts expounded, its evidences explained, and its glorious principles of morality inculcated." The Court asked rhetorically:

Where can the purest principles of morality be learned so clearly or so perfectly as from the New Testament? Where are benevolence, the love of truth, sobriety, and industry, so powerfully and irresistibly inculcated as in the sacred volume?

The Bible MUST be taught in government schools, the 1844 US Supreme Court declared.

You would NEVER EVER hear language like this from the modern secularist Court. But you ALWAYS heard language like this from the Founding Fathers.

The "separation of church and state" is a myth.

Appendix Two: Supplementary Material for Section One

Acts of Uniformity

(taken from Hanover Historical Texts Projects. History Department, Hanover College, Hanover, IN. http://history.hanover. edu/texts.)

First Act of Uniformity 1549 (2 & 3 Edward VI, c. 1)

Where of long time there has been had in this realm of England and in Wales divers forms of common prayer, commonly called the service of the Church; that is to say the Use of Sarum, of York, of Bangor, and of Lincoln; and besides the same now of late much more divers and sundry forms and fashions have been used in the cathedral and parish churches of England and Wales, as well concerning the Matins or Morning Prayer and the Evensong, as also concerning the Holy Communion, commonly called the Mass, with divers and sundry rites and ceremonies concerning the same, and in the administration of other sacraments of the Church: and as the doers and executors of the said rites and ceremonies, in other form than of late years they have been used, were pleased therewith, so others, not using the same rites and ceremonies, were thereby greatly offended; And albeit the king's majesty, with the advice of his most entirely beloved uncle, the lord protector, and other of his highness's council, has heretofore divers times essayed to stay innovations or new rites concerning the premises; yet the same has not had such good success as his highness required in that behalf:

Whereupon his highness by the most prudent advice-aforesaid, being pleased to bear with the frailty and weakness of his subjects in that behalf, of his great clemency has not been only content to abstain from punishment of those that have offended in that behalf, for that his highness taketh that they did it of a good zeal; but also to the intent a uniform quiet and godly order should be had concerning the premises, has appointed the Archbishop of Canterbury, and certain of the most learned and discreet bishops, and other learned men of this realm, to consider and ponder the premises; and thereupon having as well eye and respect to the most sincere and pure Christian religion taught by the Scripture, as to the usages in the primitive Church, should draw and make one convenient and meet order, rite, and fashion of common and open prayer and administration of the sacraments, to be had and used in his majesty's realm of England and in Wales; the which at this time, by the aid of the Holy Ghost, with one uniform agreement is of them concluded, set forth, and delivered to his highness, to his great comfort and quietness of mind, in a book entitled, 'The Book of the Common Prayer and Administration of the Sacraments, and other Rites and Ceremonies of the Church, after the Use of the Church of England':

Wherefore the lords spiritual and commons, in this present parliament assembled, considering as well the most godly travail of the king's highness, of the lord protector, and of other his highness's council, in gathering and collecting the said Archbishop, bishops, and learned men together, as the godly prayers, orders, rites, and ceremonies in the said book mentioned, and the considerations of altering those things which be altered and retaining those things which be retained in the said book, but also the honour of God and great quietness, which by the grace of God shall ensue upon the one and uniform rite and order in such common prayer and rites and external ceremonies to be used throughout England and in Wales, at Calais and the marches of the same, do give to his highness most hearty and lowly thanks for the same; and humbly pray, that it may be ordained and enacted by his majesty, with the assent of the lords and commons in this present parliament assembled, and by the authority of the same, that all and singular person and persons that have offended concerning the premises, other than such person and persons as now be and remain in ward in the Tower of London, or in the Fleet, may be pardoned thereof; and that all and singular ministers in any cathedral or parish church or other place within this realm of England, Wales, Calais, and the marches of the same, or other the king's dominions, shall, from and after the feast of Pentecost next coming, be bound to say and use the Matins, Evensong, celebration of the Lord's Supper, commonly called the Mass, and administration of each of the sacraments, and all their common and open prayer, in such order and form as is mentioned in the same book, and none other or otherwise. And albeit that the same be so godly and good, that they give occasion to every honest and conformable man most willingly to embrace them, yet lest any obstinate person who willingly would disturb so godly order and quiet in this realm should not go unpunished, that it may also be ordained and enacted by the authority aforesaid that if any manner of parson, vicar, or other whatsoever minister, that ought or should sing or say common prayer mentioned in the said book, or minister the sacraments, shall after the said feast of Pentecost next coming refuse to use the said common prayers, or to minister the sacraments in such cathedral or parish church or other places as he should use or minister the same, in: such order and form as they be mentioned and set forth in the said book; or shall use, wilfully and obstinately standing in the same, any other rite, ceremony, order, form, or manner of Mass openly or privily, or Matins, Evensong, administration of the sacraments, or other open prayer than is mentioned and set forth in the said book (open prayer in and throughout this Act, is meant that prayer which is for other to come unto or hear either in common churches or private chapels or oratories, commonly called the service of the Church); or shall preach, declare, or speak anything in the derogation or depraving of the said book, or anything therein contained, or of any part thereof; and shall be thereof lawfully convicted according to the laws of this realm, by verdict of twelve men, or by his own confession, or by the notorious evidence of the fact: shall lose and forfeit to the king's highness, his heirs and successors, for his first offence, the profit of such one of his spiritual benefices or promotions as it shall please the king's highness to assign or appoint, coming and arising in one whole year next after his conviction: and also that the same person so convicted shall for the same offence suffer imprisonment by the space of six months, without bail or mainprize: and if any such person once convicted of any offence concerning the premises, shall after his first conviction again offend and be thereof in form aforesaid lawfully convicted, that then the same person shall for his second offence suffer imprisonment by the space of one whole year, and also shall therefore be deprived ipso facto of all his spiritual promotions; and that it shall be lawful to all patrons, donors, and grantees of all and singular the same spiritual promotions, to present to the same any other able clerk, in like manner and form as though the party so offending were dead: and that if any such person or persons, after he shall be twice convicted in form aforesaid, shall offend against any of the premises the third time, and shall be thereof in form aforesaid lawfully convicted, that then the person so offending and convicted the third time shall suffer imprisonment during his life. And if the person that shall offend and be convicted in form aforesaid concerning any of the premises, shall not be beneficed nor have any spiritual promotion, that then the same person so offending and convicted shall for the first offence suffer imprisonment during six months, without bail or mainprize: and if any such person not having any spiritual promotion, after his first conviction shall again offend in anything concerning the premises, and shall in form aforesaid be thereof lawfully convicted, that then the same person shall for his second offence suffer imprisonment during his life.

II. And it is ordained and enacted by the authority abovesaid, that if any person or persons whatsoever, after the said feast of Pentecost next coming, shall in any interludes, plays, songs, rhymes, or by other open words declare or speak anything in the derogation, depraving, or despising of the same book or of anything therein contained, or any part thereof; or shall by open fact, deed, or by open threatenings, compel or cause, or otherwise procure or maintain any parson, vicar, or other minister in any cathedral or parish church, or in any chapel or other place, to sing or say any common and open prayer, or to minister any sacrament otherwise or in any other manner or form than is mentioned in the said book; or that by any of the said means shall unlawfully interrupt or let any parson, vicar, or other ministers in any cathedral or parish church, chapel, or any other place, to sing or say common and open prayer, or to minister the sacraments, or any of them, in any such manner and form as is mentioned in the said book; that then every person being thereof lawfully convicted in form abovesaid, shall forfeit to the King our sovereign lord, his heirs and successors, for the first offence ten pounds. And if any person or persons, being once convicted of any such offence, again offend against any of the premises, and shall in form aforesaid be thereof lawfully convicted, that then the same persons so offending and convicted shall for the second offence forfeit to the King our sovereign lord, his heirs and successors, twenty pounds; and if any person after he, in form aforesaid, shall have been twice convicted of any offence concerning any of the premises, shall offend the third time, and be thereof in form abovesaid lawfully convicted, that then every person so offending and convicted shall for his third offence forfeit to our sovereign lord the King all his goods and chattels, and shall suffer imprisonment during his life: and if any person or persons, that for his first offence concerning the premises shall be-convicted in form aforesaid, do not pay the sum to be paid by virtue of his conviction, in such manner and form as the same ought to be paid, within six weeks next after his conviction, that then every person so convicted, and so not paying the same, shall for the same first offence, instead of the said tell pounds, suffer imprisonment by the space of three months without bail or mainprize. And if any person or persons, that for his second offence concerning the premises shall be convicted in form aforesaid, do not pay the sum to be paid by virtue of his conviction, in such manner and form as the same ought to be paid, within six weeks next after his said second conviction, that then every person so convicted, and not so paying the same, shall for the same second offence, instead of the said twenty pounds, suffer imprisonment during six months without bail or mainprize.

III. And it is ordained and enacted by the authority aforesaid, that all and every justices of oyer and terminer, or justices of assize, shall have full power and authority in every of their open and general sessions to inquire, hear, and determine all and all manner of offences that shall be committed or done contrary to any article contained in this present Act, within the limits of the commission to them directed, and to make process for the execution of the same, as they may do against any person being indicted before them of trespass, or lawfully convicted thereof.

IV. Provided always, and be it enacted by the authority aforesaid, that all and every Archbishop and Bishop shall or may at all time and times at his liberty and pleasure join and associate himself, by virtue of this Act, to the said justices of oyer and terminer, or to the said justices of assize, at every of the said open and general sessions to be holden in any place within his diocese, for and to the inquiry, hearing, and determining of the offences aforesaid.

V. Provided always, that it shall be lawful to any man that understands the Greek, Latin, and Hebrew tongue, or other strange tongue, to say and have the said prayers, heretofore specified, of Matins and Evensong in Latin, or any such other tongue, saying the same privately, as they do understand;

VI. And for the further encouraging of learning in the tongues in the Universities of Cambridge and Oxford, to use and exercise in their common and open prayer in their chapels (being no parish churches) or other places of prayer, the Matins, Evensong, Litany, and all other prayers (the Holy Communion, commonly called the Mass, excepted) prescribed in the said book, in Greek, Latin, or Hebrew; anything in this present Act to the contrary notwithstanding.

VII. Provided also, that it shall be lawful for all men, as well in churches, chapels, oratories, or other places, to use openly any psalm or prayer taken out of the Bible, at any due time, not letting or omitting thereby the service or any part thereof mentioned in the said book.

VIII. Provided also, and be it enacted by the authority aforesaid, that the books concerning the said services shall at the costs and charges of the parishioners of every parish and cathedral church be attained and gotten before the feast of Pentecost next following, or before; and that all such parish and cathedral churches, or other places where the said books shall be attained and gotten before the said feast of Pentecost, shall within three weeks next after the said books so attained and gotten use the said service, and put the same in use according to this Act.

IX. And be it further enacted by the authority aforesaid, that no person or persons shall be at any time hereafter impeached or otherwise molested of or for any of the offences above mentioned, hereafter to be committed or done contrary to this Act, unless he or they so offending be thereof indicted at the next general sessions to be holden before any such of the justices of oyer and terminer or justices of assize, next after any offence committed or done contrary to the tenor of this Act.

X. Provided always, and be it ordained and enacted by the authority aforesaid, that all and singular lords in the Parliament, for the third offence above mentioned, shall be tried by their peers.

XI. Provided also, and be it ordained and enacted by the authority aforesaid, that the Mayor of London, and all other Mayors, bailiffs, and other head officers of all and singular cities, boroughs, and towns corporate within this realm, Wales, Calais, and the marches of the same, to the which justices of assize do not commonly repair, shall have full power and authority by virtue of this Act to inquire, hear, and determine the offences abovesaid, and every of them yearly, within fifteen days after the feasts of Easter and St. Michael the Archangel, in like manner and form as justices of assize and oyer and terminer may do.

XII. Provided always, and be it ordained and enacted by the authority aforesaid, that all and singular archbishops and bishops, and every of their chancellors, commissaries, archdeacons, and other ordinaries, having any peculiar ecclesiastical jurisdiction, shall have full power and authority by virtue of this Act, as well to inquire in their visitations, synods, and elsewhere within their jurisdiction, [or] at any other time or place, to take accusations and informations of all and every the things above mentioned, done, committed, or perpetrated, within the limits of their jurisdiction and authority, and to punish the same by admonition, excommunication, sequestration, or deprivation, and other censures and process, in like form as heretofore has been used in like cases by the king's ecclesiastical laws.

XIII. Provided always, and be it enacted, that whatsoever person offending in the premises shall for the first offence receive punishment of the ordinary, having a testimonial thereof under the said ordinary's seal, shall not for the same offence again be summoned before the justices; and likewise receiving for the said first offence punishment by the justices, he shall not for the same offence again receive punishment of the ordinary; anything contained in this Act to the contrary notwithstanding.

Elizabeth's Act of Uniformity (1559)

Where at the death of our late sovereign lord King Edward VI there remained one uniform order of common service and prayer, and of the administration of sacraments, rites, and ceremonies in the Church of England, which was set forth in one book, entitled: The Book of Common Prayer, and Administration of Sacraments, and other rites and ceremonies in the Church of England; authorized by Act of Parliament holden in the fifth and sixth years of our said late sovereign lord King Edward VI, intituled: An Act for the uniformity of common prayer, and administration of the sacraments; the which was repealed and taken away by Act of Parliament in the first year of the reign of our late sovereign lady Queen Mary, to the great decay of the due honour of God, and discomfort to the professors of the truth of Christ's religion: Be it therefore enacted by the authority of this present Parliament, that the said statute of repeal, and everything therein contained, only concerning the said book, and the service, administration of sacraments, rites, and ceremonies contained or appointed in or by the said book, shall be void and of none effect, from and after the feast of the Nativity of St. John Baptist next coming; and that the said book, with the order of service, and of the administration of sacraments, rites, and ceremonies, with the alterations and additions therein added and appointed by this statute, shall stand and be, from and after the said feast of the Nativity of St. John Baptist, in full force and effect, according to the tenor and effect of this statute; anything in the aforesaid statute of repeal to the contrary notwithstanding. And further be it enacted by the queen's highness, with the assent of the Lords (sic) and Commons in this present Parliament assembled, and by authority of the same, that all and singular ministers in any cathedral or parish church, or other place within this realm of England, Wales, and the marches of the same, or other the queen's dominions, shall from and after the feast of the Nativity of St. John Baptist next coming be bounden to say and use the Matins, Evensong, celebration of the Lord's Supper and administration of each of the sacraments, and all their common and open prayer, in such order and form as is mentioned in the said book, so authorized by Parliament in the said fifth and sixth years of the reign of King Edward VI, with one alteration or addition of certain lessons to be used on every Sunday in the year, and the form of the Litany altered and corrected, and two sentences only added in the delivery of the sacrament to the communicants, and none other or otherwise. And that if any manner of parson, vicar, or other whatsoever minister, that ought or should sing or say common prayer mentioned in the said book, or minister the sacraments, from and after the feast of the nativity of St. John Baptist next coming, refuse to use the said common prayers, or to minister the sacraments in such cathedral or parish church, or other places as he should use to minister the same, in such order and form as they be mentioned and set forth in the said book, or shall wilfully or obstinately standing in the same, use any other rite, ceremony, order, form, or manner of celebrating of the Lord's Supper, openly or privily, or Matins, Evensong, administration of the sacraments, or other open prayers, than is mentioned and set forth in the said book (open prayer in and throughout this Act, is meant that prayer which is for other to come unto, or hear, either in common churches or private chapels or oratories, commonly called the service of the Church), or shall preach, declare, or speak anything in the derogation or depraving of the said book, or anything therein contained, or of any part thereof, and shall be thereof lawfully convicted, according to the laws of this realm, by verdict of twelve men, or by his own confession, or by the notorious evidence of the fact, shall lose and forfeit to the queen's highness, her heirs and successors, for his first offence, the profit of all his spiritual benefices or promotions coming or arising in one whole year next after his conviction; and also that the person so convicted shall for the same offence suffer imprisonment by the space of six months, without bail or mainprize. And if any such person once convicted of any offence concerning the premises, shall after his first conviction eftsoons offend, and be thereof, in form aforesaid, lawfully convicted, that then the same person shall for his second offence suffer imprisonment by the space of one whole year, and also shall therefore be deprived, ipso facto, of all his [Page 461] spiritual promotions; and that it shall be lawful to all patrons or donors of all and singular the same spiritual promotions, or of any of them, to present or collate to the same, as though the person and persons so offending were dead. And that if any such person or persons, after he shall be twice convicted in form aforesaid, shall offend against any of the premises the third time, and shall be thereof, in form aforesaid, lawfully convicted, that then the person so offending and convicted the third time, shall be deprived, ipso facto, of all his spiritual promotions, and also shall suffer imprisonment during his life. And if the person that shall offend, and be convicted in form aforesaid, concerning any of the premises, shall not be beneficed, nor have any spiritual promotion, that then the same person so offending and convicted shall for the first offence suffer imprisonment during one whole year next after his said conviction, without bail or mainprize. And if any such person, not having any spiritual promotion, after his first conviction shall eftsoons offend in anything concerning the premises, and shall be, in form aforesaid, thereof lawfully convicted, that then the same person shall for his second offence suffer imprisonment during his life. And it is ordained and enacted by the authority aforesaid, that if any person or persons whatsoever, after the said feast of the Nativity of St. John Baptist next coming, shall in any interludes, plays, songs, rhymes, or by other open words, declare or speak anything in the derogation, depraving, or despising of the same book, or of anything therein contained, or any part thereof, or shall, by open fact, deed, or by open threatenings, compel or cause, or otherwise procure or maintain, any parson, vicar, or other minister in any cathedral or parish church, or in chapel, or in any other place, to sing or say any common or open prayer, or to minister any sacrament otherwise, or in any other manner and form, than is mentioned in the said book; or that by any of the said means shall unlawfully interrupt or let any parson, vicar, or other minister in any cathedral or parish church, chapel, or any other place, to sing or say common and open prayer, or to minister the sacraments or any of them, in such manner and form as is mentioned in the said book; that then every such person, being thereof lawfully convicted in form abovesaid, shall forfeit to the queen our sovereign lady, her heirs and successors, for the first offence a hundred marks. And if any person or persons, being once convicted of any such offence, eftsoons offend against any of the last recited offences, and shall, in form aforesaid, be thereof lawfully convicted, that then the same person so offending and convicted shall, for the second offence, forfeit to the queen our sovereign lady, her heirs and successors, four hundred marks.

And if any person, after he, in form aforesaid, shall have been twice convicted of any offence concerning any of the last recited offences, shall offend the third time, and be thereof, in form abovesaid, lawfully convicted, that then every person so offending and convicted shall for his third offence forfeit to our sovereign lady the queen all his goods and chattels, and shall suffer imprisonment during his life. And if any person or persons, that for his first offence concerning the premises shall be convicted, in form aforesaid, do not pay the sum to be paid by virtue of his conviction, in such manner and form as the same ought to be paid, within six weeks next after his conviction; that then every person so convicted, and so not paying the same, shall for the same first offence, instead of the said sum, suffer imprisonment by the space of six months, without bail or mainprize. And if any person or persons, that for his second offence concerning the premises shall be convicted in form aforesaid, do not pay the said sum to be paid by virtue of his conviction and this statute, in such manner [Page 463] and form as the same ought to be paid, within six weeks next after his said second conviction; that then every person so convicted, and not so paying the same, shall, for the same second offence, in the stead of the said sum, suffer imprisonment during twelve months, without bail or mainprize. And that from and after the said feast of the Nativity of St. John Baptist next coming, all and every person and persons inhabiting within this realm, or any other the queen's majesty's dominions, shall diligently and faithfully, having no lawful or reasonable excuse to be absent, endeavour themselves to resort to their parish church or chapel accustomed, or upon reasonable let thereof, to some usual place where common prayer and such service of God shall be used in such time of let, upon every Sunday and other days ordained and used to be kept as holy days, and then and there to abide orderly and soberly during the time of the common prayer, preachings, or other service of God there to be used and ministered; upon pain of punishment by the censures of the Church, and also upon pain that every person so offending shall forfeit for every such offence twelve pence, to be levied by the churchwardens of the parish where such offence shall be done, to the use of the poor of the same parish, of the goods, lands, and tenements of such offender, by way of distress. And for due execution hereof, the queen's most excellent majesty, the Lords temporal (sic), and all the Commons, in this present Parliament assembled, do in God's name earnestly require and charge all the archbishops, bishops, and other ordinaries, that they shall endeavour themselves to the uttermost of their knowledges, that the due and true execution hereof may be had throughout their dioceses and charges, as they will answer before God, for such evils and plagues wherewith Almighty God may justly punish His people for neglecting this good and wholesome law. And for their authority in this behalf, be it further enacted by the authority aforesaid, that all and singular the same archbishops, bishops, and all other their officers exercising ecclesiastical jurisdiction, as well in place exempt as not exempt, within their dioceses, shall have full power and authority by this Act to reform, correct, and punish by censures of the Church, all and singular persons which shall offend within any their jurisdictions or dioceses, after the said feast of the Nativity of St. John Baptist next coming, against this Act and statute; any other law, statute, privilege, liberty, or provision heretofore made, had, or suffered to the contrary notwithstanding. And it is ordained and enacted by the authority aforesaid, that all and every justices of oyer and terminer, or justices of assize, shall have full power and authority in every of their open and general sessions, to inquire, hear, and determine all and all manner of offences that shall be committed or done contrary to any article contained in this present Act, within the limits of the commission to them directed, and to make process for the execution of the same, as they may do against any person being indicted before them of trespass, or lawfully convicted thereof. Provided always, and be it enacted by the authority aforesaid, that all and every archbishop and bishop shall or may, at all time and times, at his liberty and pleasure, join and associate himself, by virtue of this Act, to the said justices of oyer and terminer, or to the said justices of assize, at every of the said open and general sessions to be holden in any place within his diocese, for and to the inquiry, hearing, and determining of the offences aforesaid. Provided also, and be it enacted by the authority aforesaid, that the books concerning the said services shall, at the cost and charges of the parishioners of every parish and cathedral church, be attained and gotten before the said feast of the Nativity of St. John Baptist next following; and that all such parishes and cathedral churches, or other places where the said books shall be attained and gotten before the said feast of the Nativity of St. John Baptist, shall, within three weeks next after the said books so attained and gotten, use the said service, and put the same in use according to this Act. And be it further enacted by the authority aforesaid, that no person or persons shall be at any time hereafter impeached or otherwise molested of or for any the offences above mentioned, hereafter to be committed or done contrary to this Act, unless he or they so offending be thereof indicted at the next general sessions to be holden before any such justices of oyer and terminer or justices of assize, next after any offence committed or done contrary to the tenor of this Act. Provided always, and be it ordained and enacted by the authority aforesaid, that all and singular lords of the

Parliament, for the third offence above mentioned, shall be tried by their peers. Provided also, and be it ordained and enacted by the authority aforesaid, that the mayor of London, and all other mayors, bailiffs, and other head officers of all and singular cities, boroughs, and towns corporate within this realm, Wales, and the marches of the same, to the which justices of assize do not commonly repair, shall have full power and authority by virtue of this Act to inquire, hear, and determine the offences abovesaid, and every of them, yearly within fifteen days after the feasts of Easter and St. Michael the Archangel, in like manner and form as justices of assize and oyer and terminer may do. Provided always, and be it ordained and enacted by the authority aforesaid, that all and singular archbishops and bishops, and every their chancellors, commissaries, archdeacons, and other ordinaries, having any peculiar ecclesiastical jurisdiction. shall have full power and authority by virtue of this Act, as well to inquire in their visitation, synods, and elsewhere within their jurisdiction at any other time and place, to take occasions (sic) and informations of all and every the things above mentioned, done, committed, or perpetrated within the limits of their jurisdictions and authority, and to punish the same by admonition, excommunication, sequestration, or deprivation, and other censures and processes, in like form as heretofore has been used in like cases by the queen's ecclesiastical laws.

Provided always, and be it enacted, that whatsoever person offending in the premises shall, for the offence, first receive punishment of the ordinary, having a testimonial thereof under the said ordinary's seal, shall not for the same offence eftsoons be convicted before the justices: and likewise receiving, for the said offence, first punishment by the justices, he shall not for the same offence eftsoons receive punishment of the ordinary;

anything contained in this Act to the contrary notwithstanding.

Provided always, and be it enacted, that such ornaments of the church, and of the ministers thereof, shall be retained and be in use, as was in the Church of England, by authority of Parliament, in the second year of the reign of King Edward VI, until other order shall be therein taken by the authority of the queen's majesty, with the advice of her commissioners appointed and authorized, under the great seal of England, for causes ecclesiastical, or of the metropolitan of this realm.

And also, that if there shall happen any contempt or irreverence to be used in the ceremonies or rites of the Church, by the misusing of the orders appointed in this book, the queen's majesty may, by the like advice of the said commissioners or metropolitan, ordain and publish such further ceremonies or rites, as may be most for the advancement of God's glory, the edifying of His Church, and the due reverence of Christ's holy mysteries and sacraments.

And be it further enacted by the authority aforesaid, that all laws, statutes, and ordinances, wherein or whereby any other service, administration of sacraments or common prayer, is limited, established, or set forth to be used within this realm, or any other the queen's dominions or countries, shall from henceforth be utterly void and of none effect.

An Act For the Uniformity of Publick Prayers; and Administration of Sacraments, and other Rites and Ceremonies: And for the establishing the Form of Making, Ordaining, and Consecrating Bishops, Priests, and Deacons in the Church of England.

Third Act of Uniformity Charles 1662

HEREAS in the first year of the late Queen Elizabeth there was one Uniform Order of Common Service and

Prayer, and of the Administration of Sacraments, Rites and Ceremonies in the Church of England (agreeable to the Word of God, and usage of the Primitive Church) compiled by the Reverend Bishops and Clergy, set forth in one Book, Entituled, The Book of Common Prayer, and Administration of Sacraments, and other Rites and Ceremonies in the Church of England, and enjoyned to be used by Act of Parliament, holden in the said first year of the said late Queen, Entituled, An Act for the Uniformity of Common Prayer, and Service in the Church, and Administration of the Sacraments, very comfortable to all good people desirous to live in Christian conversation, and most profitable to the Estate of this Realm, upon the which the Mercy, Favour and Blessing of Almight God is in no wise so readily and plentifully poured, as by Common Prayers, due using of the Sacraments, and often Preaching of the Gospel, with devotion of the hearers: And yet this notwithstanding, a great number of people in divers parts of this Realm, following their own sensuality, and living without knowledge and due fear of God, do willfully and Schismatically abstain, and refuse to come to their Parish Churches and other Publick places where Common Prayer, Administration of the Sacraments, and Preaching of the Word of God is used upon the Sundays and other days ordained and appointed to be kept and observed as Holy days: And whereas by the great and scandalous neglect of Ministers in using the said Order, or Liturgy so set forth and enjoyned as aforesaid, great mischiefs and inconveniences, during the times of the late unhappy troubles, have arisen and grown; and many people have been led into Factions and Schisms, to the great decay and scandal of the Reformed Religion of the Church of England, and to the hazard of many souls: for prevention whereof in time to come, for settling the Peace of the Church, and for allaying the present distempers, which the indisposition of the time hath contracted, The Kings Majesty (according to His

Declaration of the Five and twentieth of October, One thousand six hundred and sixty) granted His Commission under the great Seal of England to several Bishops and other Divines to review the Book of Common Prayer, and to prepare such Alterations and Additions, as they thought fit to offer; And afterwards the Convocations of both the Provinces of Canterbury and York, being by his Majesty called and assembled (and now sitting) His Majesty hath been pleased to Authorize and require the Presidents of the said Convocations, and other Bishops and Clergy of the same, to review the said Book of Common Prayer, and the Book of the Form and manner of the Making and Consecrating of Bishops, Priests and Deacons; And that after mature consideration, they should make such Additions and Alterations in the said Books respectively, as to them should seem meet and convenient; And should exhibit and present the same to His Majesty in writing, for his further allowance or confirmation; since which time, upon full and mature deliberation, they the said Presidents, Bishops, and Clergy of both Provinces have accordingly reviewed the said Books, and have made some Alterations which they think fit to be inserted to the same; and some Additional Prayers to the said Book of Common-Prayer, to be used upon proper and emergent occasions; and have exhibited and presented the same unto his Majesty in writing, in one Book, Entituled, The Book of Common Prayer, and Administration of the Scaraments, and other Rites and Ceremonies of the Church, according to the use of the Church of England, together with the Psalter, or Psalms of David, Pointed as they are to be sung or said in Churches; and the Form and Manner of Making, Ordaining, and Consecrating of Bishops, Priests, and Deacons: All which His Majesty having duely considered hath fully approved and allowed the same, and recommended to this present Parliament, that the said Book of Common Prayer, and of the Form of Ordination and Concecration of Bishops, Priests, and Deacons, with the Alterations and Additions, which have been so made and presented to His Majesty by the said Convocations, be the Book, which shall be appointed to be used by all that Officiate in all Cathedral and Collegiate Churches and Chappels, and in all Chappels of Colleges and Halls in both the Universities, and the Colledges of Eaton and Winchester, and in all Parish-Churches and Chappels within the Kingdom of England, Dominion of Wales, and Town of Berwick upon Tweed, and by all that Make, or Consecrate Bishops, Priests or Deacons in any of the said Places, under such Sanctions and Penalties as the Houses of Parliament shall think fit: Now in regard that nothing conduceth more to the feeling of the Peace of this Nation (which is desired of all good men) nor to the honour of our Religion, and the propagation thereof, than an Universal agreement in the Publick Worship of Almighty God; and to the intent that every person within this Realm, may certainly know the rule, to which be is to conform in Publick Worship, and Administration of Sacraments, and other Rites and Ceremonies of the Church of England, and the manner how, and by whom Bishops Priests and Deacons are, and ought to be Made, Ordained and Consecrated;

Be it Enacted by the Kings most Excellent Majesty, by the advice, and with the consent of the Lords Spiritual and Temporal, and of the Commons in this present Parliament assembled, and by the Authority of the same, That all and singular Ministers, in any Cathedral, Collegiate, or Parish-Church or Chappel, or other Place of Publick Worship within this Realm of England, Dominion of Wales, and Town of Berwick upon Tweed, shall be bound to say and use the Morning Prayer, Evening Prayer, Celebration and Administration of both the Sacraments, and all other the Publick, and Common Prayer, in such order and form as is mentioned in the said Book, annexed and joined to this present Act, and

Entituled, The Book of Common Prayer, and Administration of the Sacraments, and other Rites and Ceremonies of the Church, according to the use of the Church of England: together with the Psalter or Psalms of David, Pointed as they are to be sung or said in Churches; and the form or manner of Making, Ordaining, and Consecrating of Bishops, Priests and Deacons; and That the Morning and Evening Prayers, therein contained, shall upon every Lords day, and upon all other days and occasions, and at the times therein appointed, be openly and solemnly read by all and every Minister or Curate in every Church, Chappel, or other place of Publick Worship within this Realm of England, and places aforesaid.

And to the end that Uniformity in the Publick Worship of God (which is so much desired) may be speedily effected, Be it further Enacted by the Authority aforesaid, that every Parson, Vicar, or other Minister whatsoever, who now hath, and enjoyeth any Ecclesiastical Benefice, or Promotion, within this Realm of England, or places aforesaid, shall in the Church, Chappel, or place of Publick Worship belonging to his said Benefice or Promotion, upon some Lords day before the Feast of Saint Bartholomew, which shall be in the year of our Lord God, One thousand six hundred sixty and two, openly; publickly, and solemnly read the Morning and Evening Prayer appointed to be read by, and according to the said Book of Common Prayer at the times thereby appointed, and after such reading thereof shall openly and publickly, before the Congregation there assembled, declare his unfeigned assent, and consent to the use of all things in the said Book contained and prescribed, in these words, and no other;

I, A. B. Do here declare my unfeigned assent, and consent to all, and every thing contained, and prescribed in, and by the Book intituled, The Book of Common Prayer and Administration of the Sacraments, and other

Rites, and Ceremonies of the Church, according to the use of the Church of England; together with the Psalter, or Psalms of David, Pointed as they are to be sung, or said in Churches, and the form, or manner of Making, Ordaining, and Consecrating of Bishops, Priests, and Deacons;

And, That all and every such person, who shall (without some lawful Impediment, to be allowed and approved of by the Ordinary of the place) neglect or refuse to do the same within the time aforesaid, or (in case of such Impediment) within one Moneth after such Impediment removed, shall ipso facto be deprived of all his Spiritual Promotions; And that from thenceforth it shall be lawful to, and for all Patrons, and Donors of all and singular the said Spiritual Promotions, or of any of them, according to their respective Rights, and Titles, to present, or collate to the same; as though the person, or persons, so offending or neglected were dead.

And be it further Enacted by the Authority aforesaid, That every person, who shall hereafter be presented, or collated, or put into any Ecclesiastical Benefice, or Promotion within this Realm of England and places aforesaid, shall in the Church, Chappel, or Place of Publick Worship, belonging to his said Benefice or Promotion, within two Moneths next after that he shall be in the actual possession of the said Eccelsiastical Benefice or Promotion, upon some Lords day openly, publickly, and solemnly Read the Morning and Evening Prayers, appointed to be Read by, and according to the said Book of Common Prayer, at the times thereby appointed, and after such reading thereof, shall openly, and publickly before the Congregation there assembled, declare his unfeigned assent, and consent to the use of all things therein contained and prescribed, according to the form before appointed: and That all and every such person, who shall (without some lawful Impediment, to be allowed and approved by the Ordinary of the place) neglect or refuse to do the same within the time aforesaid, or (in case of such Impediment) within one month after such Impediment removed shall ipso facto be deprived of all his said Ecclesiastical Benefices and Promotions; and That from thenceforth, it shall and may be lawful to, and for all Patrons, and Donors of all and singular the said Ecclesiastical Benfices and Promotions, or any of them (according to their respective Rights and Titles) to present, or collate to the same, as though the person or persons so offending, or neglecting, were dead.

And be it further Enacted by the Authority aforesaid, That in all places, where the proper Incumbent of any Parsonage, or Vicarage, or Benefice with Cure doth reside on his Living, and keep a Curate, the Incumbent himself in person (not having some lawful impediment, to be allowed by the Ordinary of the place) shall once (at the least) in every month openly and publickly Read the Common prayers and Service, in, and by the said Book prescribed, and (if there be occasion) Administer each of the Sacraments and other Rites of the Church, in the Parish Church or Chappel, of, or belonging to the same Parsonage, Vicarage, or Benefice, in such order, manner and form, as in, and by the said Book is appointed, upon pain to forfeit the sum of Five poiunds to the use of the poor of the Parish for every offence, upon conviction by confession, or proof of two credible Witnesses upon Oath, before two Justices of the Peace of the County, City, or Town-Corporate where the offence shall be committed, (which Oath the said Justices are hereby Impowred to Administer) and in default of payment within ten days, to be levied by distress, and sale of the goods and chattels of the Offender, by the Warrant of the said Justices, by the Churchwardens, or Over-seers of the Poor of the said Parish, rendering the surplusage to the party.

And be it further Eacted by the Authority aforesaid, That every Dean, Canon, and Prebendary of every Cathedral, or Collegiate Church, and all Masters, and other Heads, Fellows, Chaplains, and Tutors of, or in any Colledge, Hall, House of Learning, or Hospital, and every Publick Professor, and Reader in either of the Universities, and in every Colledge elsewhere, and every Parson, Vicar, Curate, Lecturer, and every other person in holy Orders, and every School-master keeping any publick, or private School, and every person Instructing, or Teaching any Youth in any House or private Family as a Tutor, or School-master, who upon the first day of May, which shall be in the year of our Lord God, One thousand six hundred sixty two, or at any time thereafter shall be Incumbent, or have possession of any Deanry, Canonry, Prebend, Mastership, Headship, Fellow-ship, Professors-place, or Readers place, Parsonage, Vicarage, or any other Ecclesiastical Dignity or Promotion, or of any Curates place, Lecture, or School; or shall instruct or teach any Youth as Tutor, or School-master, shall before the Feast-day of Saint Bartholomew, which shall be in the year of our Lord One thousand six hundred sixty two, or at or before his, or their respective admission to be Incumbent, or have possession aforesaid, subscribe the Declaration or Acknowledgement following, Scilicet,

I, A. B. Do declare that it is not lawful upon any pretence whatsoever to take Arms agains the King; and that I do abhor that Traiterous Position of taking Arms by His Authority against His Person, or against those that are Commissionated by him; and that I will conform to the Liturgy of the Church of England, as it is now by Law established. And I do declare that I do hold, there lies no Obligation upon me, or on any other person from the Oath, commonly called the Solemn League and Covenant, to endeavor any change, or alteration of Government, either in Church, or State; and that the same was in itself an unlawful Oath, and imposed upon the Subjects of this Realm against the known Laws and Liberties of this Kingdom.

Which said Declaration and Acknowledgement shall be subscribed by every of the said Masters and other Heads, Fellows, Chaplains, and Tutors of, or in any Colledge, Hall, or House of Learning, and by every publick Professor and Reader in either of the Universities, before the Vice-Chancellor of the respective Universities for the time being, or his Deputy; And the said Declaration or Acknowledgement shall be subscribed before the respective Arch-bishop, Bishop or Ordinary of the Diocess, by every other person hereby injoyned to subscribe the same, upon pain, that all and every of the persons aforesaid, failing in such subscription, shall lose and forfeit such respective Deanry, Canonry, Prebend, Mastership, Headship, Fellowship, Professors place, Readers place, Parsonage, Vicarage, Ecclesiastical Dignity, or Promotion, Curates place, Lecture, and School and shall be utterly disabled, and ipso facto deprived of the same; and that every such respective Deanry, Canonry, Prebend, Mastership, Headship, Fellowship, Professors place, Readers place, Parsonage, Vicarage, Ecclesiastical Dignity, or Promotion, Curates place, Lecture and School shall be void, as if such person so failing were naturally dead.

And if any Schoolmaster or other person, Instructing or teaching Youth in any private House or Family, as a Tutor or Schoolmaster, shall Instruct or Teach any Youth as a Tutor or Schoolmaster, before License obtained from his respective Archbiship, Bishop, or Ordinary of the Diocess, according to the Laws and Statutes of this Realm, (for which he shall pay twelve-pence onely) and before such subscription and acknowledgement made as aforesaid; Then every such School-master and other, Instructing and Teaching as aforesaid, shall for the first offence suffer three months Imprisonment without bail or mainprize; and for every second and other such offense shall suffer three months Imprisonment without bail or mainprize, and also forfeit to His Majesty the sum of five pounds.

And after such subscription made, every such Parson, Vicar, Curate, and Lecturer shall procure a certificate under the Hand and Seal of the respective Archbishop, Bishop, or Ordinary of the Diocess, (who are hereby enjoyned and required upon demand to make and deliver the same) and shall publickly and openly Read the same, together with the Declaration, or Acknowledgement aforesaid, upon some Lords day within three months next following, in his Parish Church where he is to officiate, in the presence of the Congregation there assembled, in the time of Divine Service; upon pain that every person failing therein shall lose such Parsonage, Vicarage, or Benefice, Curates place, or Lecturers place respectively, and shall be utterly disabled, and ipso facto deprived of the same; And that the said Parsonage, Vicarage, or Benefice, Curates place, or Lecturers place shall be void, as if he was naturally dead.

Provided always that from and after the Twenty fifth day of March, which shall be in the year of our Lord God, One thousand six hundred eighty two, there shall be omitted in the said Declaration, or Acknowledgement so to be Subscribed and Read, these words following, Scilicet,

AND I do declare that I do hold, there lies no obligation on me, or on any other person from the Oath, commonly called the Solemn League and Covenant, to endeavor any change, or alteration of Government either in Church, or State; And that the same was in itself an unlawful Oath, and imposed upon the Subjects of this Realm against the known Laws and Liberties of this Kingdom; So as none of the persons aforesaid shall from thenceforth be at all obliged to Subscribe or Read that part of the said Declaration or Acknowledgement.

Provided always, and be it Enacted, That from and after the Feast of Saint Bartholomew, which shall be in the year of our Lord, One thousand six hundred sixty and two, no person, who now is Incumbent, and in possession of any Parsonage, Vicarage, or Benefice, and who is not already in holy Orders by Episcopal Ordination, or shall not before the said Feast-day of Saint Bartholomew be Ordained Priest, or Deacon, according to the form of Episcopal Ordination, shall have, hold, or enjoy the said Parsonage, Vicarage Benefice with Cure or other Ecclesiastical Promotion within this Kingdom of England, or the Dominion of Wales, or Town of Berwick upon Tweed; But shall be utterly disabled, and ipso facto deprived of the same; And all his Ecclesiastical Promotions shall be void, as if he was naturally dead.

And be it further Enacted by the Authority aforesaid, That no person whatsoever shall thenceforth be capable to be admitted to any Parsonage, Vicarage, Benefice, or other Ecclesiastical Promotion or Dignity whatsoever, nor shall presume to Consecrate and Administer the holy Sacrament of the Lords Supper, before such time as he shall be Ordained Priest, according to the form, and manner in, and by the said Book prescribed, unless he have formerly been made Priest by Episcopal Ordination, upon pain to forfeit for every offence the sum of One hundred pounds; (one moiety thereof to the Kings Majesty, the other moiety thereof to be equally divided between the poor of the Parish where the offence shall be committed, and such person, or personas as shall sue for the same by Action of Debt, Bill, Plaint, or Information in any of his Majesties Courts of Record, wherein no Essoign, Protection, or Wager of Law shall be allowed) And to be disabled from taking, or being admitted into the Order of Priest, by the space of one whole year next following.

Provided that the Penalties of this Act shall not extend to the Foreigners or Aliens of the Forein Reformed

Churches allowed, or to be allowed by the Kings Majesty, His Heirs and Successors, in England.

Provided always, That no title to confer, or present by lapse shall accrue by any avoidance, or deprivation ipso facto by vertue of this Statute, but after six months after notice of such voidance, or deprivation given by the Ordinary to the Patron, or such sentence of deprivation openly and publickly read in the Parish Church of the Benefice, Parsonage, or Vicarage becoming void, or whereof the Incumbent shall be deprived by vertue of this Act.

And be it further Enacted by the Authority aforesaid, That no Form, or Order of Common Prayers, Administration of Sacraments, Rites or Ceremonies, shall be openly used in any Church, Chappel, or other Publick place of [Worship] or in any Colledge, or Hall in either of the Universities, the Colledges of Westminster, Winchester, or Eaton, or any of them, other than what is prescribed and appointed to be used in and by the said Book; and That the present Governour, or Head of every Colledge and Hall in the said Universities, and of the said Colleges of Westminster, Winchester, and Eaton, within one month after the Feast of Saint Bartholomew, which shall be in the year of our Lord, One thousand six hundred sixty and two: And every Governour or Head of any of the said Colledges, or Halls, hereafter to be elected, or appointed, within one month next after his Election, or Collation, and Admission into the same Government, or Headship, shall openly and publickly in the Church, Chappel, or other Publick place of the same Colledge, or Hall, and in the presence of the Fellows and Scholars of the same, or the greater part of them then resident, Subscribe unto the Nine and thirty Articles of Religion, mentioned in the Statute made in the thirteenth year of the Reign of the late Queen Elizabeth, and unto the said Book, and declare his unfeigned assent and consent unto, and approbation of the said Articles, and of the same Book, and to the use of all the Prayers, Rites, and Ceremonies, Forms, and Orders in the said Book prescribed, and contained according to the form aforesaid; and that all such Governours, or Heads of the said Colledges and Halls, or any of them as are, or shall be in holy Orders, shall once at least in every Quarter of the year (not having a lawful Impediment) openly and publickly Read the Morning Prayer, and Service in and by the said Book appointed to be Read in the Church, Chappel, or other Publick place of the same Colledge or Hall, upon pain to lose, and be suspended of, and from all the Benefits and Profits belonging to the same Government or Headship, by the space of Six months, by the Visitor or Visitors of the same Colledge or Hall; And if any Governour or Head of any Colledge or Hall, Suspended for not Subscribing unto the said Articles and Book, or for not Reading of the Morning Prayer and Service as aforesaid, shall not at, or before the end of Six months next after such suspension, Subscribe unto the said Articles and Book, and declare his consent thereunto as aforesaid, or Read the Morning Prayer and Service as aforesaid, then such Government or Headship shall be ipso facto void.

Provided always, That it shall and may be lawful to use the Morning and Evening Prayer, and all other Prayers and Service prescribed in and by the said Book, in the Chappels and other Publick places of the respective Colledges and Halls in both the Universities, in the Colledges of Westminster, Winchester, and Eaton, and in the Convocations of the Clergies of either Province in Latine; Any thing in this Act contained to the contrary notwithstanding.

And be it further Enacted by the Authority aforesaid, That no person shall be, or be received as a Lecturer, or permitted, suffered, or allowed to Preach as a Lecturer, or to Preach, or Read any Sermon or Lecture in any Church, Chappel, or other place of Publick worship, within this Realm of England, or the Dominion of Wales, and Town of Berwick upon Tweed, unless he be first approved and thereunto Licensed by the Archbishop of the Province, or Bishop of the Diocess, or (in case the See be void) by the Guardian of the Spiritualities, under his Seal, and shall in the presence of the same Archbishop, or Bishop, or Guardian Read the Nine and thirty Articles of Religion, mentioned in the Statute of the Thirteenth year of the late Queen Elizabeth, with Declaration of his unfeigned assent to the same; and That every person, and persons who now is, or hereafter shall be Licensed, Assigned, Appointed, or Received as a Lecturer, to preach upon any day of the week in any Church, Chappel, or place of Publick worship within this Realm of England, or places aforesaid, the first time he Preacheth (before his Sermon) shall openly, publickly, and solemnly Read the Common Prayers and Service in and by the said Book appointed to be Read for that time of the day, and then and there publickly and openly declare his assent unto, and approbation of the said Book, and to the use of all the Prayers, Rites and Ceremonies, Forms and Orders therein contained and prescribed, according to the Form before appointed in this Act; And also shall upon the first Lecture-day of every month afterwards, so long as he continues Lecturer, or Preacher there, at the place appointed for his said Lecture or Sermon, before his said Lecture or Sermon, openly, publickly, and solemnly Read the Common Prayers and Service in and by the said Book appointed to be read for that time of the day, at which the said Lecture or Sermon is to be Preached, and after such Reading thereof, shall openly and publickly, before the Congregation there assembled, declare his unfeigned assent and consent unto, and approbation of the said Book, and to the use of all the Prayers, Rites and Ceremonies, Forms and Orders therein contained and prescribed, according to the form aforesaid; and, That all and every such person and persons who shall neglect or refuse to do the same, shall from thenceforth be disabled to Preach the sad, or any other Lecture or Sermon in the said, or any other Church, Chappel, or place of Publick worship, until such time as he and they shall openly, publickly, and solemnly Read the Common-Prayers and Service appointed by the said Book, and Conform in all points to the things therein appointed and prescribed, according to the purport, tru intent, and meaning of this Act.

Provided always, that if the said Sermon or Lecture be to be Preached or Read in any Cathedral, or Collegiate Church or Chappel, it shall be sufficient for the said Lecturer openly at the time aforesaid, to declare his assent and consent to all things contained in the said Book, according to the form aforesaid.

And be it further Enacted by the Authority aforesaid, That if any person who is by this Act disabled to Preach any Lecture or Sermon, shall during the time that he shall continue and remain so disabled, Preach any Sermon or Lecture; That then for every such offence the person and persons so offending shall suffer Three months Imprisonment in the Common Gaol without Bail or mainprise, and that any two Justices of the Peace of any County of this Kingdom and places aforesaid, and the Mayor or other chief Magistrate of any City, or Town-Corporate, within the same, upon Certificate from the Ordinary of the place made to him or them of the offence committed, shall, and are hereby required to commit the person or persons so offending to the Gaol of the Same County, City, or Town Corporate accordingly.

Provided always, and be it further Enacted by the Authority aforesaid, That at all and every time and times, when any Sermon or Lecture is to be Preached, the Common Prayers and Service in and by the said Book appointed to be Read for that time of the day, shall be openly, publickly, and solemnly Read by some Priest, or Deacon, in the Church, Chappel, or place of Publick worship, where the said Sermon or Lecture be Preached, before such Sermon or Lecture is to be Preached; And that the Lecturer then to Preach shall be present at the Reading thereof.

Provided nevertheless, That this Act shall not extend to the University-Churches in the Universities of this Realm, or either of them, when or at such times as any Sermon or Lecture is Preached or Read in the same Churches, or any of them, for, or as the publick University-Sermon or Lectures but that the same Sermons and Lectures may be Preached or Read in such sort and manner as the same have been heretofore Preached or Read; This Act, or any thing herein contained to the contrary thereof in any wise notwithstanding.

And be it further Enacted by the Authority aforesaid, That the several good Laws, and Statutes of this Realm, which have been formerly made, and are now in force for the Uniformity of Prayer and Administration of the Sacraments, within this Realm of England, and places aforesaid, shall stand in full force and strength to all intents and purposes whatsoever, for the establishing and confirming of the said Book; Entituled, The Book of Common Prayer, and Administration of the Sacraments, and other Rites and Ceremonies of the Church, according to the use of the Church of England; together with the Psalter or Psalms of David, Pointed as they are to be sung or said in Churches; and the form or manner of Making, Ordaining, and Consecrating of Bishops, Priests and Deacons; herein before mentioned to be joined and annexed to this Act; and shall be applied, practiced, and put in use for the punishing of all offences contrary to the said Laws, with relation to the Book aforesaid, and no other.

Provided alwaies, and be it further Enacted by the Authority aforesaid, That in all those Prayers, Litanies, and Collects, which do any way relate to the King, Queen, or Royal Progeny, the Names be altered and changed from time to time, and fitted to the present occasion, according to the direction of lawful Authority.

Provided also, and be it Enacted by the Authority aforesaid, That a true Printed Copy of the said Book, Entituled, The Book of Common Prayer, and Administration of the Sacraments, and other Rites and Ceremonies of the Church, according to the use of the Church of England; together with the Psalter or Psalms of David, Pointed as they are to be sung or said in Churches; and the form or manner of Making, Ordaining, and Consecrating of Bishops, Priests and Deacons, shall at the costs and charges of the Parishoners of every Parish-Church, and Chappelry, Cathedral Church, Colledge, and Hall, be attained and gotten before the Feast-day of Saint Bartholomew, in the year of our Lord, One thousand six hundred sixty and two, upon pain of forfeiture of Three pounds by the months for so long time as they shall then after be unprovided thereof, by every Parish, or Chappelry, Cathedral Church, Colledge, and Hall, making default therein.

Provided alwaies, and be it Enacted by the Authority aforesaid, That the Bishops of Hereford, Saint Davids, Asaph, Bangor, and Landaff, and their Successors shall take such order among themselves, for the souls health of the Flocks committed to their Charge within Wales, That the Book hereunto annexed be truly and exactly Translated into the Brittish or Welsh Tongue, and that the same so Translated and being by them, or any three of them at the least viewed, perused, and allowed, be Imprinted to such number at least, so that one of the said Books so Translated and Imprinted may be had for every Cathedral, Collegiate, and Parish-Church; and Chappel of Ease in the said respective Diocesses, and places in Wales, where the Welsh is commonly spoken or used before the First day of May, One thousand six hundred sixty five; and, That from and after the Imprinting and publishingof the said Book so Translated, the whole Divine Service shall be used and said by the Ministers and Curates thoughout all Wales within the said Diocesses where the Welsh Tongue is commonly used, in the Brittish, or Welsh Tongue, in such manner and form as is prescribed according to the Book hereunto annexed to be used in the English Tongue, differing nothing in any Order or Form from the said English Book; for which Book, so Translated and Imprinted, the Church-wardens of every of the said Parishes shall pay out of the Parish-money in their hands for the use of the respective Churches, and be allowed the same on their Accompt; and, That the said Bishops and their Successors, or any Three of them, at the least, shall set and appoint the price, for which the said Book shall be sold; And one other Book of Common Prayer in the English Tongue shall be bought and had in every Church throughout Wales, in which the Book of Common Prayer in Welsh is to be had, by force of this Act, before the First day of May, One thousand six hundred sixty and four, and the same Book to remain in such convenient places, within the said Churches, that such as understand them may resort at all convenient times to read and peruse the same, and also such as do not understand the said Language, may by conferring both Tongues together, the sooner attain to the knowledge of the English Tongue; Any thing in this Act to the contrary notwithstanding; And until Printed Copies of the said Book so to be Translated may be had and provided, the Form of Common Prayer, established by Parliament before the making of this Act, shall be used as formerly in such parts of Wales, where the English Tongue is not commonly understood.

And to the end that the true and perfect Copies of this Act, and the said Book hereunto annexed may be safely kept, and perpetually preserved, and for the avoiding of all disputes for the time to come; Be it therefore Enacted by the Authority aforesaid, That the respective Deans and Chapters of every Cathedral, or Collegiate Church, within England and Wales shall at their proper costs and charges, before the twenty fifth day of December, One thousand six hundred sixty and two, obtain under the Great Seal of England a true and perfect Printed Copy of this Act, and of the said Book annexed hereunto, to be by the said Deans and Chapters, and their Successors kept and preserved in safety for ever, and to be also produced, and shewed forth in any Court of Record, as often as they shall be thereunto lawfully required; And also there shall be delivered true and perfect Copies of this Act, and of the same Book into the respective Courts at Westminster, and into the Tower of London, to be kept and preserved for ever among the Records of the said Courts, and the Records of the Tower, to be also produced and shewed forth in any Court as need shall require; which said Books so to be exemplified under the Great Seal of England, shall be examined by such persons as the Kings Majesty shall appoint under the Great Seal of England for that purpose, and shall be compared with the Original Book hereunto annexed, and shall have power to correct, and amend in writing any Error committed by the Printer in the printing of the same Book, or of any thing therein contained, and shall certifie in writing under their Hands and Seals, or the Hands and Seals of any Three of them at the end of the same Book, that they have examined and compared the same Book, and find it to be a true and perfect Copy; which said Books, and every one of them so exemplified under the Great Seal of England, as aforesaid, shall be deemed, taken, and adjudged, and expounded to be good, and available in the Law to all intents and purposes whatsoever, and shall be accounted as good Records as this Book it self hereunto annexed; Any Law or Custom to the contrary in any wise notwithstanding.

Provided also, That this Act or any thing therein contained shall not be prejudicial or hurtful unto the Kings Professor of the Law within the University of Oxford, for, or concerning the Prebend of Shipton, within the Cathedral Church of Sarum, united and annexed unto the place of the same Kings Professor for the time being, by the late King James of blessed memory.

Provided always, That whereas the Six and thirtieth Article of the Nine and thirty Articles agreed upon by the Arch-bishops, and Bishops of both Provinces, and the whole Clergy in the Convocation holden at London, in the year of our Lord, One thousand five hundred sixty two, for the avoiding of diversities of Opinions, and for establishing of consent, touching true Religion, is in these words following, viz.

That the Book of Consecration of Archbishops, and Bishops, and Ordaining of Priests and Deacons, lately set forth in the time of King Edward the Sixth, and confirmed at the saem time by Authority of Parliament, doth contain all things necessary to such Consecration and Ordaining, neither hath it any thing that of it self is superstitious, and ungodly; And therefore whosoever are Consecrated or Ordered according to the Rites of that Book, since the second year of the aforenamed King Edward unto this time, or hereafter shall be Consecrated or Ordered according to the same Rites; We decree all such to be rightly, orderly, and lawfully Consecrated and Ordered;

It be Enacted, and be it therefore Enacted by the Authority aforesaid, That the Subscriptions hereafter to be had or made unto the said Articles, by any Deacon, Priest, or Ecclesiastical person, or other person whatsoever, who by this Act or any other Law now in force is required to Subscribe unto the said Articles, shall be construed and taken to extend, and shall be applied (for and touching the said Six and thirtieth Article) unto the Book containing the form and manner of Making, Ordaining, and Consecrating of Bishops, Priests, and Deacons in this Act mentioned, in such sort and manner as the same did heretofore extend unto the Books set forth in the time of King Edward the Sixth, mentioned in the said Six and thirtieth Article; Any thing in the said Article, or in any Statute, Act, or Canon heretofore had or made, to the contrary thereof in any wise notwithstanding.

Provided also, That the Book of Common Prayer, and Administration of the Sacraments and other Rites and Ceremonies of this Church of England, together with the form and manner of Ordaining, and Consecrating Bishops, Priests, and Deacons heretofore in use, and respectively established by Act of Parliament in the First and Eighth years of Queen Elizabeth, shall be still used and observed in the Church of England, untilt he Feast of Saint Bartholomew, which shall be in the year of our Lord God, One thousand six hundred sixty and two.

Antidisestablishmentarianism

Antidisestablishmentarianism is a word that most Americans come across for the first time in high school. Because it is so long and since most people do not hear of it before a teacher introduces it to them, it is considered funny. Though technical and scientific terms can be much longer, it is usually considered the longest nontechnical word in the Standard English language. It comes from the English Established Church. The American version of the English Established Church is the Episcopal Church. Historically, the English Established Church subsidized through taxation as well as donations and was responsible for welfare, such as the running of orphanages (as an example read Charles Dickens's Oliver Twist), education, such as Oxford and Cambridge, and public worship. Unlike the bishops and priests of Rome, the bishops, priests and other members of the Established Church of England were allowed to marry and were responsible to the English crown. Since they were paid by the crown, the Established Church had loyalties to the English crown and responsibilities to support the English crown.

Various Acts of Uniformity have attempted to force the entire English population into the Established Church, with little success. For hundreds of years, those who have removed themselves from the Established Church of England were known as Separatists. However, those within the Established Church of England who wanted to keep their pastors, churches and property but dissolve their ties to the Church of England were known as disestablishmentarians. In the nineteenth century the Disestablishmentarian Movement became quite strong with the attempts to remove the Churches of Scotland and Wales from the Church of England. Those opposed to the Disestablishmentarians, who wanted to keep the Churches of Scotland and Wales under the Archbishop of Canterbury in the Church of England were known as Antidisestablishmentarians and their movement Antidisestablishmentarianism. The word is not, however, confined to the Church of England. Antidisestablishmentarianism means any opposition to the withdrawal of any state support or recognition from any established church.

These words have fallen into disuse and would be completely ignored by Americans except for two things. The first, which almost all American with a high school education know, is that Antidisestablishmentarianism is a big funny sounding word which is not used in every day conversation. The second use of the word is virtually unknown to the average American. It is, however, the foundation of every American freedom. The first amendment to the United States Constitution states Congress shall make no law respecting an establishment of religion, or prohibiting the free exercise thereof; or abridging the freedom of speech, or of the press; or the right of the people peaceably to assemble, and to petition the government for a redress of grievances. Those who are part of the American Establishment of Religion demand that they continue receiving their federal government checks and that they continue enforcing their will on others through the unconstitutional police power of the Federal Government.

Antidisestablishmentarians want to keep Secular Humanism as America's Established Religion. The Established Religion of Secular Humanism America forbids any form of Christianity in education and welfare. The Established Religion of Secular Humanism both collects taxes and enforces law. Those who want the first amendment of the US Constitution enforced by removing federal taxation and law enforcement from education and welfare are Disestablishmentarians.

John Foxe's Book of Martyrs

John Foxe (1517-1587) wrote a book that he entitled *Actes and Monuments of these Latter and Perillous Days, Touching Matters of the Church*. It is known today as *Foxe's Book of Martyrs*. It is a series of brief biographies that include graphic details of Christians who were tortured and murdered for their faith. John Foxe was called an evangelical during the reign of Henry VIII, however his beliefs might be more in line with what we would call Quakers. He personally compiled and wrote about events up through the reign of Queen Mary.

Though first published in 1563, it was updated many times. Foxe completed a fourth edition in 1583. It comprised three volumes, a total of 3000 folio pages (one folio page equals eight regular pages). The work was filled with woodcut illustrations. It was reprinted several times during John Foxe's lifetime both in Latin and English. After his death various editors revised and expanded the work to include later protestant history.

The edition edited by William Byron Forbush is most readily available today in online editions and goes through approximately 1819, the beginnings of American Missions. This text is around 400 8 ½ x 11 sheets if printed out. As a print book it would probably be nearer 800 total pages of text. One severely abridged print edition available at Amazon.com has approximately 400 pages. The Oxford University Press edition, called Foxes Book of Martyrs: Select Narratives has 322 pages.

It is as influential as John Calvin's Institutes of the Christian Religion and John Bunyan's Pilgrim's Progress.

Appendix of Documents related to Colonial Founding

These documents can be obtained from the National Archives website or the Yale Law Library Site, the Avalon Project or from individual state archives online.

Magna Carta 1215

From English Bill of Rights 1689

Mayflower Compact : 1620

Connecticut Oath of Fidelity (1640)

Fundamental Orders of 1639

Fundamental Agreement, or Original Constitution of the Colony of New Haven, June 4, 1639

Government of New Haven Colony October 27/November 6, 1643

Fundamental Constitutions of Carolina : March 1, 1669

Constitution of North Carolina : December 18, 1776

Constitution of South Carolina - March 26, 1776

The Fundamental Constitutions for the Province of East New Jersey in America, Anno Domini 1683

Constitution of New Jersey; 1776

Frame of Government of Pennsylvania May 5, 1682

Constitution of Pennsylvania - September 28, 1776

Charter of Delaware - 1701

Constitution of Delaware; 1776

Constitution of Georgia; February 5, 1777

Maryland Toleration Act; September 21, 1649

Constitution of Maryland November 11, 1776

The Charter of Massachusetts Bay : 1629

Constitution of Massachusetts 1780

Agreement of the Settlers at Exeter in New Hampshire, 1639

Constitution of New York April 20, 1777

Queen Elizabeth I

Queen Elizabeth I ruled England after a period of considerable turmoil. She was the last of the line of Tudors. Her father, Henry VIII, had her declared illegitimate so he could execute her mother and marry again. He severed ties with Rome by convincing the English church that the *Magna Carta* did not allow for foreign control of the "free English Church." Elizabeth's brother, Henry VI, had her cut out of the succession, but died before sufficiently strengthening the English church to withstand the onslaught of their sister, Bloody Mary, who tried to reintroduce Catholicism. After Mary's death Elizabeth was placed on the throne with the understanding that she would restore England to protestantism. She executed Mary Stuart "Queen of Scotts" as a rival to her throne and as a Catholic threat to the protestant revitalization of England. She reigned from 1558 to her 1603.

Elizabeth supported the establishment of an English protestant church, of which she became the Supreme

Governor. This "Elizabethan Religious Settlement" consisted of two aspects: one, the reestablishment of the Church of England separate from Rome, and two, the Act of Uniformity of 1559, rigidly codifying the form of worship. She related church worship to national identity and loyalty and demanded conformity to the Church and its prescribed forms, considering it treason to do otherwise. Separatists, among others, were imprisoned and executed under her reign for dissenting from her Act of Uniformity.

The defeat of the Spanish Armada in 1588 was considered an act of God's miraculous intervention. Catholicism had tried to re-insert itself into England and God had sent a storm to destroy Spain's physically superior fleet. He had also enabled the English navy to build smaller but vastly more maneuverable and efficient ships to defeat the Spanish galleons not destroyed in the storm. This also established the reputation of English seafarers such as Francis Drake.

Elizabeth's reign is known as the Elizabethan era, a golden age of literature and language, the time when Shakespeare wrote and the language of the King James Bible was being created, though she personally forbade the making of a new translation of the Scriptures into English. The poet Edmund Spenser, in his allegory The Faerie Queene, taught spiritual lessons to various knights in training through Gloriana the Queen of Faerieland. He dedicated the work to Queen Elizabeth and explained that it was a strongly nationalistic work as well as a promotion of Christian virtue. In it he has Queen Glorianna (who represents Elizabeth) marry King Arthur, symbolizing the merging of ancient and modern England and promoting religious and national unity.

Many idealized Elizabeth's "perpetual virginity," calling her the "virgin queen" and even equating her with the Virgin Mary, though it is a Catholic tradition, not a biblical reality, that Mary remained a virgin. The colony of Virginia was named for her, and she was also nicknamed "Gloriana," the name appropriated by Spenser for his tribute work.

Geoffrey Chaucer, the English Vernacular, and the Wycliffe Bible

Geoffrey Chaucer lived from about 1343 to 1400. He was the first to refine the English Language and use it for literary purposes. Most writing had been done in Latin or French before this time. He is sometimes called the father of English Literature and the source of the vernacular tradition (writing in one's native language). Chaucer proved the vernacular language could speak beautifully and powerfully to and for the English people. His family was upper class and had connections to royalty. He was friends with John of Gaunt (son of King Edward III and close advisor to Gaunt's nephew King Richard II) and enjoyed his patronage.

Chaucer traveled extensively and mingled at court, serving as a varlet de chamber, yeoman or esquire to nobility on some of the occasions of his travel. These were general terms for many positions held by courtiers. Exactly what Chaucer did is unknown, though he sometimes apparently served as an envoy on secret missions attempting to arrange alliances by marriage or other means in various places.

In Italy he discovered the medieval poetry that would inspire his later work, and throughout his travels met people who would form the basis for the characters of his most famous but unfinished work, the Canterbury Tales. The Canterbury Tales is a fictional frame tale about a group of stories told by pilgrims traveling to Canterbury Cathedral. Chaucer may have traveled to *Santiago de Compostela, Spain,* on the "Way of St. James Pilgrimage," as was the custom of well-to-do Catholics of the time period. Chaucer wrote original works and translated others into English. His work to refine the English language was invaluable and paralleled that of a few others, notably in Scotland.

Some translation work of the Bible into English had been done earlier, but most were relatively brief passages of actual Scripture burdened with lengthy commentaries. Wycliffe's translation of the Scriptures from the Latin Vulgate occurred between 1382 and 1395. Wycliffe was an early reformer. Little is known about the translation work because the Council of Constance (1414 to 1418) ordered the destruction of all records concerning the work and tried to destroy all copies, burning heretics with fragments of Scriptures around their necks and digging up the bones of Wycliffe to burn them. It is unknown how many people may have been involved in the work, though Wycliffe and Nicholas of Hereford were certainly involved. It was orthodox according to Roman Catholic belief, but produced without the church's sanction or control, and therefore declared heretical. Thomas More, Lord Chancellor of England under Henry VIII (1478-1535), who was beheaded for opposing Henry's installation of himself as head of the Church of England, used portions of Wycliffe's Bible because it could not be distinguished from "approved" translations.

Chaucer pays tribute to Wycliffe in his Canterbury Tales, basing the character of the Poor Parson on Lollardy preachers (traveling preachers taught by Wycliffe), or possibly Wycliffe himself. Following is a modern English version of the description of the Parson from the Tales, and next the poem much as Chaucer originally wrote it, with a few modernizations of spelling and punctuation. Both are from the website http://www.msgr.ca/msgr-3/church_of_england.htm and the subpage http://www.msgr.ca/msgr-3/canterbury_tales_parson.htm

There was a good man of religion, too,
A country parson, poor, I warrant you;
But rich he was in holy thought and work.
He was a learned man also, a clerk,
Who Christ's own gospel truly sought to preach;
Devoutly his parishioners would he teach.
Benign he was and wondrous diligent,
Patient in adverse times and well content,
As he was oft times proven; always blithe,
He was right loath to curse to get a tithe,
But rather would he give, in case of doubt,
Unto those poor parishioners about,
Part of his income, even of his goods.
Enough with little, coloured all his moods.
Wide was his parish, houses far asunder,
But never did he fail, for rain or thunder,
In sickness, or in sin, or any state,
To visit to the farthest, small and great,
Going afoot, and in his hand, a stave.
This fine example to his flock he gave,
That first he wrought and afterwards he taught;
Out of the gospel then that text he caught,
And this figure he added thereunto
That, if gold rust, what shall poor iron do?
For if the priest be foul, in whom we trust,
What wonder if a layman yield to lust?
And shame it is, if priest take thought for keep,
A shitty shepherd, shepherding clean sheep.
Well ought a priest example good to give,
By his own cleanness, how his flock should live.
He never let his benefice for hire,
Leaving his flock to flounder in the mire,
And ran to London, up to old Saint Paul's
To get himself a chantry there for souls,
Nor in some brotherhood did he withhold;
But dwelt at home and kept so well the fold
That never wolf could make his plans miscarry;
He was a shepherd and not mercenary.

And holy though he was, and virtuous,
To sinners he was not impiteous,
Nor haughty in his speech, nor too divine,
But in all teaching prudent and benign.
To lead folk into Heaven but by stress
Of good example was his busyness.
But if some sinful one proved obstinate,
Be who it might, of high or low estate,
Him he reproved, and sharply, as I know.
There is nowhere a better priest, I trow.
He had no thirst for pomp or reverence,
Nor made himself a special, spiced conscience,
But Christ's own lore, and His apostles' twelve
He taught, but first he followed it himself.

A good man was ther of religioún,
And was a poore Parson of a town;
But riche he was of holy thought and werk.
He was also a lernèd man, a clerk
That Cristes gospel gladly wolde preach;
His parishioners devoutly wolde he teach.
Benigne he was, and wondrous diligent,
And in adversitee ful pacient;
And such he was i-provèd ofte to be.
To cursen for his tithes ful lothe was he,
But rather wolde he given out of doute,
Unto his pore parishioners aboute,
Of his offrynge, and eek of his substaunce.
He coude in litel thing have sufficience.
Wyd was his parish, and houses far asonder,
But yet he lafte not for reyne or thonder,
In siknesse and in meschief to visíte
The ferthest in his parisshe, smal and great
Uppon his feet, and in his hand a staf.
This noble ensample unto his sheep he gaf,
That ferst he wroughte, and after that he taughte,
Out of the gospel he those wordes caughte,

And this figúre he addid yet therto,
That if gold ruste, what shulde iron do?
For if a priest be foul, on whom we truste,
No wonder if the ignorant shulde ruste;
And shame it is, if that a priest take kepe,
A dirty shepperd and a clene shepe;
Wel oughte a priest ensample for to give,
By his clennesse, how that his sheep shulde lyve.
He sette not his benefice to hire,
And lefte his sheep encombred in the myre,
And ran to Londone, unto seynte Paules,
To seeken him a chaunterie for soules,
Or with a brothurhood to be withholde;
But dwelte at hoom, and kepte wel his folde,
So that the wolfe made it not myscarye.
He was a shepperde and no mercenarie;
And though he holy were, and vertuous,
He was to sinful man ful piteous,
Nor of his speche wrathful nor yet fine,
But in his teching díscret and benigne.
To drawe folk to heven by clenenesse,
By good ensample, was his busynesse:
But were it eny person obstinat,
What-so he were of high or lowe estat,
Him wolde he snubbe sharply for the nonce.
A bettre priest I trowe ther nowher non is.
He wayted after no pompe nor reverence,
Nor made himself spicèd in conscience,
But Cristes love, and his apostles twelve,
He taught, and ferst he folwed it himselve.

The Great Awakening

In the middle of the 1700s, the English colonies in America experienced a moving of God's Spirit which came to be known as the Great Awakening. Unlike many other religious movements, the Great Awakening was not simply based on emotion. The term Awakening simply meant that people awoke to the moving of God's

Holy Spirit. Today we might mean the same thing by saying that people stopped quenching the Holy Spirit. Throughout New England, New York and the middle colonies churches, often very small churches, saw men and women repenting of sin and turning to God. Entire communities experienced massive reduction in crime and drunkenness. People paid old debts. Fathers returned to children they had abandoned. Broken down buildings were repaired. Churches were filled, not just for a few weeks as when a charismatic evangelist came to town, but for years. Slaves were freed and slavery renounced. Charitable contributions of food and clothing increased dramatically.

These and other acts of God slowly moved from community to community. Though there never was any one man or any group of men who led the Great Awakening, Pastor Jonathan Edwards is the one man we generally associate with it. His sermon, Sinners In The Hands Of An Angry God will always be thought of as the sermon of the Great Awakening. The Great Awakening began in other places before this sermon was preached for the first time in Northampton, Massachusetts and continued in other places after Jonathan Edwards preached it for his last time.

Jonathan Edwards said, “True liberty consists only in the power of doing what we ought to will, and in not being constrained to do what we ought not to will.”

Sinners In The Hands Of An Angry God was a written sermon and delivered word for word as it was written. It was delivered in darkness by the light of flickering candles in a monotone. Yet people genuinely repented of their sins and led changed lives. The Great Awakening established the moral climate of America’s founding fathers.

Jonathan Edwards is credited with beginning the Great Awakening, an enormous revival throughout the colonies, with the following sermon. Benjamin Franklin describes the effects of this type of preaching on the population in the case of George Whitfield in Philadelphia (see below). Edwards was not known for being a great orator but the power of his preaching as used by God changed the hearts and lives of thousands in the colonies. The sermon still applies today, since it is directed at people who have known God but been indifferent or disobedient to His teachings. The founders knew America could not stand without the faithful adherence to Christian principles. At one time they were routinely taught as part of America's educational system. What is being taught to our students today is Secular Humanism, and our feet are just as "ready to slip" as were the careless of Edwards' day.

The English Evangelists George Whitfield and John and Charles Wesley had much wider influence in the Great Awakening. Their ministries included orphanages, financial help to families of prisoners, the spread of music, the founding of schools and the greatly needed ministries to American Indians. John Wesley laid the foundation for the ministry of circuit-riding preachers. Jonathan Edwards wrote many other works and was known as the theologian of the Great Awakening.

Established churches frequently saw it as threatening their power. George Whitefield was forbidden from preaching in these churches and tried preaching in the fields. Benjamin Franklin relates the story of how God provided a building for Whitefield in his *Autobiography*. (See author's note at the end of this appendix for the publication history of the *Autobiography*.)

The following excerpt from Franklin's *Autobiography* concerns the Great Awakening preacher George Whitfield, who was a great friend of Franklin's for many years. "The clergy" at first allowed Whitfield to preach in regular churches but later forced him out. It concerns the building of a meetinghouse to accommodate Whitfield after he tried to hold outdoor meetings. Though Franklin asserts that he was never converted to Whitfield's belief, his deep admiration of Whitfield's effectiveness as a preacher cannot be missed. The building described, which was built so rapidly and entirely by private offerings, to accommodate Whitfield's gatherings, is a remarkable tribute to America's commitment to religious liberty.

> *"In 1739 arrived among us from Ireland the Reverend Mr. Whitefield, who had made himself remarkable there as an itinerant preacher. He was at first permitted to preach in some of our churches; but the clergy, taking a dislike to him, soon refus'd him their pulpits, and he was oblig'd to preach in the fields. The multitudes of all sects and denominations that attended his sermons were enormous, and it was matter of speculation to me, who was one of the number, to observe the extraordinary influence of his oratory on his hearers, and bow much they admir'd and respected him, notwithstanding his common abuse of them, by assuring them that they were naturally half beasts and half devils. It was wonderful to see the change soon made in the manners of our inhabitants. From being thoughtless or indifferent about religion, it seem'd as if all the world were growing religious, so that one could not walk thro' the town in an evening without hearing psalms sung in different families of every street.*
>
> *"And it being found inconvenient to assemble in the open air, subject to its inclemencies, the building of a house to meet in was no sooner propos'd, and persons appointed to receive contributions, but sufficient sums were soon receiv'd to procure the ground and erect the*

> *building, which was one hundred feet long and seventy broad, about the size of Westminster Hall; and the work was carried on with such spirit as to be finished in a much shorter time than could have been expected. Both house and ground were vested in trustees, expressly for the use of any preacher of any religious persuasion who might desire to say something to the people at Philadelphia; the design in building not being to accommodate any particular sect, but the inhabitants in general; so that even if the Mufti of Constantinople were to send a missionary to preach Mohammedanism to us, he would find a pulpit at his service."*

Franklin also commented on Whitefield's ability to preach to open-air gatherings of tens of thousands and raise an offering from the most reluctant hearers. Mennonites, Moravians, Baptists and other smaller groups had a significant part in this awakening.

For more on the Great Awakening read *The Pursuit of Purity by Dr. David Beale, The History of Fundamentalism* by Dr. George Dollar and *The Story of Religion in America* by William Warren Sweet.

Author's Note: The Private Life of the Late Benjamin Franklin, LL.D. Originally Written By Himself, And Now Translated From The French. London, 1793, is one version of Franklin's unfinished *Autobiography.* (The work was not published until after he died. The notes on the publication history come from *Wikipedia.* This material is included because what we today know as the *Autobiography of Benjamin Franklin* has been published in two languages, many parts, and many versions over many years.)

The *Autobiography* remained unpublished during Franklin's lifetime. In 1791, the first edition appeared, in

French rather than English, as *Mémoires de la vie privée de Benjamin Franklin,* published in Paris. This translation of Part One only was based on a flawed transcript made of Franklin's manuscript before he had revised it. This French translation was then retranslated into English in two London publications of 1793, and one of the London editions served as a basis for a retranslation into French in 1798 in an edition which also included a fragment of Part Two.

The first three parts of the *Autobiography* were first published together (in English) by Franklin's grandson, William Temple Franklin, in London in 1818, in *Volume 1 of Memoirs of the Life and Writings of Benjamin Franklin.* W.T. Franklin did not include Part Four because he had previously traded away the original holograph of the *Autobiography* for a copy that contained only the first three parts. Furthermore, he felt free to make unauthoritative stylistic revisions to his grandfather's autobiography, and on occasion followed the translated and retranslated versions mentioned above rather than Ben Franklin's original text.

W.T. Franklin's text was the standard version of the *Autobiography* for half a century, until John Bigelow purchased the original manuscript in France and in 1868 published the most reliable text that had yet appeared, including the first English publication of Part Four. In the 20th century, important editions by Max Ferrand and the staff of the Huntington Library in San Marino, California (*Benjamin Franklin's Memoirs: Parallel Text Edition,* 1949) and by Leonard W. Labaree (1964, as part of the Yale University Press edition of *The Papers of Benjamin Franklin)* improved on Bigelow's accuracy. In 1981, J. A. Leo Lemay and P.M. Zall produced *The Autobiography of Benjamin Franklin: A Genetic Text,* attempting to show all revisions and cancellations in the holograph manuscript. This, the most accurate edition of all so far published, served as a basis for *Benjamin*

Franklin's Autobiography: A Norton Critical Edition and for the text of this autobiography printed in the Library of America's edition of Franklin's Writings.

James I and the "Authorized Version" King James Translation of the Bible

The son of Mary Queen of Scotts led a tumultuous life, torn by the religious warfare in Scotland. His mother was removed from the throne when he was thirteen months old and he never saw her again. She and her husband were both Roman Catholics, but Scotland's worship was under the auspices of the National Church of Scotland, and John Knox preached James' inauguration sermon, a strong protestant influenced by John Calvin.

The child King James VI was placed under a series of regents and tutors, some of whom were removed or killed in the continuing power struggles. Assassinations and power plays by Catholic and Protestant factions continually rocked Scotland. Among those killed was James' father. His mother tried to regain the throne and even laid claim to the English throne held by her cousin Elizabeth. Mary escaped from imprisonment and tried to lead a rebellion, but eventually was executed, after years of separation from James.

James fell under the influence of several male advisors, including Esmé Stuart, a distant relative from France, whom James made Earl of Lennox. Lennox came when James was fifteen, but Scottish Calvinists were unimpressed by Lennox's claims of conversion to Protestantism and believed he was trying to seduce James. They briefly imprisoned James and expelled Lennox. James never embraced the Scottish Church and preferred the Anglican worship.

James made it a point to secure Elizabeth's favor and as she remained unmarried and childless also became her successor. He was said to prefer the company of men, but married Anne of Denmark, seemed to love her for a time, and produced three children. He also had a mistress.

James wrote two works on the monarchy while still in Scotland. He explained the divine right of kings, believing that God had made kings higher than other men. A king had to heed tradition and God but no other authority because God would "stirre up such scourges as pleaseth him, for punishment of wicked kings."

James thought of parliaments as the king's "head court," advising his young son Henry, for whom one of the works was written, to "Hold no Parliaments but for the necesitie of new Lawes, which would be but seldome."

Kings, James believed, arose "before any estates or ranks of men, before any parliaments were holden, or laws made, and by them was the land distributed, which at first was wholly theirs. And so it follows of necessity that kings were the authors and makers of the laws, and not the laws of the kings."

James's early reign in England was spent trying to unify England and Scotland, a move both countries opposed. He also made a temporary peace with Spain. Spain wanted more toleration for Catholics and James's Privy Counsel wanted less. In 1605 A Catholic plot to blow up Parliament was uncovered when Guy Fawkes, a soldier, was discovered with wood and gunpowder in the cellars of the building. National unity was solidified as the people rejoiced that their government and king had been protected.

James made a habit of dissolving parliament and ruling without it but when the thirty years' war broke out he sought aid for his son in law and called on Parliament to provide it. He had also hoped to get monetary help from Spain by marrying his surviving son Charles to the Infanta Maria, daughter of Philip of Spain and the Duchess of Austria.

Instead of furthering either of his causes, Parliament told James he should declare war on Spain, marry Charles to a protestant and enforce the anti-catholic laws. James ordered them not to interfere with his royal rights and they protested that they had rights under English law. He tore up the record of the session and dissolved Parliament again.

Prince Charles went secretly to Spain to woo the Infanta but she rejected him. The king of Spain tried to condition the marriage on Charles' conversion to Roman Catholicism and his remaining as a political hostage for a year in Spain. Charles returned unmarried, and, to the delight of the English people, the treaty fell through. The disillusioned Charles wanted his father to ally with France and declare war on the Hapsburgs, including Spain. Parliament never officially went along with Charles to finance a war against Spain.

Parliament followed up the Gunpowder Plot discovery with the formulation of an oath of loyalty demanding that swearers affirm that the Pope had no power over the King of England. James tolerated Catholics at court who agreed to the oath but in general persecuted Romanists more intensely than Elizabeth had. He also strictly enforced uniformity, alienating and debating with Puritans, but later on relaxed his persecutions. At the Hampton Court Conference, a combination of the church and the king's court, the Millinary Petition was presented to request many things that would move the church in a more protestant direction, and included a request for a new translation of the Scriptures.

James denied all the other requests of the petition, but he disliked the Geneva Bible and permitted a new translation, though he did not actually authorize it, and only hoped it would stop the attacks on the monarchy encouraged by the notes in the Geneva translation. The king had to give permission for any publishing, and his name is attached to the work, though he did not finance or particularly support the translation. He only hoped for a translation to support his divine right and reinforce the class system.

The translation underwent thousands of revisions. A major one was done in 1629, which used the Codex Alexandranus, given to England by Archbishop Cyril of Constantinople in 1626, to protect it from the invading turks. Successive editions were discarded when the 1762 and 1769 revisions were made, both of which went back to the 1629 edition, but modernized spellings. The name "Authorized Version" never actually appeared in the printings until 1824. It was called "The New Translation" through the Restoration Period. Publication of the Geneva and Great Bibles, the previous English translations, ceased at the time the new translation appeared, though it was not incorporated into the Book of Common Prayer until 1662 and the Psalter still contains the Great Bible translation in modern times.

James' efforts to bring the Church of Scotland "so neir as can be" to the English church and reestablish the episcopacy were continually opposed. The Five Articles of Perth were passed through a General Assembly by his bishops, (including kneeling during communion, private baptism, private communion for the sick or infirm, confirmation by a Bishop, and the observance of Holy Days) but they split the church because of Puritan dissent and those who supported a presbyterian form of government. They objected to one bishop holding control as opposed to control being shared by groups of elders.

William Bradford's Plymouth Plantation

William Bradford was a leader of the Separatists of the Plymouth Colony of Colonial Massachusetts. He was the primary writer of the *Mayflower* Compact, the document that served as the colony's charter. He was elected governor thirty times and kept a diary of the events of their persecutions in England and Amsterdam as well as the voyage on the *Mayflower* and the start of the colony. His diary has become known as the official log of the voyage and the chronicle of the Separatists' journey to and settlement in the new world. The work is over 800 pages as a printed document. Bradford saw the colony through its times of extreme hardship, when half their number died, and also led them in the celebration of the first thanksgiving in gratitude to God for their later successes. Even when the successes were still small and there was still much to be done to help the colony survive and thrive, Bradford set the tone of gratitude to and dependence on God, giving little space to tragedy and misfortune, even the drowning of his own wife shortly after they arrived at Provincetown Harbor before the colony was ever established.

James I began to persecute the Separatists in 1609. By 1613 Bradford and the other Separatist had settled at Leyden in the Netherlands. John Robinson, the leader of the congregation, planned the move to the new world and Bradford was involved from the beginning. The plan was to allow them to remain Englishmen but to escape the persecution they had tried to leave behind in England but which was continuing in the Netherlands. They sailed for the new world in 1620.

The Peace of Augsburg

Lutheranism became a powerful force in Europe, to the point where Charles V, Holy Roman Emperor, though staunchly Catholic himself, sent his brother, Ferdinand I, to sign the Peace of Augsburg in 1555. Its purpose was to end conflict between Lutherans and Catholics within the empire. The Schmalkaldic League, an alliance of German princes, had gained military victories which made the compromise necessary.

Cuius regio, eius religio in the treaty meant that the prince of a particular region could determine the religion practiced by the people of that region. Families of differing religions were given a grace period of time to move to a region that practiced their beliefs.

It is important to emphasize that these were still established religions, religions to be set up and enforced by the state. That was what was meant by cuius regio, eius religio. It does not mean freedom of religion, since the prince could still enforce the practice of only the chosen state religion, and could charge with heresy and persecute any others. Such practices were common and meant confiscation of lands and burning at the stake in most cases. Both Lutherans and Catholics practiced these enforcements under the establishment of religion.

Some Catholic clergy actually held rule over some of the parts of the germanic states, "Prince-Bishops," or "Prince-Abbots," who answered only to the Emperor. If they converted to Lutheranism, they were to be replaced by Catholic clergy. This prevented the conversion of the entire region over which the clergyman ruled to Lutheranism. This provision of the treaty was called reservatum ecclesiasticum and was inserted over the objections of the Lutherans. In 1583 the Archbishop-Elector of Cologne, Gebhard Truchsess von Waldburg, became a Lutheran and the Spanish-controlled Dutch Republic and the Palatinate of the Rhine helped Ernest of Bavaria defeat him to uphold the principle of *reservatum ecclesiasticum.*

Knights who had converted to Lutheranism and had practiced it for some time were excepted from the order to move by the declaratio ferdinandei. This was a provision of the treaty kept secret for almost twenty years. The Edict of Restitution in 1629 overturned this provision and was pushed forward by confident Catholics based on their early successes in the Thirty Years' War. The effect, however, was to cause Protestants to redouble their efforts and greatly enlarge the scope of the religious conflict in Europe.

This treaty did not recognize Anabaptists, Calvinists or other religious minorities, and in fact both Catholics and Lutherans could continue to persecute them and charge them with heresy. (Article 17: "However, all such as do not belong to the two above named religions shall not be included in the present peace but be totally excluded from it.") The growth of Calvinism eventually led to the Thirty Years' War and the Peace of Westphalia.

Peace of Westphalia, 1648

The Peace of Westphalia involved many political and geographic issues throughout Europe. Its effect on religion included the provision that the Peace of Augsburg of 1555 had to be recognized by all signing parties. In that treaty, each prince had been given the right to determine the religion of his own state (the principle of *cuius regio, eius religio*). The only recognized religions at the time were Catholicism and Lutheranism. Through the Peace of Westphalia, Calvinism became a recognized religion.

It is important to emphasize that these, just as during the time of the Peace of Augsburg, were established religions, religions to be set up and enforced by the state. That was what was meant by cuius regio, eius religio. It did not mean freedom of religion, since the prince could still enforce the practice of only the chosen state religion, and could charge with heresy and persecute any others. Such practices were common and meant confiscation of lands and burning at the stake in most cases. Both Lutherans and Catholics practiced these enforcements under the establishment of religion.

The Peace of Augsburg gave people a grace period in which to move from a region where their faith was not sanctioned to one where it was, if they had the means.

But if they did not belong to the Roman Catholic or Lutheran faiths they still had to flee altogether.

After the Treaty of Westphalia provision was made for other Christian beliefs. If their practice was not that of the established church where they lived, they were still guaranteed the right to practice their faith in public during allotted hours and in private at their will. While the language of the treaty might still allow for the government to place harsh restrictions on worship practices, at least the people could hope to escape the worst persecutions of theft of property and violent death.

Puritans, Separatists and Pilgrims

(Note: Read the appendices on Elizabeth I, James I and the Authorized Version for more on specific events in their reigns and especially details on James' actions concerning the churches of England and Scotland. Also see the Appendixes on the Acts of Uniformity and the Peaces of Augsburg and Westphalia for influences on these Protestant movements.)

The Puritans were members of the Church of England who wanted to remain faithful members of the church but continue the process of "purifying" the church from the influence of Roman Catholicism. Henry VIII had separated the church in England from the Pope for more or less personal and nationalistic reasons, but these reformers were influenced by religious belief and practice by Europeans like Luther and Calvin. Protestant clergy fled Europe during the initial Thirty Years' War defeats of the Schmalkaldic League. They found academic and ecclesiastical posts in England. (See the appendices on the Peace of Augsburg and the Peace of Westphalia.)

The Eucharist, or the Communion, commemorating the Lord's Last Supper with His disciples, was a serious area of difference among the Christian faiths. The Roman

Catholics believed in Transubstantiation, or that the elements of bread and wine actually became the body and blood of Christ. Lutherans claimed that Christ was somehow spiritually or actually present in the receiving of the elements, but not literally consumed, a confusing view called Consubstantiation. Most other Reformers held to the interpretation that it was simply symbolic, and sometimes taught that receiving communion "conferred grace," as did baptism, somehow awarding the participant spiritual standing. The symbolic interpretation seems to be most in line with the Scriptures, since Paul in I Corinthians said we were to "show the Lord's death" till He come, not cause it to happen over and over or expect His literal presence in any way.

This controversy was important because the Catholics were in effect resacrificing Christ each time they held communion. This was a heresy, because the Scriptures teach that Christ's sacrifice was once for all. It allowed the church to control the people by forcing them to return for cleansing from sin over and over instead of confessing their sins to God based on the already completed work of Christ.

Thomas Cranmer emerged as a leading English reformer as a result of these European influences. His place in England is important because he wrote and rewrote the Book of Common Prayer several times during the reign of Edward VI. It was the official guide to the service in the English church. Continental Reformers had already done away with the keeping of Lent, requiring the clergy to wear vestments, and requiring kneeling at Communion, among other things). A sizeable controversy ensued when John Hooper was to become Bishop of Gloucester, but he refused to wear the vestments required by the Book of Common Prayer. He was imprisoned under house arrest because refusing consecration as a Bishop violated the Acts of Uniformity of 1549. It took a letter from John Calvin to convince Hooper to relent. The vestment controversy was a long and bitter source of contention in the English church. The reason the English Reformers held so strongly to it was that they saw the vestments as a manifestation of spiritual pride, like the condemnation of the Pharisees by Jesus in Luke 20:45-47,

Then in the audience of all the people he said unto his disciples, "Beware of the scribes, which desire to walk in long robes, and love greetings in the markets, and the highest seats in the synagogues, and the chief rooms at feasts; Which devour widows' houses, and for a show make long prayers: the same shall receive greater damnation."

The ascension of Bloody Mary to the throne saw Thomas Cranmer, Hooper and others burned at the stake as the queen tried to restore England to Catholicism. Hundreds of protestants were forced to flee England. Many retained the forms of the Anglican worship but John Knox led a congregation to further reform, including the discarding of vestments. These worshipers found many conflicts with the reformers in Europe, including the vestment issue.

The Elizabethan Religious Settlement returned England to its status as a Protestant nation but tried to appease the large population which had supported Mary. Protestant exiles returned, eager for further reform. In the 1560s these people began the official Puritan Movement. Bishops who embraced Calvinism still opposed the Puritan degree of reform. In 1563, during the first Convocation of the English Clergy of Elizabeth's reign, the Puritans asked for further reforms: 1) a reduction in the number of saints' days; 2) the elimination of vestments; 3) the elimination of kneeling at communion; 4) the elimination of "emergency baptism" of sickly newborns; and 5) the elimination of organs from churches. All were denied, but many Puritan clergymen practiced them in their own churches. They received little support from Europe, partly because there was hope Elizabeth would aid the Hugenot cause, partly because the extreme attention to the vestments controversy in England sometimes seemed like troublemaking to the Europeans. When ministers were suspended for not wearing vestments, some began conducting their own services, beginning the Separatist movement.

Elizabeth was forced to deal with rebellious Catholics in the north, a Papal pronouncement absolving Catholics of their duty to be loyal to her, and the plot to replace her with Mary Queen of Scotts. Loyalty was coupled with church practice by the requirement that all clergymen subscribe to the Thirty-Nine Articles, distinctives outlining differences in Roman Catholic, Anabaptist, Protestant and Anglican practices and spelling out what practices were permitted and what forbidden in the English method of worship; (2) all laity were required to take communion according to the rite of the Book of Common Prayer in their home parish at least once a year; and (3) it became a treasonable offense to say that the queen was a heretic or a schismatic. Elizabeth had no interest in the further reforms sought by such men as John Foxe and Norton, determined to continue the terms of the original Elizabethan Religious Settlement.

In 1571 the Book of Common Prayer included the Thirty-nine Articles and said it was a “requirement [that] no man hereafter shall either print or preach, to draw the Article aside any way, but shall submit to it in the plain and Full meaning thereof: and shall not put his own sense or comment to be the meaning of the Article, but shall take it in the literal and grammatical sense.” Bishops tied the vestment issue into the required submission to the Thirty-nine Articles, as well as swearing that obedience to the Book of Common Prayer and wearing of vestments were not contrary to the Scriptures. A bill in Parliament that would have permitted dissenters for conscience and conviction reasons was defeated. The Puritans responded with the Admonition to Parliament.

They wanted to replace the Episcopalian order with the Presbyterian, asserting that no one man had biblical authority to be spiritually superior to another man. The Puritans once again were denied their requests.

A group called the Brownists were exiled to the lowlands because they objected to the Church's stifling of original preaching. The Brownists were among the first Separatists, those who believed the Church of England could not be fixed and must be separated from, but most Puritans disagreed with leaving the church and continued to try to reform it. In 1588-89, Welsh publisher John Penry published the anonymous Marprelate tracts, calling bishops agents of Antichrist and "our vile servile dunghill ministers of damnation, that viperous generation, those scorpions." A number of influential Puritans died by the late 1580's. Imprisonment of other leaders caused the latest reform movement to disband.

A secret congregation met in the woods near Islington in 1593. John Greenwood and Henry Barrowe, their leaders, were executed by Elizabeth for advocating separatism. Their followers fled to the Netherlands, joining others to become the Pilgrims, founders of the Plymouth Colony.

In 1593 the English Parliament passes the Religion Act and the Popish Recusants Act. Directed primarily at Roman Catholics, they gave those worshiping outside the Church of England 3 months to conform or leave, forfeiting their lands and goods to the crown. Failure to comply was a capital offense. These laws as written also applied to many Puritans and Separatists. No Puritans were executed under these laws but they were a constant threat.

Lollards, early reformers and followers of Wycliffe, had been outlawed in the 14th century, partly by making it illegal for an ordained parish priest to preach to his congregation without a license from his bishop. Elizabeth preferred a church service focused on the Prayer Book liturgy but many of her bishops favored more actual preaching in the services. Soon many more preachers were licensed, but a division grew between those who used original sermons and prayers, requiring cutting out some of the liturgy of the Book of Common Prayer, and some who stuck to the prescribed service.

Some churches began to concentrate on personal holiness and see themselves as separate from other Puritans. Variations of the idea of predestination based on whether you could or could not know if you were truly one of the elect led to further divisions. Some of these groups became Separatists, but a large segment of the Puritan population remained confident that they could hope for better things as James VI of Scotland became James I of England after Elizabeth's death. They saw the Church of Scotland as already close to the presbyterian form they wanted and, in spite of some of James' writings that spoke with disfavor of Puritanism, they looked forward to his ascension.

Puritan ministers collected 1000 signatures on the Millinary Petition (meaning 1000) listing items they wished to remove and change. Many rites they considered superstitious, and they also included their objection to the wearing of vestments. They also presented their desire for the presbytery to replace the bishops.

James convened a debate at Hampton Court, first meeting with a group of bishops and then with Puritan representatives. As soon as he heard the puritans' request for the replacement of bishops, he ended the day's meeting. To James, bishops were appointed by the king and therefore a tool of his power. "No bishop, no king!" he told the Puritans.

James approved a few changes in terminology in the Book of Common Prayer ("absolution" became "remission of sins," for example). James refused the request for preaching ministers, and in fact, turned down every request of substance but one. Puritans were permitted to begin a new translation of the Scriptures into English. Otherwise, James made it clear that he preferred things as they were in the Church of England, and even appointed one of the bishops who had opposed the Puritans at the Conference as Archbishop, Richard Bancroft, when a successor was needed. Bancroft created a book of canons and had it approved by the king and the Convocations of the English Clergy. Parliament came on the scene at this point, since it had been given the authority to approve new church laws and it had not even been consulted. Parliament declared that the convocations did not have authority to approve the new canons. James was eventually forced to withdraw the new canons. The Puritans and Parliament formed an alliance that later became a defining factor in the English Civil War.

The Gunpowder Plot and the resulting strong anti-catholic sentiments it produced (see the appendix on King James and the Authorized Version) resulted in an improved position for Puritans, who opposed Catholics more than anyone, but Bancroft still blocked any real reforms. George Abbot was the next archbishop appointed by James, as part of his ongoing plan to unify the Scottish and Anglican churches. Although he managed to reinstall bishops in Scotland, they did not replace the presbytery and never had equivalent powers of bishops in England. Abbot was considered the most

Puritan Archbishop of all but he disapproved of the Puritan plan to do away with the bishops.

Most Anglicans agreed that Sunday morning should be devoted to worship but Sunday afternoons were given over to games and sports. Puritans, stern observes of the sabbath, considered it necessary to refrain from all work or non-religious activity in order to avoid breaking the fourth commandment, and in some areas managed to banish Sunday sports. Thomas Morton, Bishop of Chester, asked the king to rule on Sunday sports. King James issued a Book of Sports, specifically criticizing "Puritans and precise people," and specifying harmless sports like archery, dancing, "leaping," and vaulting, that could be played on Sundays, forbidding a few such a bear-baiting and bowling. Archbishop Abbott, as strict Sabbath-observer, forbade his clergy to follow the king's command to the ministers to read the book to their congregations.

The Five Articles of Perth pushed upon the Scottish clergy alarmed Puritans because they saw the Church of Scotland becoming more like the Anglican, while they had hoped for the opposite outcome. James, however, envisioned himself as a great mediator of peace throughout Europe, and saw the Church of England as a model of a middle ground church that could reconcile Roman Catholicism and Protestantism. His plan to marry his son Charles to the Spanish princess Maria Infanta was intended to give him financial aid and further that goal. The Thirty Years' war, caused by James' son-in-law, Frederick V, Elector Palatine, forced James instead to convene Parliament and ask for money to appease the Protestants, and especially Puritans, who clamored for aid to the European cause of Protestantism. Parliament conditioned the money on James's promise that Charles would marry a Protestant. James refused.

Charles gave England cause for rejoicing by repudiating the match with Maria but they never officially provided funding for his proposed alliance with France and war with Spain. But James continued to experience Protestant and Puritan unrest as the Calvinist-Armenian controversy arose in Europe. James decided to paint the Puritans as overly strict on Calvinism to find support for his aims of ecumenism. The Puritans had never actually split with the Anglican Church on a doctrinal matter. They were concerned with matters of Catholic ritual that they considered to be based on superstition or to encourage spiritual pride. Puritans could not be cast into one mold concerning these controversies and they did not deserve James' attack on these grounds.

When Charles I succeeded his father in 1625 he continued to favor Anglican ritual as more in line with his divine rights beliefs that Puritan reform. William Laud rose to a favored position at this time and predestination preaching was entirely forbidden. Laud's party managed to promote preaching in favor of the king's divine right coupled with a demand for Parliament's obedience to the king's orders based on their religious duty to show loyalty. They campaigned against the Puritans, drawing comparisons with European reformers who had risen up against their governments. Laud based the push for preserving church liturgy and ceremony on Psalm 29:2, "Worship the Lord in the beauty of holiness."

Laud ordered churches to be beautified, in opposition to Puritans' desire for simplicity, and reinstituted the altar rail of Roman Catholicism. The railing created a separate area only priests and altar boys could enter. Inside that area the supposed transubstantiation or change of the elements of Eucharist (bread and wine of communion) to the literal presence of the body and blood of Christ took place. Puritans believed in the priesthood of all believers, opposing the creation of a special place for special people, and said that kneeling at the rail was worshiping the elements instead of God. Laudians wanted to be called priests, which the Puritans associated with the heresy of offering Christ as a sacrifice over and over again, and wanted the name ministers.

Charles tried to arrange a marriage alliance with France and get Parliament to fund his proposed war with Spain. Parliament, and especially the Puritans, believed Charles meant to raise and army and reimpose Catholicism on England. Continued opposition from Parliament decided Charles to rule without them for eleven years. This period was called the “Caroline Captivity of the Church” and the “Eleven Years’ Tyrrany” as Laud grew in power and the Puritans experienced more repression.

1618 saw a Puritan settlement begin in Virginia. Followers of Richard Clyfton, including William Brewster and John Robinson, formed a Separatist group, evading persecution by moving when Clyfton was removed by the Archbishop of York. The group eventually fled to Holland tried to join another Separatist group, but found more controversy there. They sought a place to retain their English identity and find true freedom to worship. The *Mayflower* brought them to Plymouth in 1620.

A number of other New England settlements rose with commercial charters and their leaders convinced wealthy Puritans to invest in them and come to settle, providing havens for some Puritans. John Winthrop led the founding of the Massachusetts Bay Colony, designed for Puritans who had given up hope of establishing reform under Charles but still differed from Separatists. John Winthrop and others pointed out that the charter of the Massachusetts Bay Company did not specify where the meetings of the company stockholders should be held. Moving the directors to the location of the colony would effectively allow the directors to become a colonial legislature. The king agreed to this, probably believing it was strictly a commercial venture, not the founding of a Puritan venture. A Pilgrim migration followed, which

Charles ended at the time of the English Civil war by allowing only confirmed churchmen to emigrate.

The colonies experienced unrest due to remaining divisions between Puritans and Separatists. Roger William was cast out, partly for his contentions that the wall of separation between the world and the Church had been broken down and the church had denied itself God's protection because of its worldliness. Anne Hutchinson taught heretical views on predestination and claimed God had spoken directly to her, in opposition to the Puritan (and biblical) belief that Scripture was the only source of revelation. She was first banished, then executed when she refused to stay away.

Colonists even resettled in Massachusetts and Virginia from other British possessions in Bermuda and the Bahamas. Those Puritans who remained in England saw intensified persecution when Laud rose to the rank of Archbishop. Scotland managed to cast off the impositions of bishops and revised prayer books Charles and Laud heaped on them after two Bishops' Wars, one instigated by Charles and one by Scotland. Charles took this defeat badly and with Laud's help turned on Puritanism in England. The convocation of Clergy remained in session, even though Parliament had been dissolved, and it approved a new set of canons, including the infamous "Et Cetera Clause" oath.

"I, A. B., do swear that I do approve the doctrine, and discipline, or government established in the Church of England as containing all things necessary to salvation: and that I will not endeavour by myself or any other, directly or indirectly, to bring in any popish doctrine contrary to that which is so established; nor will I ever give my consent to alter the government of this Church by archbishops, bishops, deans, and archdeacons, &c., as it stands now established, and as by right it ought to stand, nor yet ever to subject it to the usurpations and superstitions of the see of Rome. And all these things I do plainly and sincerely acknowledge and swear, according to the plain and common sense and understanding of the same words, without any equivocation, or mental evasion, or secret reservation whatsoever. And this I do heartily, willingly, and truly, upon the faith of a Christian. So help me God in Jesus Christ."

Puritans denounced the canons as unconstitutional. They also uncovered a plan by Charles to raise an army of Irish Catholics to overpower the Scottish and force the bishops back upon them. The Puritans managed to get Charles to execute the Earl of Strafford, who was in charge of the project. The pressure they exerted included an uprising of the English army, which had long gone unpaid through Charles' refusal to deal with Parliament. Desperate for money, Charles was forced to agree to a bill banning him from dissolving Parliament. Puritans also secured an end to the Star Chamber, a secret court used for prosecuting imprisoning and punishing Puritans, and got some of their imprisoned fellows released.

Puritans introduced a "Root and Branch" petition to Parliament asking for sweeping reforms in the church and government practices relating to religious issues. Archbishop Laud was impeached and imprisoned, and a Bill based on the Root and Branch petition was drafted. This was defeated, but conflict intensified as Puritans again sought to abolish the bishopric, inciting a mob to force them away from their seats in Parliament.

The Irish threw off British control, leading to protestant fears that a Catholic army of Irish would attack them. Charles heard that Puritans intended to impeach the Queen for pro-Catholic plotting. Back and forth suspicions resulted in Charles and Parliament raising armies of self-defense against each other. The Roundhead and Cavalier parties in Parliament quickly took sides. The Westminster Assembly, called by Parliament when they realized they had to act without royal assent if anything was to be accomplished, attempted to deal with revising the thirty-nine articles, solving the Episcopal versus Presbyterian controversy, and negotiating an agreement with Scotland. Congregationalists, as well as those who believed church organization was not a matter of doctrine or general polity, but a matter for individual churches, were also represented.

Independents exerted an influence at the Assembly. They believed that only persons who had experienced conversion and been examined by godly members of a church could be admitted. In other words, people would be "gathered" into individual churches upon a profession of faith testified to by existing church members. They favored congregational organization and said England should not have any national church, but individual congregations accepting their own members, preaching their own sermons, rejecting any sort of prayerbook or set form of worship but letting each church be free to develop its own forms or no forms. This was the beginning of the concept of religious liberty in England.

The majority positions included belief that God had especially chosen England and the English Church much as He had chosen the Israelites.

Others also argued that no one could know for certain who was saved or not saved. Still others believed that everyone needed set forms of worship to help them live as close to pleasing God as possible. Civil control was needed, said some of the delegates, when churchmen stepped out of line and needed punishment. Secular jurists sought to prohibit the Assembly from changing the established order of government supreme over the church. The independents faced too much opposition to get any of their proposals passed.

Attempts to establish a Presbyterian system were unsatisfactory because they always included some type of external official who could rule on excommunications. Eventually forms of worship loosely guiding a minister in the service, plus a catechism and confession of faith were created.

Meanwhile, Oliver Cromwell succeeded in creating an army that favored the Independent position, which he supported, by getting Parliament to pass a law saying that no one could both serve in the army and in Parliament at the same time. He did this because he suspected the Presbyterians wanted to make peace with Charles and Cromwell wanted Charles completely defeated. He succeeded in getting Charles' surrender.

Parliament then presented a Heads of Proposals to Charles: Royalists were banned from holding office for five years.

Use of the Book of Common Prayer was to become voluntary, penalties for not going to church were to be discontinued, and attending other acts of worship was to be permitted.

The present Parliament was to announce the date when it would end. In the future, Parliaments had to be called every two years, remaining in session at least 120 days but no more than 240 days. Areas of representation were to be reorganized.

Bishops and the episcopal system would remain but bishops' powers would be greatly curtailed.

For ten years Parliament had the power to appointment state officials and officers in the army and navy.

Charles rejected these proposals. He made a secret treaty with dissenting Scottish covenanters to receive an army of 20,000 to return Charles to the throne in exchange for suppressing the episcopacy for three years, after which the church system would be renegotiated. This second

English Civil War also resulted in Charles' defeat. The army independents demanded punishment for Charles, saying that his defeat was a sign of God's judgment. Parliament refused and Colonel Thomas Pride took troops in and removed the opposing members bodily. The "Rump" Parliament which remained agreed to the execution. History has variously blamed Puritans for being violent regicides or praised them for disposing of a tyrant after years of abuse. But the Protestants in this cause were deeply divided, some wishing to spare Charles, some holding sharply divergent views on what they did accomplish or should have accomplished.

Worship fragmented during the interregnum. There were no governing church authorities to enforce any of the Parliamentary orders. Many different groups, Presbyterians, those who wanted to retain some forms of the Book of Common Prayer, and Puritans of other kinds, simply worshiped as they pleased. Separatists came out of hiding and a number of sects, some placing less emphasis on the Scriptures and more on emotional perceptions of direct contact with the Holy Spirit, like Quakers, arose. Cromwell set up broad guidelines to preserve protestantism in England, most of which did little but provide officials who could throw a minister out of his office, not for matters of belief, but for moral sins. With the restoration of the Monarchy some suppression and persecution of Puritans resumed but not as much as in the past.

For a long time Puritans in the colonies had no tolerance for those who differed with them in belief. Many colonies sprung up as a result of persecution by Puritans. Separatists tended to be more tolerant and their settlements were mixed because they wanted religious freedom for themselves and they also wanted numbers in their colonies to help with issues of survival.

Virginia Declaration of Rights

The Virginia Declaration of Rights was written in 1776 to express the true natural rights of men, including the right to revolt against bad government. It influenced many later documents and was incorporated within the Virginia State Constitution.

It was written primarily by George Mason. The Declaration is the first Constitutional protection of individual rights for Americans. The Declaration views government as the servant of the people, and clearly restricts its power. The document not only spells out the legal rights of citizens, but it also describes moral principles upon which a government should be run. The text comes from the Yale University Law Library's Avalon Project.

I That all men are by nature equally free and independent, and have certain inherent rights, of which, when they enter into a state of society, they cannot, by any compact, deprive or divest their posterity; namely, the enjoyment of life and liberty, with the means of acquiring and possessing property, and pursuing and obtaining happiness and safety.

II That all power is vested in, and consequently derived from, the people; that magistrates are their trustees and servants, and at all times amenable to them.

III That government is, or ought to be, instituted for the common benefit, protection, and security of the people, nation or community; of all the various modes and forms of government that is best, which is capable of producing the greatest degree of happiness and safety and is most effectually secured against the danger of maladministration; and that, whenever any government shall be found inadequate or contrary to these purposes, a majority of the community hath an indubitable, unalienable, and indefeasible right to reform, alter or abolish it, in such manner as shall be judged most conducive to the public weal.

IV That no man, or set of men, are entitled to exclusive or separate emoluments or privileges from the community, but in consideration of public services; which, not being descendible, neither ought the offices of magistrate, legislator, or judge be hereditary.

V That the legislative and executive powers of the state should be separate and distinct from the judicative; and, that the members of the two first may be restrained from oppression by feeling and participating the burthens of the people, they should, at fixed periods, be reduced to a private station, return into that body from which they were originally taken, and the vacancies be supplied by frequent, certain, and regular elections in which all, or any part of the former members, to be again eligible, or ineligible, as the laws shall direct.

VI That elections of members to serve as representatives of the people in assembly ought to be free; and that all men, having sufficient evidence of permanent common interest with, and attachment to, the community have the right of suffrage and cannot be taxed or deprived of their property for public uses without their own consent or that of their representatives so elected, nor bound by any law to which they have not, in like manner, assented, for the public good.

VII That all power of suspending laws, or the execution of laws, by any authority without consent of the representatives of the people is injurious to their rights and ought not to be exercised.

VIII That in all capital or criminal prosecutions a man hath a right to demand the cause and nature of his accusation to be confronted with the accusers and witnesses, to call for evidence in his favor, and to a speedy trial by an impartial jury of his vicinage, without whose unanimous consent he cannot be found guilty, nor can he be compelled to give evidence against himself;

that no man be deprived of his liberty except by the law of the land or the judgement of his peers.

IX That excessive bail ought not to be required, nor excessive fines imposed; nor cruel and unusual punishments inflicted.

X That general warrants, whereby any officer or messenger may be

commanded to search suspected places without evidence of a fact committed, or to seize any person or persons not named, or whose offense is not particularly described and supported by evidence, are grievous and oppressive and ought not to be granted.

XI That in controversies respecting property and in suits between man and man, the ancient trial by jury is preferable to any other and ought to be held sacred.

XII That the freedom of the press is one of the greatest bulwarks of liberty and can never be restrained but by despotic governments.

XIII That a well regulated militia, composed of the body of the people, trained to arms, is the proper, natural, and safe defense of a free state; that standing armies, in time of peace, should be avoided as dangerous to liberty; and that, in all cases, the military should be under strict subordination to, and be governed by, the civil power.

XIV That the people have a right to uniform government; and therefore, that no government separate from, or independent of, the government of Virginia, ought to be erected or established within the limits thereof.

XV That no free government, or the blessings of liberty, can be preserved to any people but by a firm adherence to justice, moderation, temperance, frugality, and virtue and by frequent recurrence to fundamental principles.

XVI That religion, or the duty which we owe to our Creator and the manner of discharging it, can be directed by reason and conviction, not by force or violence; and therefore, all men are equally entitled to the free exercise of religion, according to the dictates of conscience; and that it is the mutual duty of all to practice Christian forbearance, love, and charity towards each other.

Adopted unanimously June 12, 1776 Virginia Convention of Delegates drafted by Mr. George Mason

Appendix Four: Recommended Reading

Websites

Heritage Foundation *askheritage.org* "To build an America where freedom, opportunity, prosperity and civil society flourish. Public policy research organization."

Cato Institute *www.cato.org* "Increase the understanding of public policies based on the principles of limited government, free markets, individual liberty, and peace."

Discovery Institute *discovery.org*. "Explore ...technology, science and culture, reform of the law, national defense, the environment and the economy, the future of democratic institutions, transportation, religion and public life, government entitlement spending, foreign affairs."

Answers in Genesis *answersingenesis.org*. "enabling Christians to defend their faith ... answers to questions surrounding the book of Genesis, ... train others to develop a biblical worldview..."

Institute for Creation Research *icr.org*. "Scientific research from a biblical perspective ...graduate-level degree program in science education, graduate-level training in biblical education and apologetics ... Publications, Events, and Media."

Ayn Rand Center for Individual Rights *aynrandcenter.org* "advance individual rights (the rights of each person to life, liberty, property, and the pursuit of happiness) as the moral basis for a fully free, laissez-faire capitalist society."

National Rifle Association *nra.org* safety and training programs for military, law enforcement, civilian, female protection and child safety, and "a major political force ... America's foremost defender of Second Amendment rights."

The Internet Sacred Text Archive *sacred-texts.com* Every kind of public-domain material remotely connected with spiritual, philosophical, and broadly religious subjects.

Creation Research Society *creationresearch.org* Education, research, journal publication, "committed to full belief in the Biblical record of creation and early history."

World Net Daily *wnd.com* Original news articles and links to outside sources for news, opinion, commentary with a conservative emphasis.

Books
James Hannam, Web site and book *God's Philosophers: How the Medieval World Laid the Foundations of Modern Science*. Icon Books, London, 2009.

Allan Bloom, *The Closing of the American Mind*. Documentation on secular humanist influence from non-Christian but conservative perspective with extensive research and proofs.

Francis Schaeffer *The God Who Is There, The Christian Manifesto, How Should We Then Live, True Spirituality, Escape from Reason, Back to Freedom and Dignity*. Schaeffer is reformed in theology, evangelical rather than fundamentalist, left America for Switzerland. He was the first evangelical to advocate political activism opposing abortion.

Aleksandr Solzhenitsyn *Gulag Archipelago* (3 volumes) Believer imprisoned under Stalin. collected stories of other prisoners massive, well-documented work on the effects of communism on its own people.

Dr. Don DeYoung, *Thousands, Not Billions: Challenging an Icon of Evolution Questioning the Age of the Earth.* Disproves uniformitarianism by collection of individual scientific studies

George W. Dollar, *A History of Fundamentalism in America.* Church history in America from founding to early 70's emphasis on the 20th century.

David O Beale, *In Pursuit of Purity.* American church history up to 1980's emphasizing conflicts between belief and unbelief, as it affects the church.

William Evans. *The Great Doctrines of the Bible.* Brief easy to read basic Bible doctrines.

John Foxe. Foxe's Book of Martyrs. History of martyrs up to Foxe's time sections added mid-16th century.

Humphreys, D. Russell, Ph.D. *Starlight and Time, Solving the Puzzle of Distant Starlight in a Young Universe.*

Josephus, *Antiquities of the Jews.* Roman General and Jewish historian. Late first century writer from Creation to his lifetime.

Josh MacDowell, *The New Evidence that Demands a Verdict.* Conservative evangelical Christian apologist, evidence in support of the Bible's truth.

G. Campbell Morgan. Commentator Baptist preacher English, lived in America.

Michael Oard. *Frozen in Time: The Wooly Mammoth, The Ice Age and the Bible.* Recent information refuting uniformitarianism.

Antonin Scalia. Supreme Court Justice, Conservative constitutional jurisprudence.

William Warren Sweet. *The Story of Religions in America.* Well-documented, honest but liberal perspective.

J.C Whitcomb and H. M. Morris. *The Genesis Flood.* Classic scientific treatise on Earth geology.

Bibliography for Antidisestablishmentarianism

Scripture references are as follows: The Bible: The King James Version, public domain. A few verses for comparison purposes are from other translations as follows: The New International Version, from the HOLY BIBLE, NEW INTERNATIONAL VERSION Registered. NIV Registered. Copyright 1973, 1978, 1984 by International Bible Society. Used by permission of Zondervan. All rights reserved. The New American Standard Version: Scripture quotations taken from the New American Standard Bible Registered, Copyright 1960, 1962, 1963, 1968, 1971, 1972, 1973, 1975, 1977, 1995 by The Lockman Foundation Used by permission.

Antidisestablishmentarianism references hundreds of authors and works, yet one source needs special mention. The website Sacred Texts by J.B. Hare is the largest collection of public domain material of which we are aware. The entire website of over one thousand books is available for purchase on either CD ROM or DVD ROM. Most of the ancient texts used in this work are public domain books from this collection. A problem with this or any other collection is proving the validity of the primary sources. Though we do not know anything about John B. Hare, except the information posted on his website, we believe that he faithfully and accurately scanned the texts. The problem is, are the texts reliable? Since they are public domain, they are older and sometimes not the latest translations. We are confident, however, that they are acceptable. Some sources we use are books where Westerners lived among a tribe and wrote down oral traditions. Though we trust that the authors accurately recorded the oral traditions, how much 'contamination' with outside influences shaped these oral traditions? The Lore of the Whare-Wananga, a New Zealand tribe, is well documented by the translator S. Percy Smith to be older than outside influences and free of 'contamination.' Myths of the Cherokee by James Mooney, however, was published in 1900 after more than 250 years of wars and close contact with outsiders. The level of outside influence on the oral traditions of the North American Indians is impossible to measure or deny.

It should also be noted that some of the authors listed here have been accused of being pseudoarchaeologists or pseudoscientists and are largely discounted by many as scholarly sources because of the conclusions they drew from their research or the inability to substantiate some of their claims. Examples of these authors are Graham Hancock, Emmanuel Velikovsky and Thor Heyerdahl. Their conclusions are in some cases not worthy of serious consideration and some of their findings are unverifiable. However, the research they conducted and the discoveries they claim to have made, when verifiable, bear serious consideration. It is necessary to go back to verifiable evidence uncovered by archaeology, exploration and scientific discovery and to draw realistic conclusions from this evidence based on biblical understanding.

Material used from these books includes discoveries verified by repeated similar references in primary sources, documented archaeological sites which beyond question exist and testimony of ancient manuscripts accepted by scholars for hundreds of years. Some evidence cannot be substantiated because it exists in off-limits areas like the interior of China or other countries experiencing dangerous travel conditions. Presenting such claims does not attest to their truth, but in most cases these finds are part of an established pattern repeated throughout the *world.*

___________. *"1549, 1559, 1662 Acts of Uniformity." Hanover Historical Texts Projects.* History Department, Hanover College, Hanover, IN. *history.hanover.edu.*

___________. Access Research Network (*ARN.org*). (A scholarly website containing scientific research articles.)

___________. *The American Heritage® Dictionary of the English Language*, Fourth Edition. ©2000 Houghton Mifflin Company. Updated in 2003.

___________. *americanpresbyterianchurch.org*

___________. "Ancient temple found under Lake Titicaca." *BBC News.* Wednesday, 23 August, 2000, 11:04 GMT 12:04 UK.

___________. *answersingenesis.org.*

___________. *Assyrian Kings' Lists.* Various translators, various public domain texts with sources including Google Books, Wikipedia, The Internet Ancient History Sourcebook, (http://www.fordham.edu halsall/ ancient/asbook.html), and various universities which have placed public domain works online.

___________. (Atheist poster compilation) From the website *scottklarr.com.*

___________. Bethel Lutheran Church, Cupertino, CA website.

___________. *Biblefacts.org*

___________. The Book of Enoch. Translated by R.H. Charles, 1917. *The Apocrypha and Pseudepigrapha of the Old Testament*. Oxford: The Clarendon Press, 1913.

____________. *BBC online*, updated April 10, 2002.

____________. "Bible Answers." Like the Master Ministries. (Mathematical calculation from proves that 10,000 people could have been born before Adam and Eve died.) *Never Thirsty.org* website.

____________. "Boat People, a Refugee Crisis." *cbc.ca digital archives*. Broadcast May 1, 2000.

____________. "PART I THE BUNDAHIS-BAHMAN YAST, AND SHÂYAST LÂ-SHÂYAST." *Sacred Books of the East, Volume 5,* 1860. Taken from the Internet Sacred Text Archive, www.sacred-texts.com, managed by John Bruno Hare.

____________. "Cave Reveals Southwest's Abrupt Climate Swings During Ice Age." *Science Daily.com,* January 25, 2010.

____________. Church Community Services, Elkhart, IN website.

____________. *Church of the Holy Trinity v. United States. U.S. Supreme Court:* 143 U.S. 457 (1892). *www.talkorigins.org*.

____________. *CNN.com*.

____________. "Coal, Volcanism and Noah's Flood," *TJ (Technical Journal)* 1(1):11–29, Creation Ministries International, April 1984.

____________. Committee on the Judiciary House of Representatives, Prohibiting Detention Camps, March 18, 1971.

____________. *Corpus Aristotelicum,* collected works of Aristotle preserved by Medieval manuscript transmission. They are studies of philosophy made

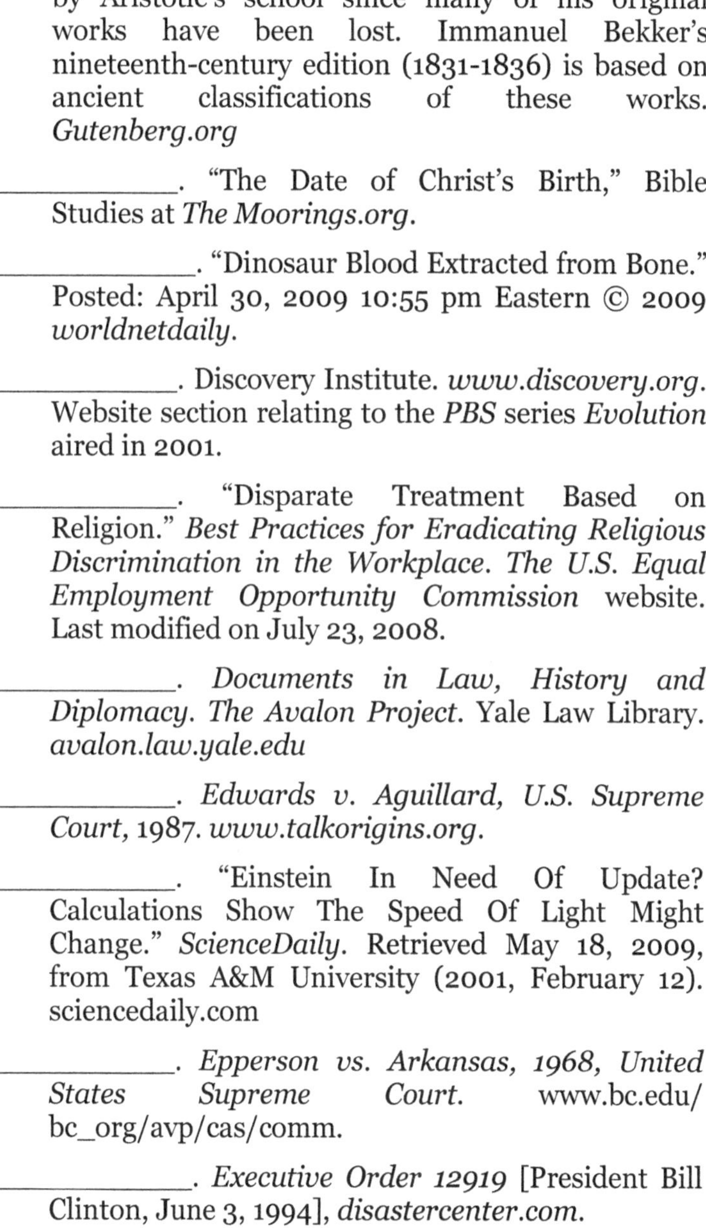

by Aristotle's school since many of his original works have been lost. Immanuel Bekker's nineteenth-century edition (1831-1836) is based on ancient classifications of these works. *Gutenberg.org*

___________. "The Date of Christ's Birth," Bible Studies at *The Moorings.org*.

___________. "Dinosaur Blood Extracted from Bone." Posted: April 30, 2009 10:55 pm Eastern © 2009 *worldnetdaily*.

___________. Discovery Institute. *www.discovery.org*. Website section relating to the *PBS* series *Evolution* aired in 2001.

___________. "Disparate Treatment Based on Religion." *Best Practices for Eradicating Religious Discrimination in the Workplace. The U.S. Equal Employment Opportunity Commission* website. Last modified on July 23, 2008.

___________. *Documents in Law, History and Diplomacy. The Avalon Project*. Yale Law Library. *avalon.law.yale.edu*

___________. *Edwards v. Aguillard, U.S. Supreme Court*, 1987. *www.talkorigins.org*.

___________. "Einstein In Need Of Update? Calculations Show The Speed Of Light Might Change." *ScienceDaily*. Retrieved May 18, 2009, from Texas A&M University (2001, February 12). sciencedaily.com

___________. *Epperson vs. Arkansas, 1968, United States Supreme Court*. www.bc.edu/ bc_org/avp/cas/comm.

___________. *Executive Order 12919* [President Bill Clinton, June 3, 1994], *disastercenter.com*.

__________. "Expelled Exposed: Why Expelled Flunks." *National Center for Science Education.* (website)

__________. *Fellowship of Humanity v. County of Alameda,* 1956.

__________. *GeorgiaEncyclopedia.org* Background on Providence Canyon.

__________. *GORP.com* (Great Outdoor Recreation Page.)

__________. *Greek Apocalypse of Baruch iii.* English translations were published from the Slavonic by W. R. Morfill (Apocrpyha Anecdota II, ed. M. R. James [T&S 5.1] Cambridge: CUP, 1987. Pp. 95-102) and from the Slavonic and Greek by H. M. Hughes (APOT 2. Pp. 533-41). The pseudepigraphon was composed in the beginning of the second century A.D., but it is difficult to discover whether it was written in Greek, Hebrew, or Aramaic. (Background note from Charlesworth, James H. The Pseudepigrapha and Modern Research: with a Supplement. SBLSCS 7. Chico, Ca.: Scholars Press, 1981.)M. R. James's publication of the Greek text, until then entirely unknown, in "Texts and Studies: Contributions to Biblical and Patristic Literature," edited by J. Armitage Robinson, v., No. i., pp. 84-94, Cambridge, 1897.

__________. *gulaghistory.org.*

__________. "How Old are Kimberlites and Diamonds?" *American Museum of Natural History* website.

__________. "Judge Says UC (University of California) Can Deny Religious Course Credit. "*Answers in Genesis News to Note.* From the *San Francisco Chronicle,* Aug 16, 2008.

__________. "Kim Jong Il." *BBC news online.* Asia/Pacific Profile: Page last updated at 11:14 GMT, Friday, 16 January 2009.

__________. "Letter of Oct. 7, 1801 from Danbury (CT) Baptist Assoc. to Thomas Jefferson," *Thomas Jefferson Papers*, Manuscript Division, Library of Congress, Wash. D.C.

__________. Library of Congress website.

__________. *McLean v. Arkansas Board of Education*, 1982. www.talkorigins. org/faqs/mclean-v-arkansas.

__________. *Magna Carta*, 1215 AD, from *The Avalon Project. Documents in Law, History and Diplomacy*. Yale Law Library. *avalon.law.yale.edu.*

__________. The Mahabharata. "Santiparva," cclx.20, 21, 23 and cxxiv.67, translated by Friedrich Max Müller and others *in Sacred Books of the East* (50 volumes), Oxford University Press, 1879-1910.

__________. *Mayflower* 1620.com (website).

__________. The National Archives. *archives.gov.*

__________. *National Geographic,* photo caption, March 1, 2010.

__________. National Park Services Website.

__________. National Park Service report on Wall Arch collapse August 4-5, 2008.

__________. *The New York Times.* News item published September 14, 1999.

__________. "NC State Paleontologist Discovers Soft Tissue in Dinosaur Bones." North Carolina State University News Release from *www.ncsu.edu/ news/press* /05-03/05 March 24, 2005.

__________. Novori.com. History and manufacture of synthetic diamonds.

___________. "Parents Fuming as Texas Schools Let Gideons Provide Bibles to Students." *Foxnews.com,* Tuesday, May 19, 2009.

___________. *Peloza v. Capistrano School District,* 1994. *www.talkorigins.org.*

___________. "Prohibiting Detention Camps." U. S. House of Representatives, Committee on the Judiciary, March 18, 1971.

___________. "Superbridge." *NOVA. PBS.* November 12, 1997.

___________. Public Information Office, Jet Propulsion Laboratory, California Institute of Technology, NASA, press release, July 21, 1994.

___________. "Question and Answer with Dr. Mary Schweitzer." *Nova* online. July 31, 2007.

___________. *Ramayana.* [Charvaka teachings (ancient Indian skeptic philosophy) quoted in, the Ramayana, approximately 600 BC. (Most original source material of the Charvaka beliefs were destroyed, and fragments are preserved in Hindu texts, where they are denounced as heresy.)] Ravi Prakash Arya, (ed.). *Ramayana of Valmiki: Sanskrit Text and English Translation.* (English translation according to M. N. Dutt, introduction by Dr. Ramashraya Sharma, 4-volume set) Parimal Publications: Delhi, 1998.

___________. Reports on the Antarctic research stations at *Antarctic Connection.com.*

___________. Review of the book *Mayflower*: *A Story of Courage Community and War* by Nathaniel Philbrick, 2007, Penguin. Bookmarks Magazine, Phillips & Nelson Media, Inc., from *Amazon.com.*

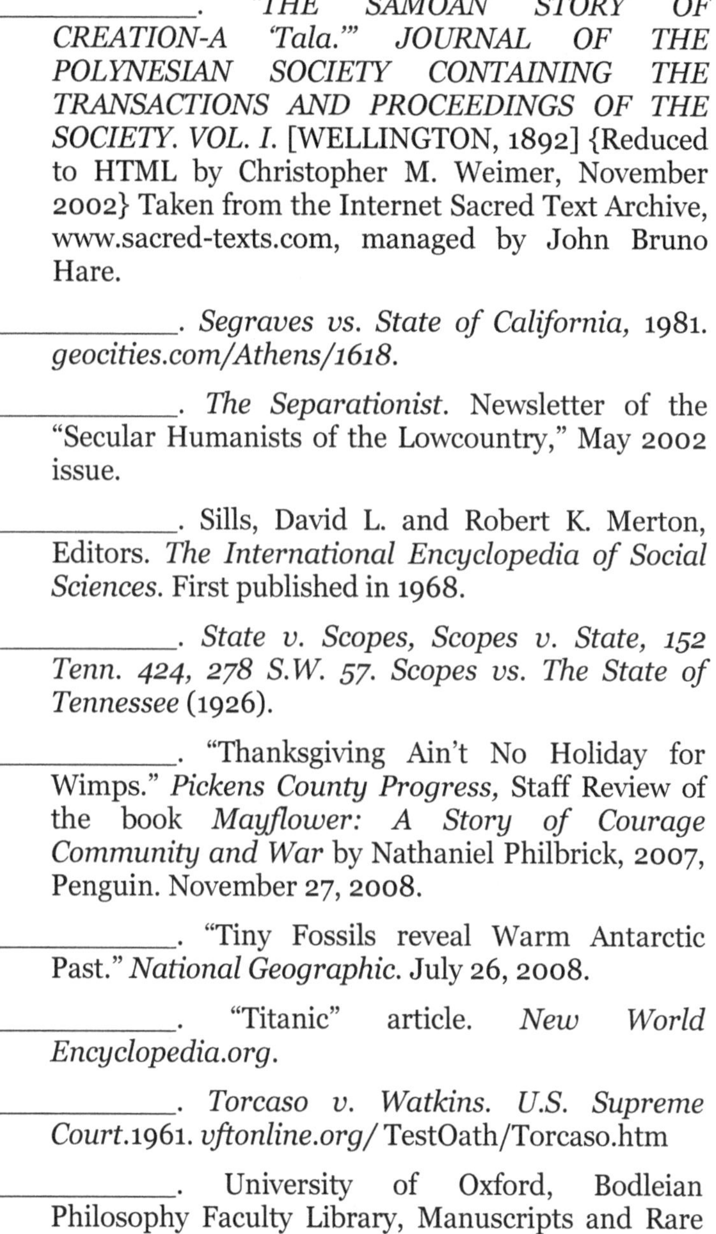

___________. *"THE SAMOAN STORY OF CREATION-A 'Tala.'" JOURNAL OF THE POLYNESIAN SOCIETY CONTAINING THE TRANSACTIONS AND PROCEEDINGS OF THE SOCIETY. VOL. I.* [WELLINGTON, 1892] {Reduced to HTML by Christopher M. Weimer, November 2002} Taken from the Internet Sacred Text Archive, www.sacred-texts.com, managed by John Bruno Hare.

___________. *Segraves vs. State of California,* 1981. *geocities.com/Athens/1618.*

___________. *The Separationist.* Newsletter of the "Secular Humanists of the Lowcountry," May 2002 issue.

___________. Sills, David L. and Robert K. Merton, Editors. *The International Encyclopedia of Social Sciences.* First published in 1968.

___________. *State v. Scopes, Scopes v. State, 152 Tenn. 424, 278 S.W. 57. Scopes vs. The State of Tennessee* (1926).

___________. "Thanksgiving Ain't No Holiday for Wimps." *Pickens County Progress,* Staff Review of the book *Mayflower: A Story of Courage Community and War* by Nathaniel Philbrick, 2007, Penguin. November 27, 2008.

___________. "Tiny Fossils reveal Warm Antarctic Past." *National Geographic.* July 26, 2008.

___________. "Titanic" article. *New World Encyclopedia.org.*

___________. *Torcaso v. Watkins. U.S. Supreme Court.*1961. *vftonline.org/* TestOath/Torcaso.htm

___________. University of Oxford, Bodleian Philosophy Faculty Library, Manuscripts and Rare

Books "Medieval Manuscript Sources and Incunabula." *ox.ac.uk.*

____________. Utah Geological Survey, *Utah.gov.*

____________. *varchive.org.* A scholarly archive of Immanuel Velikovsky's unpublished works.

____________. *Voices for Evolution* (website).

____________. *Washington Ethical Society v. District of Columbia,* 249 F.2d 127 (D.C. Cir. 1957).

____________. *Web of Science* (Formerly Science Citation Index). Guillermo Gonzalez - publication record at ISU.

____________. *Webster v. New Lenox School District,* 1990, the Seventh Circuit Court of Appeals. *geocities.com/Athens/618/Webster_vs._New_Lenox.html*

____________. *Wikipedia.org*

____________. The *Wisconsin University website,* overview of the Laramide/ Yellowstone mountain ranges with aerial maps designating geologic ages.

____________. World Net Daily. *wnd.com.*

____________. Youth Ministry Entertainment (or Y-ME ministries). *y-ment.com.*

____________. Abbott, Frank Frost and Alan Chester Johnson (authors, translators and editors). *Municipal Administration in the Roman Empire [concerning the The Law of the Twelve Tables (Duodecim Tabulae), the ancient foundation of Roman law*]. Princeton University Press, Princeton, NJ, 1926.

Adams, John. "Argument in defence of the soldiers in the Boston Massacre trial." December 1770.

____________. "Letter to Abigail Adams." July 7, 1775.

__________. "Letter to the 1st Brigade of the 3rd Division of the Militia of Massachusetts." October 11, 1798.

__________. "Letter to a friend." 1805.

__________. "Letter to Benjamin Waterhouse," 29 October 1805.

Adams, Samuel. "Letter to John Pitts." 21 January 1776.

__________. "The Report of the Committee of Correspondence to the Boston Town Meeting" Nov. 20, 1772. *history.hanover. edu/texts/adamss.html.*

Ahlstrom. Sydney F. *A Religious History of the American People.* New Haven: Yale University Press, 1972.

Aquinas, Thomas. *Summa Theologica* 1265-1274 AD Sixth Article [I-II, Q. 94, Art. 6] Objection 3. Translated by Fathers of the English Dominican Province. Benziger Brothers, New York. 1947.

Archer, Gleason Leonard, Jr. *A Survey of Old Testament Introduction.* Chicago: Moody, c. 1974. Updated and revised ed., c1994.

Arndt, William F. and F. Wilbur Gingrich, trans. Bauer, Walter. *A Greek-English Lexicon of the New Testament and Other Early Christian Literature.* University of Chicago Press: Chicago, 1967.

Asimov, Isaac. *The Roving Mind.* Prometheus Books, 1997.

Athenagoras of Athens. *Legatio pro Christianis* ["Supplication for the Christians"]. (Letter to Marcus Aurelius), 177 A.D. Translated by B. P. Pratten in "Athenagoras." *The Ante-Nicene Fathers, vol. 2*, Wm. B. Eerdmans, Grand Rapids: Michigan, 1954.

Augustine of Hippo. *City of God.* Selections. series 1, vol. 2 of the Nicene and Post-Nicene Fathers. Translated

Henry Bettenson. Pelican Books, England, Clay's LTD, St. Ives Place, 1972.

Austin, Steven. Citing Hamilton Hicks. "Mineralized sodium silicate solutions for artificial petrification of wood," United States Patent Number 4,612,050, September 16, 1986, pp. 1-3. *CatastroRef*--'Catastrophe Reference Database: Catastrophes in Earth History, Geologic Evidence, Speculation and Theory', Institute for Creation Research, San Diego. Entry no. 267.

Austin, S.A. (editor). *Grand Canyon: Monument to Catastrophe.* Institute for Creation Research, Santee, California, 1994.

Ayer. A.J. (editor) *The Humanist Outlook.* Rationalist Press Association, Ltd. 1968.

Bakunin Mikhail. *God and the State.* written 1871. First published 1882 (Discovered posthumously by Carlo Cafiero and Elisée Reclus). Translated by Benjamin R. Tucker. Published by Mother Earth Publishing Association, New York, 1916.

Baldwin, James. *The Fire Next Time.* 1963 by the Dial Press. Copyright renewed 1990, 1991 by Gloria Baldwin Karefa-Smart. Published in the United States by Vintage Books, a division of Random House, first Vintage International Edition, February 1993.

Baldwin, Roger Nash. "Thirty Years Later." *Harvard Class Book of 1935.* "Baldwin's Class of 1905 on its thirtieth anniversary," Insight on the News 1997.

Balmer, Randall and John R. Fitzmier. *The Presbyterians.* Westport, CT: Praeger, 1994.

Balter, Michael. "How Human Intelligence Evolved—Is It Science or 'Paleofantasy'?" *Science* magazine, 2008.

Barnett, Randy E. "The Case for a Federalism Amendment." *Wall Street Journal,* April 23, 2009.

Bates, Mike. "Aleksandr Solzhenitsyn: The Power of One," *The National Ledger, an Eclectic Mix.* August 7, 2008. The article quotes from Aleksandr Solzhenitsyn's *The Gulag Archipelago,* 1918-1956, Volume 1, English translation by Thomas P. Whitney and Harry Willetts, Harper & Row, New York, NY, 1973.

Beale, David O. *In Pursuit of Purity.* Bob Jones University Press: Greenville, SC, 1986.

Beckford, Martin, Antony Flew, Richard Dawkins. "Flew Speaks Out: Professor Antony Flew reviews The God Delusion." (Flew's review is copyrighted as follows) Antony Flew, 2008, *bethinking.org. www.telegraph.co.uk/ science/science-news,* 9:30 PM BST 02 Aug 2008.

Bentham, Jeremy. *The Works of Jeremy Bentham,* vol. 4, Edinburgh: William Tait. 1838-1843. 11 vols, 1843.

Bhartruhari, Neeti Shatakan (spelling varies; a work of Sanskrit philosophical verse). The empire in which he lived lasted from 185 B.C. to 135 A.D. Sahu Dharanidhar published *An English Verse Translation of Three Shatakas of Bhartruhari* in 2003.

Bierce, Ambrose. *The Enlarged Devil's Dictionary.* 1906.

Billington, Ray Allen. *Westward Expansion: A History of the American Frontier,* Macmillan, New York, NY, 1974.

Blackburn, Simon. "Independent on Sunday." *National Secular Society Newsline,* 12 May 2002.

Blackstone, William. Commentaries on the Law of England, 1765–1769.

Bonomi, Patricia U. "Religious Pluralism in the Middle Colonies." *Divining America: Religion in American History,* New York University, National Humanities Center. *nationalhumanitiescenter.org* accessed May 6, 2010.

Bowden, Thomas A. "Your Child Is Not State Property," *FrontPage* Magazine, April 4, 2008. Reproduced at Ayn Rand Center for Individual Rights Website. (Thomas A. Bowden is an analyst at the Ayn Rand Institute, focusing on legal issues.)

Bradford, William. *History of Plymouth Plantation. Bradford's History of 'Plimoth Plantation' From the Original Manuscript. With a Report of the Proceedings Incident to the Return of the Manuscript to Massachusetts.* c. 1650. *Gutenberg.org*

Breasted, James Henry. *Ancient Records of Egypt: Historical Documents from the Earliest Times to the Persian Conquest,* collected, edited, and translated, with Commentary. Chicago: University of Chicago Press, 1906–1907.

Brian, Denis. Adapted from *Einstein, A Life*. John Wiley and Sons, New York, 1996.

Briggs, Charles Augustus. *American Presbyterianism.* New York, NY: Charles Scribner's Sons, 1885

Brown, Brian. *The Wisdom of the Egyptians* (1923). Taken from the Internet Sacred Text Archive, *www.sacred-texts.com*, managed by John Bruno Hare.

Budge, E. A. Wallis. "Legends of the Gods. THE HISTORY OF CREATION." *The Egyptian Texts, edited with Translation.* (Brit. Mus. Papyrus No 10,188). [1912] Taken from the Internet Sacred Text

Archive, *www.sacred-texts.com,* managed by John Bruno Hare.

Butt, Kyle, M.A. "'So We Make Up Stories' About Human Evolution." Apologetics' Press. 2008. *www.apologeticspress.org*.

Byrnes, Ryan. "Private Sector Jobs Decline, Government Jobs Increase." Quoting Bill Beach, director of the Center for Data Analysis at the Heritage Foundation. *CNS News,* Monday, March 09, 2009.

Calvin, John. Commentary on Luke 24:45. *Commentary On A Harmony of the Evangelists, Matthew, Mark, and Luke.* Translator from Latin and collator with the French version Rev. William Pringle. Edinburgh, Calvin Translation Society, 1847-1850. Calvin's Commentaries, Vol. 33: Matthew, Mark and Luke, Part III, translated by John King, 1847-50.

__________. *Institutes of the Christian Religion.* Thomas Norton, Translator. 1581.

Calabresi, Guido. *A Common Law for the Age of Statutes.* Copyright by the President and Fellows of Harvard College, 1982.

Callaway, Henry. *The Religious System of the Amazulu.* Springville, Natal, 1870.

Carson, Jonathan David. "Science's Sins of the Eyes." *New Oxford Review,* November 2001.

Castillo, Bernal Diaz Del. *The Discovery And Conquest Of Mexico* 1517-1521. Edited by Genaro Garcia, Translated with an Introduction and Notes, A. P. Maudslay. first pub 1928. Taken from the Internet Sacred Text Archive, *www.sacred-texts.com,* managed by John Bruno Hare.

Catullus, Gaius Valerius (c. 84 – c. 54 BC). *Carmina.* Translated by Leonard C. Smithers. 1894.

Chamberlain, B.H. translator. [1882] *THE KOJIKI PART I.- THE BIRTH OF THE DEITIES. THE BEGINNING OF HEAVEN AND EARTH* Taken from the Internet Sacred Text Archive, www.sacred-texts.com, managed by John Bruno Hare.

Charron Pierre. *De la sagesse* ("Of Wisdom," In Three Parts). French version, 1601. Translated by Samson Lennard, Eliot's Court Press for Edward Blount and Will, Aspley, London, c.1615.

Chaucer, Geoffrey. "Prologue." *The Canterbury Tales.* 14th century. (Description of the Poor Parson). *msgr.ca/msgr-3/church_of_england.htm and the subsite msgr.ca/msgr-3/canterbury_tales_parson.htm.*

Clarke, Arthur C. *90th Birthday Reflections,* 2007.

__________. *Greetings, Carbon-Based Bipeds! : Collected Essays,* 1934-1998 including "Credo" (1991). St. Martin's Press, New York, NY, 1999

Cline, Aaron. Agnosticism/atheism columnist for ten years. *About.com.*

Clinton, Hillary. Speech. Global Business Coalition on HIV/AIDS Annual Awards for Business Excellence Gala at the Kennedy Center in Washington, D.C. Wednesday, Sept. 28, 2005.

__________. Speech in San Francisco, CA. June 28th, 2004.

Coe, R.S. and M. Prevot. "Evidence suggesting extremely rapid field variation during a geomagnetic reversal." *Earth and Planetary Science Letters,* Elsevier, Amsterdam, Netherlands. Vol. 92, pp. 296-297, 1989.

Coomaraswamy, Rama. "The Conflict Between Science and Faith," from his online archives, 2001.

Covey, Stephen. *Principle-Centered Leadership.* Fireside, Simon and Schuster, Rockefeller Center, New York, NY, 1992.

Cunningham, G., Fluckiger-Hawker, E, Robson, E., and Zólyomi, G.,*The Epic of Gilgamesh, The Electronic Text Corpus of Sumerian Literature,* Oxford 1998-.

Curtis, Adrian. *Oxford Bible Atlas,* Fourth Edition. Oxford University Press: London, 2009.

Custer, Stewart. *A Treasury of New Testament Synonyms.* Bob Jones Univ. Press: Greenville, SC, 1975.

Cyprian of Carthage (3rd century AD). Letter LXXII, *Ad Jubajanum de haereticis baptizandis.* Translated by Robert Ernest Wallis. From *Ante-Nicene Fathers, Vol. 5.* Edited by Alexander Roberts, James Donaldson, and A. Cleveland Coxe. (Buffalo, NY: Christian Literature Publishing Co., 1886.)

Dalrymple, G. Brent. *The Age of the Earth.* Stanford University Press: Stanford, CA, 1991.

Darwin, Charles. *The Correspondence of Charles Darwin. 1821-1860. Vol. 8* Cambridge University Press, 1993.

___________. *The Descent of Man.* Princeton University Press, Princeton NJ, 1981.

___________. "Charles Darwin's Natural Selection," Being the Second Part of his *Big Species Book* Written from 1856 to 1858, ed. R.C. Stauffer Cambridge, 1975.

Davidson, J. P., W. E. Reed, and P. M. Davis. "The Rise and Fall of Mountain Ranges." *Exploring Earth: An Introduction to Physical Geology,* Upper Saddle River, New Jersey, Prentice Hall, 1997.

Davies, A. Powell. *America's Real Religion.* Boston: Beacon Press, 1965.

Dawkins, Richard. *The Ancestor's Tale: A Pilgrimage to the Dawn of Evolution.* (Editorial research by Yan Wong) Boston, N.Y.: A Mariner Book, Houghton Mifflin, 2004.

___________. quoted in "The Evolutionary Future of Man." *The Economist.* 1993-09-11, vol. 328.

___________. The Extended Phenotype: The Long Reach of the Gene. London: Oxford University Press, 1982, 1999.

___________. quoted in "The Flying Spaghetti Monster." Steve Paulson. *Salon.com*, October 13, 2006.

___________. *The Greatest Show on Earth.* Free Press, Simon and Schuster, New York, NY, also by Bantam Press Transworld Publishers in Great Britain, 2009.

___________. *River Out of Eden.* Basic Books, the Perseus Book Group, New York, NY, 1995.

___________. *The Root of All Evil.* Television documentary, January 2006.

___________. "Science, Delusion and the Appetite for Wonder." *The Richard Dimbleby Lecture.* BBC1 Television, November 12,1996.

___________. *The Selfish Gene.* London: Oxford University Press, 30th Edition, 2006.

___________. "Slaves to Superstition," *The Enemies of Reason.* [1.01], timecode 00:46:47ff, aired 13 August 2007.

___________. "From Tail to Tale On the Path of Pilgrims In Life." *The Scotsman.* April 9, 2005.

__________. Speech at the Edinburgh International Science Festival, April 15, 1992.

__________. Speech following the 9/11/2001 Islamic-led terrorist attacks on targets in the United States.

__________. *Unweaving the Rainbow: Science, Delusion and the Appetite for Wonder*. Houghton-Mifflin, New York, NY, 1998.

DeYoung, Dr. Don. *Thousands, Not Billions: Challenging an Icon of Evolution Questioning the Age of the Earth.* Green Forest, AR: Master Books, Inc., 2005.

Dickens, Charles. *Bleak House.* originally published serially from March 1852 to September 1853.

__________. *A Tale of Two Cities*. 1859.

Dickinson, Emily. "The Bible Is an Antique Volume," poem # 1545, Johnson, Thomas H., editor. *Complete Poems*. Boston: Little, Brown, 1960.

Dillard, Annie. *Pilgrim at Tinker Creek.* Harper's Magazine Press, New York, NY, 1974.

Disney, Walt. Quoted on *justDisney.com*.

Dollar, George W. *A History of Fundamentalism in America*. Greenville, SC: Bob Jones University Press, 1973.

Douglass, Frederick. "What, to the Slave, is the Fourth of July?" address given to a women's anti-slavery society in Rochester, New York. July 4, 1852.

DuBois, W.E.B. essay on birth control in Margaret Sanger's *Birth Control Review*. 1932.

Dunphy, John J. Quoted in *Humanist Magazine,* January-February 1983.

Dyer, B.D. and R.A. Obar. *Tracing the History of Eukaryotic Cells*. Columbia University Press, 1994.

Edison, Thomas A. "The Philosophy of Paine," a June 7, 1925 essay from the book, *The Diary and Sundry Observations,* edited by Dagobert D. Runes (1948).

Edwards, Chris. "Federal Pay Continues Rapid Ascent." *The Cato Institute Website. Cato At Liberty.org*. The Bureau of Economic Analysis annual data on compensation levels by industry. August 24, 2009 11:57 am.

Edwards, Jonathan. "Sinners in the Hands of an Angry God." Enfield, Connecticut, July 8, 1741.

Eisenhower, Dwight David. Speech when installed as president of Columbia University in 1948.

Epicurus, from the *40 Sovran Maxims* (or "Sovereign Maxims"), 341-270 BC, as translated by Robert Drew Hicks, 1925.

___________. *Orestes*. Translated by E. P. Coleridge, 1910. Taken from the Internet Sacred Text Archive, www.sacred-texts.com, managed by John Bruno Hare.

___________. Recorded by Seneca the Younger in his *Epistle XX. From Lucius Annaeus Seneca. Moral Essays*. Translated by John W. Basore. The Loeb Classical Library. London: W. Heinemann, 1928-1935. 3 vols.

Epictetus. *The Encheiridion.* Transcribed by Flavius Arrianus. Translated by Sanderson Beck, 1911.

Eskridge, William Jr. *Dynamic Statutory Interpretation.* Copyright by the President and Fellows of Harvard College, 1994.

Eusebius of Caesarea. *Church History or Ecclesiastical History* (Hist. Ecc viii 2.) written by in the 4th century. Translated by Arthur Cushman McGiffert, From Nicene and Post-Nicene Fathers, Second

Series, Vol. 1. Edited by Philip Schaff and Henry Wace. Christian Literature Publishing Co., Buffalo, NY, 1890.

Evans, William. *The Great Doctrines of the Bible*. Moody Publishers: Chicago, IL, 1995.

Fa-Hien (or Fa-Xien)). *A Record of Buddhistic Kingdoms, Being an Account by the Chinese Monk Fa-Hien of his Travels in India and Ceylon in Search of the Buddhist Books of Discipline*. Written between A.D. 399 and 412. Translated by James Legge, 1886.

Fange, Erich A. Von. "Time Upside Down." *Creation Research Quarterly*. June 1974.

Farabee, M.J. *The Online Biology Book*. Estrella Mountain Community College, Avondale, Arizona. emc.maricopa.edu.1992-2002.

Faure, G. *Principles of Isotope Geology*. 2nd. edition. John Wiley and Sons: New York, NY, 1986.

Fowler, Regi (Church/ Community Vice President). "Tolerating Thoughts On Tolerance," *Texas Sings*, Volume 13, number 2, Fall 1997.

Foxe, John. *Foxe's Book of Martyrs*. Written ca. 1560, revised in the 1700s edited by William Byron Forbush. Taken from the Internet Sacred Text Archive, www.sacred-texts.com, managed by John Bruno Hare.

Franklin, Benjamin. *Autobiography*. First English version published London, 1793. (Please see the Great Awakening Appendix for publication history.)

____________. From his speech at the Constitutional Convention Philadelphia, PA. June 28, 1787.

Freud, Sigmund. *The Future of an Illusion*. 1927. Translated by W.D Robson-Scott. English translation published by Horace Liveright and the Institute of Psychoanalysis. 1928.

Gibbs, Phil (original writer, 1996) and Sugihara Hiroshi (1997 update). "Occam's (or Ockham's) razor." University of California, Riverside, *Math.ucr.edu.*

Gibson, Rebecca. "Canyon Creation." *Answers in Genesis,* September 2000.

Gilley,Gary E. *This Little Church Went to Market–Is the Modern Church Reaching Out of Selling Out?* Evangelical Press, Carlisle, PA, July 2005.

Gish, Duane T. "A Decade of Creationist Research" (Part I). *Creation Research Society Quarterly.* 12 (1): 34-46 June, 1975.

Goetz, Delia, and Sylvanus Griswold Morley. *The Book of the People: POPOL VUH.* from Adrián Recino's translation from Quiché into Spanish. 1954. Taken from the Internet Sacred Text Archive, *www.sacred-texts.com,* managed by John Bruno Hare.

Goldberg, Justice Arthur J. The Supreme Court of the United States No. 02-1574 UNITED STATES OF AMERICA, PETITIONER v. MICHAEL A. NEWDOW, ET AL. ON PETITION FOR A WRIT OF CERTIORARI TO THE UNITED STATES COURT OF APPEALS FOR THE NINTH CIRCUIT REPLY BRIEF FOR THE UNITED STATES. June 26. 2003.

Grant, Peter R. and B. Rosemary Grant. "Genetics and the origin of bird species." *The National Academy of Sciences of the USA Colloquium Paper,* 1997.

Green, Joey, editor. *Philosophy on the Go.* Joey Green and Alan Corcoran, Running Press, Philadelphia, PA, 2007.

Green, Nathan, Dr. *Course overview for GEO.101,"Introduction to Geology,"* University of Alabama. Spring 2006.

Grinspoon, Lester. *Marihuana Reconsidered.* Quick American Archives. Quick Trading Company, Oakland, CA, 1971.

Hall, Edward T. *Beyond Culture.* Anchor Books, Random House, New York, NY, 1976.

Hall, Fred. "Ice Cores Not All That Simple." *AEON II*: 1, 1989:199.

Haeckel, Ernst. *The History of Creation.* Vol. 1, 6-9. 1876. Translated by Joseph McCabe, Watts & Company, London, 1912.

Hamilton, Alexander. Letter to James Bayard. 1802.

Hamilton, Alexander and James Madison. *The Federalist Papers.* Signet Classics, Penguin, Putnam: New York, NY, 2003.

Hammond, James Henry (Senator of South Carolina) "Reply to Senator William H. Seward of New York." 1858.

Hancock, Graham. *Fingerprints of the Gods.* Three Rivers Press, New York, NY: Crown Publishing Group, Random House, 1995.

____________. *Underworld: The Mysterious Origins of Civilization,* Three Rivers Publishing, Crown, Random House, New York, NY, 2003.

Han Fei. c 200 BC. *The Five Vermin.* W. K. Liao (translator and annotator), The Complete Works of Han Fei Tzu. 2 vols, London, 1939-59.

Hannam, James. "Medieval Science and Philosophy" and "Science and Church in the Middle Ages." (From his Web site for the book.) *God's Philosophers: How the*

Medieval World Laid the Foundations of Modern Science. Icon Books, London, 2009.

Hapgood, Charles H., J.B. Delair and E.F. Oppe. *The Path of the Pole*. Chilton Books, Philadelphia, PA, 1970.

Harris, Sam. *The End of Faith*. W.W. Norton & Company New York, NY, 2004.

Haught, James A. *2000 Years of Disbelief: Famous People with the Courage to Doubt*. Prometheus Books, Amherst, NY, 1998.

Hawking, Stephen. *The Illustrated A Brief History of Time*. New York, NY: Bantam Dell, a division of Random House, 1996.

Heinlein, Robert A. *The Notebooks of Lazarus Long,* 1978, Pomegranate Publications, Inc., 1999.

Herndon, William and Jesse W. Weik. *Herndon's Lincoln: The True Story of a Great Life,* a three volume edition published by Belford, Clarke & Company beginning in 1889.

Herodotus (484-ca. 425 BC). *Histories*. English translation G. C. Macaulay. Macmillan, London and NY, 1890.

Hesiod. *Theogeny*. Translated by Hugh G. Evelyn-White. 1914. Taken from the Internet Sacred Text Archive, www.sacred-texts.com, managed by John Bruno Hare.

Heyerdahl, Thor. *Kon-Tiki: Across the Pacific in a Raft* (The Kon-Tiki Expedition: By Raft Across the South Seas) F.H. Lyon, Translator. Rand McNally & Company: Skokie, IL, 1950.

____________. *Aku-Aku: The Secret of Easter Island.* 1958.

Hitler, Adolph. Speech given May 1, 1937.

____________. Speech given at Elbing, Germany. November 6, 1939.

Hoagland, Peter. American lawyer and congressman (US House of Representatives, Democrat, Nebraska), in a radio speech with Pastor Everett Silevan, 1983, documented in Bill Clinton: Friend or Foe? Ann Wilson, J. W. Publishing Company, 1993.

Hodges, Charles. *Systematic Theology.* 3 Volumes. Hendrickson Publishers: Peabody, MA, 1999.

Holmes, Oliver Wendell. "The Theory of Legal Interpretation." 12 Harvard Law Review. 417, 419 (1899).

Homer. *The Iliad.* C. 850 BC Translated by Samuel Butler, 1900. Gutenberg.org.

____________. *The Odyssey.*

Hornberger, Jacob G. "Your Children Are the Property of the State," *The Future of Freedom Foundation Website.* April 2000.

Howorth, H.H. *The Mammoth and the Flood: An Attempt to Confront the Theory of Uniformitarianism with the Facts of Recent Geology.* London: Sampson Low, Marston, Searle & Livingston. 1887. Reproduced by the Sourcebook Project, Glen Arm, Maryland.

Humphreys, D. Russell, Steven A. Austin, John R. Baumgardner, and Andrew A. Snelling. "Helium Diffusion Age of 6,000 Years Supports Accelerated Nuclear Decay." *Creation Research Society Quarterly Journal.* (CRSQ) Vol 41 No 1 June 2004. Creation Research.org, Copyright © 2004 by Creation Research Society.

Humphreys, D. Russell, Ph.D. *Starlight and Time, Solving the Puzzle of Distant Starlight in a Young Universe*. Green Forest, AR: Master Books, Inc., 2004, Ninth Printing.

Huxley, Aldous. "Confessions of a Professed Atheist," Report: *Perspective on the News,* Vol. 3, June 1966, p. 19.

Huxley, Julian. "At Random," a television preview on Nov. 21, 1959.

Huxley, Thomas Henry. Letter to Charles Kingsley (23 September 1860).

Ingersoll, Robert G. *Thomas Paine*. 1892. Thomas Paine National Historical Association website, http://www.thomaspaine.org/bio/ingersoll1892.html.

Iype, George. First press conference of Indian Prime Minister Manmohan Singh. *Rediff, India Abroad*, May 20, 2004.

Jay, William. "Charge to the Grand Jury of Ulster County" on Sept. 9, 1777. from *The Life of John Jay*. J. & J. Harper, New York, NY, 1833.

Jefferson, Thomas. *Autobiography*. 1821.

__________. "Draft for a Bill for Establishing Religious Freedom. Proposed to the Virginia Assembly," 1779. odur.let.rug.nl ~usa/P/tj3/writings/draft1779.htm

__________. "Letter to the Secretary of the Treasury, Albert Gallatin," 1802.

__________. *The Writings of Thomas Jefferson,* Albert E. Bergh, ed. (Washington, D. C.: The Thomas Jefferson Memorial Association of the United States, 1904), Vol. XVI, pp. 281-282.

____________. University of Virginia Library Collection of the letters and papers of Thomas Jefferson.

Jensen, Carl, *http://web.archive.org/web/20050831053419 /www.pbnnews*.reposted on the website *D.program.net* October 1, 2008,

Johnson, Allen H. "James Dale, the Supreme Court and fond memories of Troop 148," *News and Record I,* July 30, 2000. *Gay Straight Advocates for Education Website (gsafe.org).*

Johnson, Samuel. *The History of Rasselas, Prince of Abissinia.* 1759.

Josephus, Flavius. *Against Apion.* William Whiston, Translator, 1737. Taken from the Internet Sacred Text Archive, www.sacred-texts.com, managed by John Bruno Hare.

____________. *Antiquities of the Jews.*

____________. *Autobiography.*

____________. *Hades.*

____________. *Wars of the Jews.*

Justin Martyr. *First Apology.* Translated by Alexander Roberts and James Donaldson. 1867.

Keil, C. F. and F. Delitzsch. *Commentary on the Old Testament. 10 Volumes* Hendrickson Publishers: Peabody, MA, Updated Edition 1996.

King, Coretta Scott. Speech at the Palmer House Hilton in Chicago April 1, 1998.

King, Leonard William, translator. *ENUMA ELISH: THE EPIC OF CREATION (from The Seven Tablets of Creation,* London 1902) Public Domain. Taken from the Internet Sacred Text Archive, www.sacred-texts.com, managed by John Bruno Hare.

Kipling, Rudyard. *The Jungle Book.* originally published serially, 1893-1894.

Kurtz, Paul, Editor. *A Secular Humanist Declaration,* issued by The Council for Democratic and Secular Humanism (now the Council for Secular Humanism). Published in Free Inquiry Magazine, 1980.

LaBahn, Jeri. "Education and Parental Involvement in Secondary Schools: Problems, Solutions, and Effects," *Educational Psychology Interactive.* Valdosta, GA: Valdosta State University, 1995.

Landor, Walter Savage. "Melanchthon and Calvin," *Imaginary Conversations.* 1824-29.

Lee, Harper. *To Kill A Mocking-Bird.* Harper and Row, New York, NY, 1961 (copyright 1960 by the author, renewed 1988).

Lee, Robert E. (General Lee's son). *Recollections and Letters of General Robert E. Lee.* Rod and Black Publishers, St. Petersburg, Fl, 1904.

Leeuw, Nick De. Posting by contributor Monday, Nov. 10, 2008 on the *Right Michigan.com website,* email by Mount Hope Church in Lansing, Michigan attendee who witnessed the infiltration and actions of Bash Back (A Michigan-based pro-gay and lesbian organization) at the church November 9, 2008.

Lenin, Vladimir Ilyich. *Two Tactics of Social-Democracy in the Democratic Revolution.* Written June-July 1905, first published as a pamphlet in Geneva, July 1905, translated by Abraham Fineburg and Julius Katzer, published in Lenin's Collected Works, Volume 9, 1962, Moscow. Taken from Marxist Internet archive.

Lennon, John. “Imagine.” Title song from the *Imagine album.* Ascot Sound Studios Tittenhurst Park and The Record Plant, New York, NY. Apple/EMI Label. 1971.

Lerner Lawrence S. *Good Science, Bad Science: Teaching Evolution in the States,* Thomas B. Fordham Foundation, Washington, DC, 2000.

Lewis, Charles. “Gay Altar Server Contests Firing Human Rights Tribunal asked to intervene.” *National Post* (Canada). Tuesday, July 14, 2009.

Lewis, C.S. *The Abolition of Man or Reflections on education with special reference to the teaching of English in the upper forms of schools.* 1943. Available online at *www.columbia.edu/cu/augustine/arch/ lewis/abolition1.htm.*

Lewis, Joseph. *Ingersoll the Magnificent,* a compilation of Ingersoll’s quotations, dedicated at a memorial address in 1954, published American Atheist Press, Austin TX, 1983.

Lewontin, Richard. Quoted in a review,”Billions and Billions of Demons,” *The New York Review,* p. 31, January 9, 1997.

Lial, Margaret L., Charles David Miller and E. John Hornsby. *Beginning Algebra,* Harper-Collins College Division, New York, NY, 1992.

Liddell, H.G. and R. Scott, eds. *A Greek-English Lexicon.* Oxford University Press: London, 1982.

Lincoln, Abraham. “Response to Horace Greeley’s abolitionist editorial.” *New York Tribune,* August 22, 1862.

Linder, Douglas O. “Speech on the Occasion of the 25th Anniversary of the Scopes Trial,” July 10, 2000. “State v. John Scopes” (“The Monkey Trial”) *http://www.law.umkc.edu/faculty/projects/ftrials /scopes/evolut.htm.*

Lisle, Jason, Ph.D. "God and Natural Law." *Answers in Genesis,* August 28, 2006.

Livingston, Dr. David P. "Nimrod: Who Was He? Was He Godly or Evil?" *Associates for Biblical Research.* Originally published in *ABR's BIBLE AND SPADE,* 2001.

Lowder, Jeffery Jay, ed. Farrell Till et. al. "The Jury Is In: The Ruling on McDowell's 'Evidence.'" 1997-2001. *www.infidels.org.*

Lubicz, Isha Schwaller, de. *Her-Bak: The Living Face of Ancient Egypt and Her-Bak: Egyptian Initiate.* Inner Traditions, Santa Fe, New Mexico, 1978.

Lucian of Samosata. c. A.D. 125 – after A.D. 180. An Assyrian rhetorician, and satirist who wrote in the Greek language, translated by A. M. Harmon, 1936.

Lucretius (Titus Lucretius Carus). *Of The Nature of Things.* (c 95-55 BC) Translator: William Ellery Leonard, 1916. Gutenberg.org.

Lundstrom, Laurel. "Students Free to Thank Anybody Except God." *Fox News.com.* Monday, November 22, 2004,

MacAuliffe, Max Arthur (Author and translator of Sikh texts). *The Sikh Religion, DIVINE SERVICES BY GURU NANAK AND OTHER GURUS THE JAPJI, Volume 1.* Oxford University Press: London, 1909. Taken from the Internet Sacred Text Archive, www.sacred-texts.com, managed by John Bruno Hare.

McCafferty, Phil. "Instant petrified wood?" *Popular Science.* October 1992.

MacDowell, Josh. *The New Evidence that Demands a Verdict.* Thomas Nelson: Nashville, TN, 1999.

MacRae, Andrew. *Radiometric Dating and the Geological Time Scale Circular Reasoning or Reliable Tools?* Copyright 1997-2004 [Text last updated: October 2, 1998] *Talk Origins.org.*

Madison, James. *Federalist No. 47,* quoting Montesquieu (Charles de Secondat, Baron de Montesquieu, 1689-1755), *The Spirit of the Laws, vol. 1,* trans. Thomas Nugent (London: J. Nourse, 1777).

___________. "Letter to Robert Walsh." March 2, 1819. *http://www.stephenjaygould. org/ ctrl/church-state.html.*

Malthus, Thomas Robert. *An Essay on the Principle of Population.* 1798.

Manning, Richard and Hans Beimler, writers. Directed By: Robert Wiemer. Executive Producer: Rick Berman. Created by Gene Roddenberry,"Who Watches the Watchers?" *Star Trek the Next Generation,* Season Three, Episode Four, first aired October 16, 1989.

Marcus Aurelius. *Meditations.* 167 AD. Translated by George Long. 1862.

Marx, Karl and Friedrich Engles. "Address of the Central Committee to the Communist League." London, 1850. Translated from German in the Soviet Union, individual translators not given. Foreign Languages Publishing House, Moscow, 1951.

___________. "Contribution to the Critique of Hegel's Philosophy of Right," 1843. Published Cambridge University 1970, editor Joseph O'Malley, translators Annette Jolin and Joseph O'Malley.

Matson, Dave E. "How Good Are Those Young-Earth Arguments?" copyright 1995.on *Infidels.org*.

Maududi, Sayeed Abdul A'la. From an address given on April 13, 1939, translation on the site *IslamistWatch.org,* no translator credited.

Merrill, Eugene H. *An Historical Survey of the Old Testament*. Baker Books: Grand Rapids, MI, 1991.

Maxwell, Bill. "Intolerance as policy." *St. Petersburg Times*. August 9, 1998.

Mill, John Stuart. *Autobiography*. 1873.

Miller, Kevin and Ben Stein, writers. *Expelled: No Intelligence Allowed*. Prod. Logan Craft, Walt Ruloff and John Sullivan. Dir. Nathan Frankowski. Assoc. Prod. Mark Mathis. Ed. Simon Tondeur. © 2008 Premise Media Corporation, Rampart Films Production.

Morgan, G. Campbell. *Acts of the Apostles*. 1924.

Morton, G.R. "Young-Earth Arguments: A Second Look," 1998. *home.entouch.net*.

Montgomery, Peter. Article on *AlterNet.org*. Feb. 10, 2010.

Mooney, Chris. "Survival of the Slickest: How Anti-Evolutionists are Mutating Their Message." *The American Prospect, Liberal Intelligence*. December 2, 2002.

Mooney, James. *MYTHS OF THE CHEROKEE. From Nineteenth Annual Report of the Bureau of American Ethnology 1897-98, Part I. COSMOGONIC MYTHS*. Taken from the Internet Sacred Text Archive, www.sacred-texts.com, managed by John Bruno Hare.

Morris, Henry M. *The Genesis Record: a Scientific and Devotional Commentary on the Book of Beginnings.* Grand Rapids, MI. Baker Book House, 1976.

Mulsow, Martin and Jan Rohls. *Socinianism And Arminianism : Antitrinitarians, Calvinists, And Cultural Exchange in Seventeenth-Century Europe,* part of the series *Brills Studies of Intellectual History,* edited by A.J. Vanderjagt, University of Gronigen, Netherlands, 2005.

Newton, Isaac. Unpublished notes for the *Preface to Opticks* (1704) quoted in *Never at Rest: A Biography of Isaac Newton* by Richard S. Westfall, Cambridge Paperback Library, 1983.

Nicholls, David. *Atheist Foundation of Australia,* undated article on the Foundation's website.

Nietzsche, Friedrich. Human, *All-Too-Human, A Book for Free Spirits.* German version 1878. Translated by Marion Faber and Stephen Lehmann. English version published by Lincoln: University of Nebraska Press, 1984.

Oard, Michael. *Frozen in Time: The Wooly Mammoth, The Ice Age and the Bible.* Green Forest, AR: Master Books, Inc., 2004.

Ovid (Publius Ovidius Naso). *Metamorphoses.* Completed in AD 8.Translated by Henry Thomas Riley, 1851.

Paine. Thomas. *The Age of Reason,* in 3 parts, 1794, 1795, 1807. *Gutenberg.org*

___________. *Agrarian Justice,* printed in English by W. Adlard in Paris, and in London for T. Williams, No. 8 Little Turnstile, Holborn, 1797.

___________. "Answer to the Bishop of Lladaff." (Concerning The Age of Reason) published in the

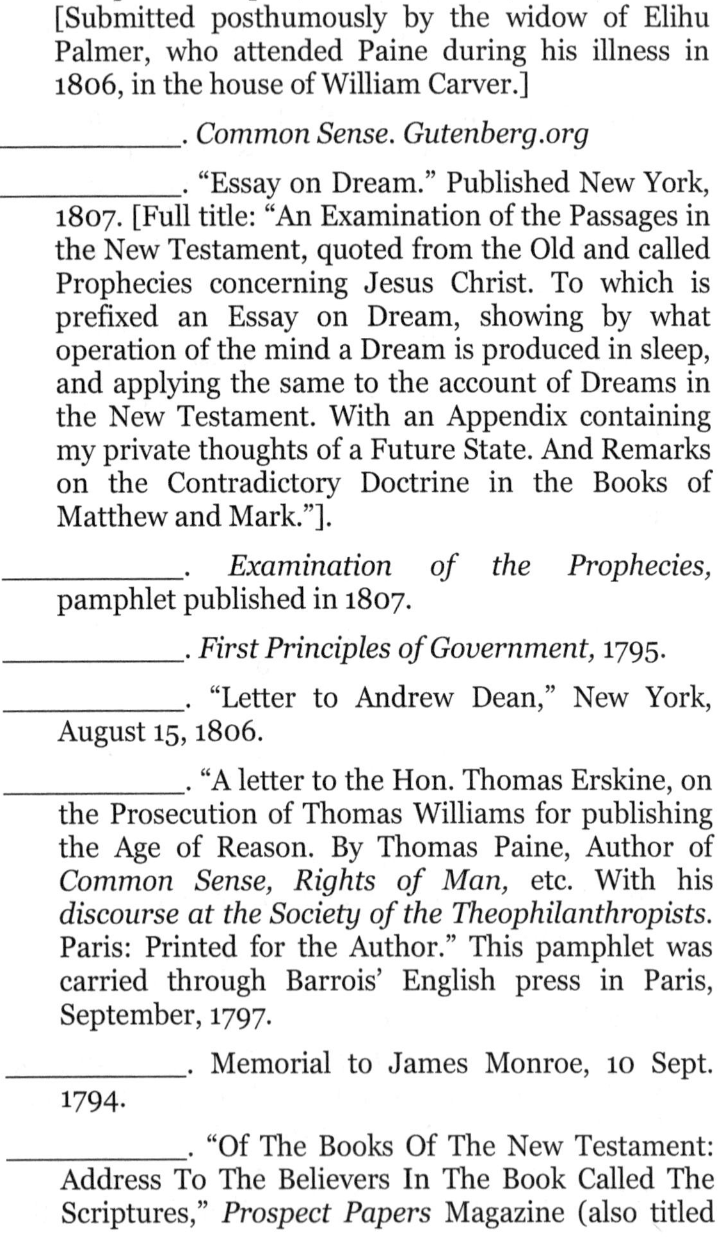

Theophilanthropist, New York, NY, 1810. [Submitted posthumously by the widow of Elihu Palmer, who attended Paine during his illness in 1806, in the house of William Carver.]

___________. *Common Sense. Gutenberg.org*

___________. "Essay on Dream." Published New York, 1807. [Full title: "An Examination of the Passages in the New Testament, quoted from the Old and called Prophecies concerning Jesus Christ. To which is prefixed an Essay on Dream, showing by what operation of the mind a Dream is produced in sleep, and applying the same to the account of Dreams in the New Testament. With an Appendix containing my private thoughts of a Future State. And Remarks on the Contradictory Doctrine in the Books of Matthew and Mark."].

___________. *Examination of the Prophecies,* pamphlet published in 1807.

___________. *First Principles of Government,* 1795.

___________. "Letter to Andrew Dean," New York, August 15, 1806.

___________. "A letter to the Hon. Thomas Erskine, on the Prosecution of Thomas Williams for publishing the Age of Reason. By Thomas Paine, Author of *Common Sense, Rights of Man,* etc. With his *discourse at the Society of the Theophilanthropists.* Paris: Printed for the Author." This pamphlet was carried through Barrois' English press in Paris, September, 1797.

___________. Memorial to James Monroe, 10 Sept. 1794.

___________. "Of The Books Of The New Testament: Address To The Believers In The Book Called The Scriptures," *Prospect Papers* Magazine (also titled

"A View of the Moral World,"), 1804, published monthly by Elihu Palmer in New York.

__________. *The Rights of Man.* Gutenberg.org. 1791.

Palin, Sarah. *Going Rogue: An American Life.* Harper Collins, New York: NY, 2009.

Parsons, Thomas J., et. al. "A high observed substitution rate in the human mitochondrial DNA control region." *Nature Genetics* 15, 363 - 368 (1997).

Pasteur, Louis. Correspondence I, p. 382-383,"To the Rector of the Academia de Douai," 15 Nov. 1855. Cuny, H., *Louis Pasteur, The Man and his Theories,* Translated P. Evans, London, The Souvenir Press, 1965.

Patten, Donald W. and Samuel R. Windsor. "Catastrophic Theory of Mountain Uplifts (A Crustal Deformation Theory)." *Catastrophism and Ancient History Vol. XIII Part 1* January 1991.

Pell, George, Cardinal. "Varieties of Intolerance: Religious and Secular," Thomas More Lecture on Religion in the Public Square, hosted by the Oxford University Newman Society, *LifesiteNews,* published March 12, 2009.

Penn, William. *THE TRYAL of WILLIAM PENN and WILLIAM MEAD*, at the Sessions held at the Old Baily in London, the 1st, 3rd, 4th, and 5th of September, 1670. *Gutenberg.org.*

Pierce, Chester M. Address at Childhood International Education Seminar, 1973.

Pitman, Sean, M.D. "Ancient Ice" (a PowerPoint presentation) created in Jan 2006. Includes testimony from a telephone interview with Bob Cardin, project manager to recover "Glacier Girl."

Plato. *The Republic.* Translated by Benjamin Jowett over a period of 30 years until his death in 1893, completed by Lewis Campbell. *Gutenberg.org*.

_________. *Critias.*

_________. *Phaedrus.*

_________. *Timmaus.*

Plutarch. *Lives.* Translated by John Dryden, 1683. Gutenberg.org.

Poincaré, Henri. "Science et méthode." ("Science and Method"), 1908, English translation in *The Foundations of Science: Science and Hypothesis, The Value of Science, Science and Method,* The Science Press, translated by George Bruce Halstead, 1913.

Polo, Marco and Rustichello of Pisa, *The Travels of Marco Polo, Volume 1, THE COMPLETE YULE-CORDIER EDITION Including the unabridged third edition* (1903) of Henry Yule's annotated translation, as revised by Henri Cordier; together with Cordier's later volume of notes and addenda. 1920. Chapter XVII. Gutenberg.org.

Porter, Janet. "Forced Vaccines: Ready For Yours?" *Faith2action,* posted: August 18, 2009 1:00 am Eastern 2010 *World Net Daily. wnd.com.*

Prager, Dennis. "Breastfeeding as a Religion." *World Net Daily. wnd.com.* posted November 11, 2003 1:00 am Eastern.

Protagoras of Abdera (ca. 490-ca. 420 BC) Greek philosopher, agnostic, logician, believed to be from his lost work *On the Gods*. Included in the following work: *Aristophanes. Clouds.* Intro. and trans. by Carol Poster. In Aristophanes 3, ed. David Slavitt and Palmer Bovie. Philadelphia PA: University of Pennsylvania Press, 1999.

Radest, Howard B. "Are We Religious?" By Algernon David Black. Collected in *Understanding Ethical Religion*. Produced for the American Ethical Union Library, 1975.

Rand, Ayn. *Atlas Shrugged*, author's copyright 1957. Signet, New American Library, Penguin Group, New York, NY 1996.

Randerson, James. "We Know Nothing About Brain Evolution." *Guardian* (UK). Report on a 2008 Lewontin speech titled, "Why We Know Nothing About the Evolution of Cognition."

Rantoul, Robert. Fourth-of-July address. Scituate, Massachusetts, 1836.

Reese, Lizette. 1856-1935. From the poem "Truth." *American Women Poets of the Nineteenth Century*. Anthology edited by Cheryl Walker. Rutgers University, New Jersey, 1992.

Regnerus, Mark. "Sex and the Evangelical Teen." *Forbidden Fruit: Sex & Religion in the Lives of American Teenagers*. Oxford University Press, New York, NY, 2007). THOUGHTS, "Minority report," World magazine, Vol. 22, No. 29, August 11, 2007.

Rickman, Thomas Clio. *Life of Thomas Paine,* 1819.

Robertson, A.T. *Word Pictures of the New Testament*. Broadman Press: Nashville, TN: 1932, 33, Renewal 1960.

Rolston, Bruce. "Speed Of Light May Not Be Constant, Physicist Suggests." Report on an article co-authored by University of Toronto Physics professor John Moffat and former U of T researcher Michael Clayton and published in *Physics Letters* in 1999. *ScienceDaily,* October 6, 1999.

Rooney, Andy. *Sincerely, Andy Rooney*. Essay Productions, Public Affairs, by the Perseus Group, New York, NY, 1999.

Rosenhouse, Jason. *EvolutionBlog*, Posted March 5, 2010.

Roys, Ralph L, translator. *THE BOOK OF CHILAM BALAM OF CHUMAYEL* 1933. Taken from the Internet Sacred Text Archive, www.sacred-texts.com, managed by John Bruno Hare.

Rummel, R.J. STATISTICS OF DEMOCIDE Chapter 4 "Statistics Of Cambodian Democide Estimates, Calculations, And Sources." Prepublication excerpt 1997, *Hawaii.edu.*

Rushdoony, Rousas. *The Mythology of Science*. Nutley, NJ: Craig Press, 1967.

Rushdie, Salman. A 1996 speech.

Russell, Bertrand. "Why I am Not a Christian." Lecture March 6, 1927, delivered to the National Secular Society.

Sagan, Carl. *Contact*. Pocket Books, Simon and Schuster, NY: NY, 1985.

___________. *Cosmos* television series. PBS, 1980.

___________. *Cosmos: A Personal Voyage* (Updated), television series, PBS, 1989.

___________. Interview with Charlie Rose, late-night PBS talk show host, 1996.

___________. *The Demon-Haunted World: Science as a Candle in the Dark*, Ballantine Book, Random House, New York, NY, 1996.

Sand, George (Amantine Aurore Lucile Dupin). 1804-1876 Letter to Gustave Flaubert, 14 September, 1871. Translated by A.L. MacKenzie, 1921.

Sanderson, Terry. Address as president of the National Secular Society of the UK, Dec 17, 2009.

Sanger, Margaret. *Pivot of Civilization,* 1932.

__________. *The Woman Rebel, Volume I, Number 1.* Reprinted in *Woman and the New Race.* New York: Brentanos Publishers, 1922.

Sarfati, Jonathan. "Who's Really Pushing Bad Science?" *Creation.com,* Creation Ministries International, 26 September 2000.

Saxe, John Godfrey. (1816-1887). "The Blind Men and the Elephant."

Sayers, Dorothy L. "The Other Six Deadly Sins." *Creed or Chaos,* Harcourt, Brace and Company, New York: NY, 1994.

Scalia, Antonin. *Common-Law Courts in a Civil-Law System: The Role of United States Federal Courts in Interpreting the Constitution and Laws.* THE TANNER LECTURES ON HUMAN VALUES. Delivered at Princeton University, March 8 and 9, 1995.

Schaff, Phillip. *History of the Christian Church, Volumes 5, 6 and 7.* Charles Scribner's Sons, New York, 1910.

Schaeffer, Francis A. "A Christian Manifesto." An address delivered by Dr. Schaeffer in 1982 at the Coral Ridge Presbyterian Church, Fort Lauderdale, Florida. It is based on the book of the same title.

__________. *The God Who Is There.* InterVarsity Press: Downer's Grove, IL, 1998.

Schmid, Randolph E. (Associated Press). "Skull Suggests Interbreeding of Neanderthal and Modern Man." *The Denver Post*, January 15, 2007.

Schweitzer, Mary H. and Jennifer L. Wittmeyer, North Carolina State University; John R. Horner, Montana

State University; Jan B. Toporski, Carnegie Institution of Washington Geophysical Laboratory. "Soft-Tissue Vessels and Cellular Preservation in Tyrannosaurus rex." *Science,* March 25, 2005. NC State, the N.C. Museum of Natural Sciences and the National Science Foundation funded the research.

__________. "Soft tissue and cellular preservation in vertebrate skeletal elements from the Cretaceous to the present." *Proceedings of the Royal Society of Biological Sciences.* vol. 274 no. 1607 183-197, 22 January 2007.

Schleiermacher, Friedrich. Letter to his father. January 1787. Martin Redeker, translator, *Schleiermacher: Life and Thought.* Fortress Press. 1973.

Sedgwick, Adam (Woodwardian Professor of Geology at Cambridge). "Letter to Charles Darwin." November 24, 1859.

Sellars, Roy Wood and Raymond Bragg. *Humanist Manifesto I draft*, 1933.

Semken, Steven, et. al. "Trail of Time" Exhibit, Grand Canyon National Park. Associate Professor of Geoscience Education and Geological Sciences, School of Earth and Space Exploration at Arizona State University. From the *Arizona State University website.* 2008.

Seneca, Lucius Annaeus (Seneca the Younger. 4 BC to AD 65). "A letter to Serenus," as translated in *Tranquillity of Mind and Providence* by William Bell Langsdorf, 1900.

Serling, Rod. Last interview before his death, with Linda Brevelle, March 4, 1975.

Shakespeare, William. *Hamlet,* Act I Scene iii, Polonius to his son Laertes.

Shallit, Jeffrey. “Pamela Winnick's Science Envy.” *Blogspot.* Monday, July 10, 2006.

Shaw, George Bernard. *Androcles and the Lion.* 1913.

Shelley, Mary Wollstonecraft. *A Vindication of the Rights of Woman With Strictures on Political and Moral Subjects*, 1792.

Shelley, Percy Bysshe. *The Necessity of Atheism* (1811), to serve as a note to the line in Queen Mab,"There is no God" (1813).

Shepherd. Jessica. “Children educated at home twice as likely to be known to social services, select committee told” and “Home pupils more likely to be known by social services and be out of work, education or training.” *guardian.co.uk.* Tuesday, 13 October 2009.

Shermer, Michael. “The Fossil Fallacy: Creationists' demand for fossils that represent ‘missing links’ reveals a deep misunderstanding of science.” *Scientific American.* 21 February 2005.

Simon, Sidney. *Values Clarification.* Originally published 1972, Warner Books. Revised edition by Grand Central Publishing, September 1, 1995.

Simpson, George Gaylord. *The Meaning of Evolution.* Revised edition. New Haven: Yale University Press, 1967.

Smith, S. Percy, trans. *The Lore of the Whare-wananga; or Teachings of the Maori College On Religion, Cosmogony, and History.* Written down by H. T. Whatahoro from the teachings of Te Matorohanga and Nepia Pohuhu, priests of the Whare-wananga of the East Coast, New Zealand. (Smith was the F.R.G.S. President of the Polynesian Society.) Part I.-Te Kauwae-runga,Or ‘Things Celestial.’ New Plymouth, N.Z. Printed for the Society by Thomas

Avery. -- 1913. {Reduced to HTML by Christopher M. Weimer, February 2003} Taken from the Internet Sacred Text Archive, www.sacred-texts.com, managed by John Bruno Hare.

Snelling, Andrew. "Radiocarbon in Diamonds Confirmed." *Answers in Genesis,* November 7, 2007. (This study was conducted during the RATE (Radioisotopes and the Age of The Earth) research project at the Institute for Creation Research.)

__________. "The Earth's magnetic field and the age of the Earth," first published: *Creation* (Creation Ministries International), 13(4):44-48 September 1991.

__________. "The Recent Origin of Bass Strait Oil and Gas." *Creation,* 5 (2):43–46 March 1982.

Sparks, Muriel. *The Prime of Miss Jean Brodie.* Harper Collins, New York, NY, 1961.

Spence, Lewis. Excerpt from: *The Popol Vuh The Mythic and Heroic Sagas of the Kichés of Central America.* Published by David Nutt, at the Sign of the Phoenix, Long Acre, London [1908]. Taken from the Internet Sacred Text Archive, www.sacred-texts.com, managed by John Bruno Hare.

__________. *The Myths of Mexico and Peru.* (1913). Taken from the Internet Sacred Text Archive, www.sacred-texts.com, managed by John Bruno Hare.

Spurgeon, Charles Haddon. "Our Reply to Sundry Critics and Enquirers," *The Sword and Trowel,* Metropolitan Tabernacle, Elephant and Castle, London, Sept. 1887.

Steinem, Gloria. "Address to the Women of America," at the founding of the National Women's Political Caucus, 1971.

Sternberg, Dr. Richard. *RichardSternberg.org.*

Strong, James. *Strong's Exhaustive Concordance of the Bible.* Hendrickson Publishers: Peabody, MA, Updated Edition, 2007.

Suetonius (Gaius Suetonius Tranquillus). *The Twelve Caesars.* c. 117 138 AD. translation J. C. Rolfe, 1913-1914.

Sun Tzu, *The Art of War.* Estimated to have been written between 476-221 BC. Translated by Lionel Guiles, 1910. Gutenberg.org.

Swatt, Barbara (Preparer, Reference Intern). Adapted from,"Themis, Goddess of Justice," *Marian Gould Gallagher Law Library, University of Washington School of Law.* Updated Oct. 31, 2007.

Sweet, William Warren. *The Story of Religions in America.* Harper & Brothers, New York, N.Y., 1930.

Sykes, Bryan. *The Seven Daughters of Eve: The Science That Reveals Our Genetic Ancestry.* W.W. Norton: New York, N.Y., 2001.

Syrett, Harold C. editor. *The Papers of Alexander Hamilton.* NY: Columbia University Press, 1979. Vol. XXI, pp. 402-404.

Tacitus. *The Annals of Imperial Rome.* 109 AD, XIII. 32. Translated by Alfred John Church and William Jackson Brodribb, 1876.

___________. *The Histories,* 109 AD. Translated by Alfred John Church and William Jackson Brodribb, 1876.

Tamny, John. "Where Are the Supply-Side Democrats?" *National Review Online.* November 18, 2005.

Taylor, Paul (Series Editor) and Elizabeth Deane (Program Executive Producer). *American*

Experience, Ulysses S. Grant. PBS, WGBH Educational Foundation, 2002.

Alfred, Lord Tennyson. *In Memoriam, AAH.* 1849. http://www.online-literature.com tennyson/718/.

Tenzin Gyatzo, 14th Dalai Lama, leader of Tibetan Buddhism,"Compassion and the Individual: the Purpose of Life." From the *Dalai Lama website.*

Thapar, Prof. Romila. *Frontline* magazine. Volume 18 - Issue 19, Sep. 15 - 28, 2001.

Thayer, Joseph Henry. *Thayer's Greek-English Lexicon of the New Testament.* Zondervan: Grand Rapids, MI, 1970.

Thiele, Edwin. *The Mysterious Numbers of the Hebrew Kings.* Zondervan Publishing House, Grand Rapids, MI, 1983.

Thiessen, Henry Clarence. *Lectures in Systematic Theology.* Wm. B. Eerdmans: Grand Rapids, MI, Revised ed., 2006.

Traufetter, Gerald. "Europe's 'Human Zoos' -- Remains of Indigenous Abductees Back Home after 130 Years." *International: Zeitgeist. Archive Der Spiegel,* 1/13/2010.

Trudeau, G.B. *Doonesbury.* Strip published in November, 1995. Universal Press Syndicate. *Doonesbury* was launched October 26, 1970.

Unruh, Bob. "Homeschooler flees state custody: Melissa Busekros surprises parents at 3 a.m." Posted: April 23, 2007 12:33 pm Eastern. *World Net Daily.*

____________. "Homeschoolers on run win U.S. asylum Judge: Teaching children 'basic right no country has right to violate.'" January 26, 2010 11:02 pm Eastern. *World Net Daily.*

Ussher, James. *Annales veteris testamenti, a prima mundi origine deducti* ("Annals of the Old Testament, deduced from the first origins of the world"), 1650.

Ustinov, Peter. Interview with Mike Wallace. March 29, 1958.

Virgil. *The Aeneid.* c. 29 BC. Translated by John Dryden 1697. *Gutenberg.org.*

__________. *Georgics,* Book Two, published c. 29 BC. Poetic translation by John Dryden, 1697. Gutenberg.org

Vega, Garcilaso de la ("El Inca," real name Gómez Suárez de Figueroa). *Comentarios Reales de los Incas.* Lisbon, 1609. Translated by Harold V. Livermore. 1965.

Velikovsky, Emmanuel. *Ages in Chaos.* Doubleday, New York: New York, 1952.

Voltaire (François-Marie Arouet). "Of Modern Atheists, Reasons of the Worshipers of God." *Atheism I, Section I. C.* 1764. Selected and Translated by H.I. Woolf, Knopf, New York, NY, 1924.

Wald, George. "The Origin of Life," *Scientific American,* 191:48, May 1954.

Walvoord, John and Roy B. Zuck. *The Bible Knowledge Commentary, Old and New Testaments.* Cook Communications: Colorodo Springs, CO, 1989.

Watts, Charles. "The Secularist's Catechism." complied in an undated book published by Watts & Co. entitled: *Pamphlets by Charles Watts Vol. I.* 1896.

Weinberg, Steve. "A Designer Universe?" *Address at the Conference on Cosmic Design, American Association for the Advancement of Science,* Washington, D.C. April 1999.

West, E. W., translator. 1880. *PAHLAVI TEXTS.* (Persian language works from c. 180 to 880 AD) Taken from the Internet Sacred Text Archive, *www.sacred-texts.com*, managed by John Bruno Hare.

Willebrands, Johannes Cardinal. *Response to the Boy Scouts of America official position on the admission of homosexual members and leaders,* 2000.

Willette (Site User). *Askville.Amazon.com.* posted late 2009 or early 2010.

Williams, Roger. "Mr. Cotton's Letter Lately Printed, Examined and Answered," (1644), and "The Hireling Ministry, None of Christ's." *The Complete Writings of Roger Williams.* The Narragansett Club (1652).

Wilson, Edward Osborne. *On Human Nature.* Harvard University Press, 1979.

Winthrop, John. From "A Model of Christian Charity," 1630. *The Avalon Project. Documents in Law, History and Diplomacy.* Yale Law Library. avalon.law.yale.edu.

Whedon, Joseph Hill "Joss." Commentary on *Buffy the Vampire Slayer* series DVD, episode 5.16 ("The Body") (Season 5, released December 9, 2003), and an interview by Tasha Robinson for *The Onion,* (an online satirical magazine) September 5, 2001.

Wheeler, Charles N. Interview with Henry Ford. *Chicago Tribune,* May 25, 1916.

Whitcomb, J.C. and H. M. Morris. *The Genesis Flood.* Grand Rapids, MI: Baker Book House, 1961.

Whitman, Walt. "Song of Myself." From *Leaves of Grass,* first published 1855. Revised and republished many times until the "deathbed" edition finished in 1892. "Definitive version" published in 1900.

Wysong, Pippa. "Dinosaur Remains Yield Soft Tissue." *Access Excellence*. Raleigh, NC April 29, 2005. (Access Excellence is an online publication of The National Health Museum, Atlanta GA.)

Xenophanes, pre-Socratic philosopher (570-475 BC). Diels, Hermann. *Die Fragmente der Vorsokratiker* ("Pre-Socratic Fragments"). Translated by Rev. Walther Kranz. Berlin: Weidmann, 1972-1973.

Xenophon. "On Hunting." (430-354 BC). *Xenophon in Seven Volumes*. 7. Translated by E. C. Marchant, G. W. Bowersock. Constitution of the Athenians. Harvard University Press, Cambridge, MA; William Heinemann, Ltd., London. 1925.

Zahn, Drew. "Pastor waits for final word in Bible study citation: Couple ordered to get permit to host friends not out of woods yet." *WorldNetDaily* Posted: June 01, 2009 10:07 pm Eastern.

__________. "State moves to restrict Catholics in politics. Official contends church must register as 'lobbyist' to speak out." *Faith Under Fire,* Posted: June 01, 2009 9:30 pm Eastern, *World Net Daily*.

The best gift you can give an author

is an honest, thoughtful review. Please consider leaving one online. Help us understand what you liked and didn't like about the book and why. Help authors reach more readers and spread your influence and ours. If you liked the book, please recommend it to your spouse, friends, pastors, teachers, cashiers, employers, – anybody and everybody you see each day. If you don't know what to say, remember Proverb 16:3 – Commit thy works unto the Lord and thy thoughts shall be established. Thank you!

OTHER BOOKS AND PRODUCTS FROM FINDLEY FAMILY VIDEO PUBLICATIONS

All our books (including Historical Fiction, SciFi, contemporary relationships short stories, and an Archaeological Mystery serial) are linked on our blog.

Elk Jerky for the Soul includes posts on current issues, excerpts from our fiction and nonfiction works, Bible teaching, travel and everyday observations, and more. http://findleyfamilyvideopublications.com/

Visit our YouTube Channel

https://www.youtube.com/channel/UCGhwNpU115ARMwgYwTIJBrA/featured. Book trailers, video excerpts, project teasers, and more. Science, History, Literature, and biblical worldview studies are the focus of our book and video projects.

Historical Fiction

by Michael J. Findley

The Ephron the Hittite Series (Including boxed set of all titles)

Ephron Son of Zohar

Tawananna Daughter of Zohar

Heth Son of Canaan Son of Ham, Noah

Shelometh Daughter of Yovov Wife of Ephron

Zita Son of Ephron and Shelometh

Adult Romantic Suspense

by Mary C. Findley

The Men of the Realmlands series

Book One: The Baron's Ring

Book Two: The Captain's Blade

Send a White Rose

Chasing the Texas Wind

Carrie's Hired Hand (novella)

Young Adult Historical Adventure

by Mary C. Findley

Hope and the Knight of the Black Lion (plus illustrated version)

The Benny and the Bank Robber Series

Benny and the Bank Robber (Plus homeschool editions for student and teacher with review and vocabulary)

Doctor Dad

The Oregon Sentinel

Lines in Pleasant Places

Science Fiction and Fantasy

by Michael J. Findley

The Empire Saga (all six of the following books in one volume)

City on a Hill and Sojourner (Combined Novella and Short Story)

Nehemiah LLC (Full-length novel available as a standalone ebook, paperback, and hardcover versions)

Empire One: Humiliation

Empire Two: Repentance

Empire Three: Sanctification

Steampunk

by Sophronia Belle Lyon (pen name for Mary C. Findley)

The Alexander Legacy Steampunk Literary Tribute Series

Book One: A Dodge, a Twist, and a Tobacconist (including illustrated version)

Book Two: The Pinocchio Factor

Book Three: The Most Dangerous Game

Book Four: Beware the Bustle

Fantasy/Allegory

by Mary C. Findley

Allegorical clockwork novella inspired by Little Red Riding Hood

The Acolyte's Education

A Paranormal Urban Fantasy serial

His Sign: The Wait Is Over

His Sign 2: The Ezra Solution

Contemporary Fiction

by Mary C. Findley

Romantic Suspense Novella

Fall On Your Knees

Relationships Short Stories

Fifty Shades of Faithful

Fifty Shades of Faithful 2: In Living Color

The Great Thirst Serial Archaeological Mystery (including boxed set of all titles)

Part One: Prepared

Part Two: Purified

Part Three: Pursued

Part Four: Persecuted

Part Five: Persevering

Part Six: Protected

Part Seven: Prevailing

Murder Mystery

Mapped Out Murders

Nonfiction

by Mary C. Findley

Write for the King of Glory, 2nd Edition (updated, with tips on indie writing and publishing)

by Michael J. and Mary C. Findley

The Good, the Bad, and the Ugly: A Readers' and Writers' Guide for Believers

Biblical Studies (Teacher and student editions plus excerpts in OT and NT Manuscript History)

Antidisestablishmentarianism (illustrated and plain versions)

Serial versions, illustrated and plain

What Is an Establishment of Religion?

What Is Secular Humanism?

What Is Science?

What Are the Results of the Establishment of Secular Humanism?

The Conflict of the Ages series (All have teacher and student editions plus one combined teacher edition for 1-3)

I. The Scientific History of Origins

II. The Origin of Evil in the World that Was

III. They Deliberately Forgot: The Flood and the Ice Age

IV. Ice Age Civilizations

V. The Ancient World

by Michael J. Findley

Short Recaps of longer nonfiction works (*Antidisestablishmentarianism* and *Conflict of the Ages*)

Disestablish: An Overview from Creation to the Ice Age

Under the Sun: The Truth about History from the Beginning

*****

Christian Books in Multiple Genres. Join Christian Indie Author ~ Readers Group on Facebook. https://www.facebook.com/groups/291215317668431/

www.ingramcontent.com/pod-product-compliance
Lightning Source LLC
LaVergne TN
LVHW050528160826
845677LV00011B/1976

9798230169130